Pragmatic Impairment

Pragmatics – the way we interact using more than just language – is particularly problematic for people with communication disorders. Through an extensive analysis of how pragmatics can go wrong, this book not only provides a novel and clinically useful account of pragmatic impairment, but it also throws new light on how pragmatics functions in healthy individuals. The aim of this book is to bring mainstream and clinical pragmatics together by showing that, not only can our understanding of pragmatics be aided by the study of pragmatic impairment, but that clinical and theoretical pragmatics are better served by treating pragmatic ability and disability within a single framework. It is the first book on this topic to be aimed primarily at linguists and psycholinguists rather than clinicians, and includes illustrative material on conditions such as autism and aphasia and a wide range of other communication disorders in both children and adults.

MICHAEL PERKINS is Professor of Clinical Linguistics in the Department of Human Communication Sciences at the University of Sheffield.

Pragmatic Impairment

Michael Perkins

CAMBRIDGE
UNIVERSITY PRESS

CAMBRIDGE UNIVERSITY PRESS
Cambridge, New York, Melbourne, Madrid, Cape Town, Singapore, São Paulo, Delhi

Cambridge University Press
The Edinburgh Building, Cambridge CB2 8RU, UK

Published in the United States of America by Cambridge University Press, New York

www.cambridge.org
Information on this title: www.cambridge.org/9780521790703

© Cambridge University Press 2007

First published 2007

Printed in the United Kingdom at the University Press, Cambridge

A catalogue record for this publication is available from the British Library

ISBN 978-0-521-79070-3 hardback

Contents

List of figures   *Page* ix
List of tables   x
Acknowledgements   xi
Transcription conventions   xii

1   Introduction   1
    1.1   Aims   1
    1.2   Influences   3
    1.3   Outline   4

2   Pragmatic theory and pragmatic impairment   8
    2.1   Introduction   8
    2.2   Defining pragmatic ability and disability   9
          2.2.1   Linguistic vs non-linguistic pragmatics   9
          2.2.2   Normal vs abnormal pragmatic behaviour   10
          2.2.3   Neurological, cognitive and behavioural perspectives 13
    2.3   The clinical application of pragmatic theories and analytical methods   14
          2.3.1   Speech Act Theory   15
          2.3.2   Conversational Implicature   17
          2.3.3   Relevance Theory   19
          2.3.4   Discourse Analysis   21
          2.3.5   Conversation Analysis   27
    2.4   The need for a holistic approach   30

3   Pragmatics and modularity: components, dissociations
    and associations   33
    3.1   Introduction   33
    3.2   Modularity   34
    3.3   Modularity and pragmatics   36
    3.4   Modular dysfunction vs central capacity overload   37
    3.5   Impairments attributed to modular dysfunction   38
    3.6   Impairments attributed to central capacity limitations   41
    3.7   Background to an interactive emergentist pragmatics   44
          3.7.1   Emergence   45

3.7.2	The Competition Model	46
3.7.3	Neuroconstructivism	47
3.7.4	Joint Action Theory	48
3.8	Conclusion	50

4 Pragmatic ability and disability: an emergentist model — 51

4.1	Introduction	51
4.2	Three atypical cases of pragmatic impairment	52
4.2.1	Len	52
4.2.2	Lucy	53
4.2.3	Peter	54
4.2.4	Summary and preview	55
4.3	The scope of pragmatic ability and disability	56
4.3.1	Pragmatics as choices	57
4.3.2	Pragmatics as choices at all levels of language	58
4.3.3	Pragmatics as choices across semiotic systems and modalities	58
4.3.4	Pragmatics as choices motivated by interpersonal communication	60
4.3.5	Pragmatic impairment as compensatory adaptation	61
4.4	Elements, interactions and domains	62
4.4.1	Elements: semiotic, cognitive and sensorimotor systems	62
4.4.2	Interactions: equilibrium, disequilibrium and compensatory adaptation	64
4.4.3	Domains: the intrapersonal and interpersonal	66
4.5	Conclusion	68

5 Cognition and pragmatics — 70

5.1	Introduction	70
5.2	Inference	72
5.2.1	Introduction	72
5.2.2	Impairment of inferential reasoning and its pragmatic consequences	74
5.2.3	Inference: interactions in the intrapersonal domain	74
5.2.4	Inference: interactions in the interpersonal domain	75
5.3	Theory of mind	76
5.3.1	Introduction	76
5.3.2	Impairment of theory of mind and its pragmatic consequences	79
5.3.3	Theory of mind: interactions in the intrapersonal domain	80
5.3.4	Theory of mind: interactions in the interpersonal domain	81
5.4	Executive function	82
5.4.1	Introduction	82
5.4.2	Impairment of executive function and its pragmatic consequences	85
5.4.3	Executive function: interactions in the interpersonal domain	87
5.5	Memory	90
5.5.1	Introduction	90
5.5.2	Memory impairment and its pragmatic consequences	93

5.5.3   Memory: interactions in the intrapersonal domain   97
5.5.4   Memory: interactions in the interpersonal domain   98
5.6   Emotion and attitude   99
5.6.1   Introduction   99
5.6.2   Impairment of emotion and attitude and its pragmatic
        consequences   102
5.6.3   Emotion and attitude: interactions in the intrapersonal
        domain   104
5.6.4   Emotion and attitude: interactions in the interpersonal
        domain   105
5.7   Conclusion   106

6   Language and pragmatics   107
6.1   Introduction   107
6.2   Phonology and prosody   109
6.2.1   Introduction   109
6.2.2   Phonological and prosodic impairment and their pragmatic
        consequences   112
6.2.3   Phonology and prosody: interactions in the intrapersonal
        domain   113
6.2.4   Phonology and prosody: interactions in the interpersonal
        domain   116
6.3   Syntax and morphology   117
6.3.1   Introduction   117
6.3.2   Grammatical impairment and its pragmatic
        consequences   119
6.3.3   Syntax and morphology: interactions in the intrapersonal
        domain   120
6.3.4   Syntax and morphology: interactions in the interpersonal
        domain   122
6.4   Semantics   123
6.4.1   Introduction   123
6.4.2   Semantic impairment and its pragmatic consequences   127
6.4.3   Semantics: interactions in the intrapersonal domain   128
6.4.4   Semantics: interactions in the interpersonal domain   129
6.5   Discourse   131
6.5.1   Introduction   131
6.5.2   Discourse: interactions in the intrapersonal domain   134
6.5.3   Discourse: interactions in the interpersonal domain   136
6.6   Conclusion   138

7   Sensorimotor systems and pragmatics   139
7.1   Introduction   139
7.2   Hearing   140
7.3   Vision   141
7.4   Motor ability   143
7.5   Conclusion   145

8   Compensatory adaptation   146
    8.1   Introduction   146
    8.2   Definition of terms   147
    8.3   Brain plasticity: the neurology of intrapersonal compensation   149
    8.4   Intrapersonal and interpersonal compensation   151
    8.5   Case study   155
          8.5.1   Background   156
          8.5.2   Language   157
          8.5.3   Cognition   162
          8.5.4   Intrapersonal interactions and compensatory adaptations   165
          8.5.5   Interpersonal interactions and compensatory adaptations   171
    8.6   Conclusion   175

9   Conclusions   176
    9.1   Issues for pragmatics and pragmatic theory   176
          9.1.1   Scope   176
          9.1.2   Multimodality   177
          9.1.3   Causation as explanation   178
          9.1.4   Intrapersonal and interpersonal synergy   178
          9.1.5   Pragmatic ability and disability   179
    9.2   Issues for clinical practice   179
          9.2.1   Terminology   179
          9.2.2   The multiple causes of pragmatic impairment   180
          9.2.3   Intrapersonal and interpersonal perspectives   181
          9.2.4   The centrality of compensatory adaptation   181

Appendix   183
References   184
Index   227

Figures

2.1 The response of a child with autism to the request 'write the days of the week in these seven boxes'   *Page* 20

2.2 Narrative picture sequence   24

2.3 A child's incorrect attempt to arrange a series of pictures to tell a story   24

2.4 Corrected picture sequence   25

2.5 Cohesion without coherence in the conversation of a man with traumatic brain injury   26

8.1 Replication of a block design   163

Tables

2.1 Main category groups of three pragmatic impairment
    checklists   *Page* 12
2.2 Discourse analytic studies of communication impairment   22
4.1 Some semiotic, cognitive and sensorimotor elements of
    pragmatics   63
4.2 Interpersonal compensation for expressive and receptive
    communication impairments   68
5.1 The effect of short-term memory problems on sentence
    repetition (1)   93
5.2 The effect of short-term memory problems on sentence
    repetition (2)   94
5.3 The emotion–attitude continuum   100
6.1 A classification scheme for pragmatic impairment   108
6.2 Example of a reduced phonological system   109
6.3 Performance of a man with aphasia on lexical production tasks   125
8.1 Sample performance on a comprehension test of reversible
    passives   158
8.2 Sample performance on a test of sentence formulation   158
8.3 Sample performance on a test of word structure production   159
8.4 Sample performance on a test of social reasoning   161
8.5 Sample performance on a test of reading accuracy   161
8.6 Performance on a test of auditory selective attention aged 13;9   163
8.7 Performance on a test of auditory memory aged 13;9   164
8.8 Performance on a test of auditory and visual sequential
    memory aged 13;9   164
8.9 Sample performance on tests of syntactic processing   164

Acknowledgements

Over the years, I have been fortunate enough to have access to a large pool of data consisting of audio and video recordings and transcripts of interactions involving individuals with communication disorders. Much of this data has been generously provided by colleagues and students, and some has found its way into this book in the form of illustrations of pragmatic impairment. My sincere thanks, therefore, go to: Chris Backes, Richard Body, Liz Botly, Andrea Butler, Judy Clegg, Sushie Dobbinson, Margaret Freeman, Sara Howard, Martin Hughes, Rachel Lanz, Tamsyn Patrick, Catherine Simons, Vesna Stojanovik, Kate Tarling, Ruth Taylor, Alison Townsend, Ruth Watson and Abigail Werth for permission to make use of their data in this way.

I would also like to express my gratitude to Richard Body, Jack Damico, Hilary Gardner, Sara Howard, Mike McTear, Dariel Merrills, Ulrika Nettelbladt, Rosemary Varley and Bill Wells, who have been sounding boards for various ideas that have made their way into the book or have provided valuable feedback on draft sections. Special thanks go to Sara Howard for help with phonetics and phonology and to Richard Body for reading and commenting on the final draft in its entirety. None of these individuals are responsible for the use I have made of their comments.

Finally, I am pleased to acknowledge Taylor and Francis (http://www.tandf.co.uk) for permission to draw on material previously published as Perkins (2001, 2005b) in Chapters 3, 4 and 8.

Transcription conventions

[pʰ]	Phonetic transcription
/p/	Phonemic transcription
(.)	Very short pause
.	Short pause
-	Longer pause
(3.0)	Pause length in seconds
ˈ	Stressed syllable
ˋ	Falling tone
´	Rising tone
ˆ	Rising-falling tone
.	Falling-rising tone
↑↓	Marked rise or fall in pitch
[text]	Text enclosed in square brackets on consecutive lines of a transcript denotes overlapping talk
° °	Text between degree signs is quieter than surrounding talk
__	Underlining indicates emphasis
(– –)	Dashes in parentheses denote unintelligible syllables
↑↑	Text between up arrows is higher in pitch than surrounding talk
::	Colons indicate that a sound is prolonged

Phonetic symbols are from the International Phonetic Alphabet (IPA, 2005).

1 Introduction

1.1 Aims

This book aims to identify areas of common ground between pragmatics, pragmatic impairment, language, cognition and communication. It is unusual in that it accords equal weight to each, and focuses on the synergy between them.

Apart from recent interest in 'mind-reading' problems in autism by some practitioners of mainstream pragmatics (e.g. Wilson, 2005), the nature of pragmatic impairment and therefore its potential significance for pragmatics generally is largely unknown outside clinical circles. The few books published on pragmatic impairment (e.g. Gallagher, 1991; Leinonen, Letts and Smith, 2000; McTear and Conti-Ramsden, 1992; Müller, 2000; Smith and Leinonen, 1992) are written primarily for clinicians and for the most part aim to show how various pragmatic theories and analytical frameworks may be applied in the description, assessment and treatment of communication disorders. Furthermore, although generally excellent in meeting their stated clinical aims, their focus tends to be rather narrow – for example, concentrating exclusively on developmental disorders. In addition, because their primary interest is in application rather than theory, they also tend to be both eclectic and uncritical with regard to the pragmatic theories they make use of. The lack of two-way traffic between pragmatic theory and clinical practice is perhaps surprising given the growing number of researchers in areas such as syntax and semantics who regularly take into account language pathologies in their attempts to understand normal language processing and to evaluate linguistic theories. But it remains the case that hardly any journal articles – let alone books – have so far considered how pragmatic impairment may inform our understanding of pragmatic theory and normal language use. This is one motivation for the current book. Another is the large number of years spent by the author attempting to analyse conversations involving people with a wide range of so-called pragmatic impairments, but generally – it must be admitted – with varying levels of success. Labelling a stretch of discourse using categories derived

1

from various pragmatic theories is not particularly difficult, but what it provides is a description rather than an explanation. These motivations are addressed by the first three aims of the book, which are:

Aim 1:   to show how our understanding of pragmatics and pragmatic theory can be informed and extended by the study of pragmatic impairment

Aim 2:   to evaluate a range of pragmatic theories and analytical methods in terms of how well they account for pragmatic impairments

Aim 3:   to provide a model of pragmatics which is applicable to pragmatic ability and disability alike, and which affords a sense of explanation rather than mere description.

The sense of explanation referred to in Aim 3 stems partly from identifying the capacities and processes which underlie pragmatic behaviour. This is no easy task, and also depends on how pragmatics is defined. In the opening paragraph of a recent encyclopedia article on pragmatics, Sperber and Wilson (2005: 468) define the term in its 'broad' sense as covering 'a range of loosely related research programmes from formal studies of deictic expressions to sociological studies of ethnic verbal stereotypes', before proceeding to focus exclusively on one sense of the term. The rationale for their specific focus – namely, 'the study of how contextual factors interact with linguistic meaning in the interpretation of utterances' – is that it has 'been of interest to linguists and philosophers of language in the past thirty years or so'. This is absolutely justified in an encyclopedia article aimed at philosophers, but at the same time reflects the ease with which issues deemed extraneous (for whatever reason) to one's particular concerns can be ignored. The particular focus used in this book derives from an extensive analysis of how pragmatics may be impaired, following the maxim that we only become truly aware of the nature of a mechanism or process by examining what happens when it goes wrong. The underlying capacities which appear to be involved in pragmatic breakdown are reflected in Aim 4:

Aim 4:   to examine in detail the role of cognition, language and sensorimotor systems in pragmatic processing.

This engenders rather a broad interpretation of pragmatics, as we shall see in Chapter 2. Nonetheless, unlike the 'range of loosely related research programmes' referred to above by Sperber and Wilson, the broad view of pragmatics covered in this book aims to be holistic while at the same time being principled and coherent. Meeting Aim 4 entails a further aim:

Aim 5:   to compare modular and interactional approaches to pragmatics.

While respecting and incorporating the achievements of research on communication and communication impairment carried out within a modular paragigm, the emphasis of this book is on the interaction and co-dependency of the constituents of cognition, language, sensory input and motor output, rather than on their dissociation and discreteness. This is partly motivated by the specific focus of pragmatics on communication between individuals and, as we shall see, by the way in which language and cognition can be seen as interpersonal phenomena, extending beyond the individual. Aim 6 is a significant by-product of Aims 1–5:

Aim 6: to illustrate the nature of pragmatic impairments using a wide range of material from both developmental and acquired communication disorders (e.g. autistic spectrum disorder, specific language impairment, Williams syndrome, Down's syndrome, aphasia, traumatic brain injury, right hemisphere brain damage).

Handbooks and encyclopedias apart, it is rare to find a comprehensive range of impairments targeted in works on communication disorder and speech and language pathology. Because of this, interesting parallels and similarities and evidence of wider principles at work are sometimes missed.

1.2   Influences

To provide a flavour of where the book is coming from, and to allow readers to form an impression of what they're letting themselves in for, I would like to briefly – but gratefully – acknowledge what I see as its main intellectual antecedents and influences. One of the greatest of these has been the interactive – or what one might call the 'melting-pot' – approach of Elizabeth Bates, whose work spans not only pragmatics but also language development, psycholinguistics, cross-linguistic perspectives, developmental and adult acquired language disorders and much else besides. Bates was not too keen on the notion of pragmatics as a narrow concept and tended to avoid the term. She writes that '[w]ithin the interactive camp, pragmatics is not viewed as a single domain at all. Instead, it can be viewed as the *cause* of linguistic structure, the set of communicative pressures under which all the other linguistic levels have evolved' (Bates, 2003: 262). While similar in breadth and spirit, my own approach focuses on causation in the opposite direction, taking the stance that pragmatics may be seen as the emergent outcome of interactions between cognition, language and sensorimotor systems within and between individuals as motivated by the requirements of interpersonal communication. A related influence is the work of Annette Karmiloff-Smith (e.g. Karmiloff-Smith, 1998), whose 'neuroconstructivist' account of developmental communication disorders puts compensatory adaptation at the heart of the developmental process. Her specific focus is on cognitive neuropsychology – i.e.

the internal ecosystem of the individual. In my own approach – let us call it 'emergentist pragmatics' – the ecosystem within which compensation operates is expanded to encompass the interpersonal domain. This extension of compensation from the intrapersonal into the interpersonal is inspired by the work of cognitive scientists such as Andy Clark (e.g. Clark, 1997), whose conception of emergence and of distributed cognition I have found particularly convincing. A further powerful influence at the interpersonal level has been Conversation Analysis (CA), particularly the work of Emanuel Schegloff, Charles Goodwin and others (e.g. Goodwin, 1995; Schegloff, 2003) who have used CA to analyse interactions involving people with communication impairments, and who tend to see manifestations of the impairment as evidence of interactive solutions to underlying problems, rather than as primary deficits per se. A related influence is the work of Herb Clark (e.g. Clark, 1996), whose 'joint action theory' – a blend of CA, social psychology and reworked elements of Austin's original version of Speech Act Theory – sees communicative interaction between individuals as indivisibly conjoint, rather than being reducible to the sum of their separate contributions. A further interwoven strand is the view of Charles Goodwin and others (e.g. Goodwin, 2000a) – also taken on board by Clark – that interpersonal communication is inextricably multimodal – i.e. that separate symbolic systems such as language, gesture and facial expression fuse together into a semiotic whole during communication. Finally, although it a) is much narrower in scope, b) sees theory of mind as the sole cognitive determinant of pragmatics and c) emphasizes the perspective of the hearer over that of the speaker, I have found Sperber and Wilson's Relevance Theory (Sperber and Wilson, 1995) an impressive account of the way in which shifting focus from pragmatics as behaviour to its cognitive foundations affords a strong sense of explanation.

1.3   Outline

The main points covered in the book are summarized below.

Perhaps inevitably, though necessarily, Chapter 2 begins with terminology. For example, it appears that linguists and language pathologists tend to make rather different assumptions about the link between pragmatics and language. To accommodate both views, a semiotic definition of pragmatics is adopted. A survey of how a range of theories and analytical frameworks has been applied in the analysis of pragmatic impairment shows that they are generally more effective at description than explanation. It is concluded that, in order to provide an acccount of pragmatic ability and disability adequate for the needs of clinicians (which turn out to be far more extensive and exacting than those of linguists), a holistic account is required which is able to explain the underlying causes of pragmatic impairment in addition to its behavioural symptoms. Because of its greater comprehensiveness, such an account should also be of help in explaining normal pragmatic behaviour too.

Chapter 3 considers to what extent pragmatics may be seen either as a discrete level of language or as a mental module. Evidence is provided from a wide range of communication impairments which suggests that the modular status of various linguistic and cognitive systems which contribute to pragmatic behaviour is far from unequivocal. This is partly a function of the difference between analytical methods which aim to identify dissociations between putative modular entities, and others which focus on associations and interactions. Because pragmatics, broadly defined, appears to be implicated in the entire range of communication impairments whatever their etiology, it is concluded that it may be more helpful – at least heuristically – to see it as the emergent product of the way cognitive and linguistic processes interact, rather than as a primary modular entity.

Chapter 4 presents an emergentist model of typical and atypical pragmatic functioning, and shows that pragmatic disruption is an inescapable corollary even of communication disorders not normally seen as paradigm cases of pragmatic impairment. The notion of choice is at the heart of the model, which includes not just linguistic choice but choice across the entire range of semiotic systems together with their input and output modalities. Pragmatics is defined as the emergent consequence of interactions between cognitive, semiotic and sensorimotor systems within, and between, communicating individuals. In accounting for pragmatic ability and disability, the burden of explanation thus shifts from the communicative behaviour itself to the constitutive elements and interactions from which it emerges. These are examined in Chapters 5–8.

Chapter 5 considers the role played by inference, theory of mind, executive function, memory, emotion and attitude in pragmatics and pragmatic impairment. Each of these areas of cognition is scrutinized in terms of how its impairment affects pragmatic performance by restricting communicative choice, and how it interacts with semiotic, sensorimotor and other cognitive elements both intrapersonally (i.e. within a single individual) and interpersonally (i.e. between communicating individuals). It is concluded that pragmatics is not exclusively linked to any single cognitive process, but typically draws on multiple areas of cognition. Furthermore, there is considerable interaction and co-dependency between the various separate cognitive systems, and there are good grounds for seeing each system as the emergent product of subsidiary interactions.

Pragmatic impairment has been most strongly associated with cognitive dysfunction, but in Chapter 6 the pragmatic consequences of linguistic impairment at all levels are seen to be equally complex and extensive. The pragmatic effects of impairments of phonology, prosody, syntax, morphology, semantics and discourse are considered both separately and together. Co-dependency between all of these, both intrapersonally and interpersonally, and also between them and cognitive and sensorimotor processes, turns out to be considerable.

In Chapter 7 the use of hearing and vision to process meaning and the use of motor output systems (such as the vocal tract, hands, arms, face, eyes and body) to express meaning are examined. Reduced capacity in any of these systems restricts communicative choice, which shows them to be as implicated in pragmatic functioning as cognition and language.

Whereas Chapters 5–7 focus on the elements whose interactions determine the nature of pragmatic ability and disability, in Chapter 8 attention shifts to the interactions themselves and the way in which dysfunction at any point in the system – whether it be cognitive, semiotic or sensorimotor – triggers compensation within the system as a whole. It is argued that the importance and pervasiveness of compensatory adaptation warrants its being given centre stage in any account of pragmatic impairment. Where most accounts of compensation focus exclusively on either the intrapersonal or the interpersonal domain, it is argued that the two should be seen as acting in synergy. A detailed case study is presented of a child whose communication problems can only be satisfactorily explained once compensatory adaptation in both domains is taken into account.

Chapter 9 recapitulates the main arguments, and compares the approach of emergentist pragmatics (EP) with that of other pragmatic theories and frameworks and also considers its clinical implications. The main distinguishing features claimed for EP are that:

- it is broader in scope than most theories, but also more comprehensive
- it focuses on underlying causes of pragmatic behaviour, as well as the behaviour itself
- it sees the underlying determinants of pragmatics as complex interactions between cognitive, semiotic and sensorimotor systems rather than the outcome of a single process
- it integrates both intrapersonal and interpersonal perspectives
- it explicitly accounts for both pragmatic ability and disability.

The major clinical implications are the need to:

- reconsider the use of terms such as 'pragmatic impairment', which are too vague, and used too inconsistently, to be clinically helpful
- address the underlying causes of pragmatic impairment, rather than simply focusing on symptoms and descriptions of pragmatic behaviour

- treat the communicating dyad, as well as the individual, as a complex interactive cognitive, semiotic and sensorimotor system
- acknowledge the centrality of compensatory adaptation in pragmatic impairment
- treat compensatory adaptation as a composite of both intrapersonal and interpersonal interactions.

2   Pragmatic theory and pragmatic impairment

2.1   Introduction

To date, the study of pragmatic impairments has had virtually no impact on pragmatic theory or on mainstream pragmatics generally. This is a pity. Linguistic communication typically appears to be a single, seamless process, but it is only when it goes wrong that we tend to have any inkling that it is really a complex of interacting processes. Unlike clinicians, who need to understand a condition in its entirety in order to plan appropriate intervention, pragmatic theorists have had the luxury of being able to focus only on the specific features which are of interest to them. It is a contention of this book that a holistic and detailed understanding of pragmatic impairment can make a significant contribution to the study of normal pragmatic behaviour, and that the potential benefits for pragmatic theory are considerable.

In contrast, the impact of pragmatic theory on the study of pragmatic impairment has been extensive. However, despite the increasing clinical application of pragmatic theories over the last couple of decades, our understanding of communication disorders has, as I aim to show, not always been particularly well served by it. This is partly because of the heterogeneity and breadth of pragmatics as a discipline. Thus 'pragmatic impairment' and other cognate terms are used to describe an excessively wide range of disparate conditions, and are often used inconsistently. Problems with the clinical use of pragmatic labels have arisen because the terminology and conceptual apparatus of pragmatics is derived from disciplines such as linguistics, philosophy of language and sociology, which are more concerned with abstract models on the one hand and with the description of social behaviour on the other. This apparatus has been imported wholesale and without adaptation into clinical linguistics, but it is not always well suited to the needs of language pathologists and has led to a great deal of confusion in the clinical diagnosis of pragmatic impairment, and in regard to the nature of pragmatic impairment itself.

In this chapter, I will first of all consider some differences in the way linguists and language pathologists appear to define and conceptualize pragmatics, and then examine the application of pragmatic theories and analytical frameworks in studies of pragmatic impairment. I will conclude that a holistic approach is best suited to the needs of clinicians, and that such an approach may in turn have benefits for linguists, too.

2.2   Defining pragmatic ability and disability

2.2.1   Linguistic vs non-linguistic pragmatics

Language is central in mainstream pragmatics. Sperber and Wilson (2005: 468) define pragmatics in general terms as 'the study of the use of language' and more specifically as 'the study of how contextual factors interact with linguistic meaning in the interpretation of utterances'. Virtually all pragmatics textbooks similarly assume the centrality of language (e.g. Green, 1989; Grundy, 2000; Leech, 1983; Levinson, 1983; Mey, 2001; Thomas, 1995; Verschueren, 1999; Yule, 1996). It is rather surprising, therefore, to find that a great deal of published work on pragmatic impairment appears to make no such assumption. Rather than an exclusive focus on language, it is common instead to find non-linguistic features of communication such as gaze, gesture, posture and social rapport described as examples of pragmatics even when they occur *independently* of language use. Dronkers, Ludy and Redfern (1998), for example, assume that pragmatic behaviour is isolable and distinct from linguistic behaviour, as is evident from the title of their article, 'Pragmatics in the absence of verbal language'. Others feel a need to distinguish at least implicitly between linguistic and non-linguistic pragmatics by using terms such as 'pragmatic *language* impairment (PLI)' (Bishop, 2000) and 'pragmatic *language* disorders' (Martin and McDonald, 2003; my emphasis). It would seem that many language pathologists, despite acknowledging mainstream pragmatics as their information source, at least covertly take a much broader and less exclusively language-oriented view than linguists – far closer, in fact, to Morris's original semiotic conception of pragmatics as 'the study of the relation of signs to interpreters' (Morris, 1938: 6). Why should this be so? Firstly, clinicians frequently encounter individuals with minimal linguistic capacity – for example, following a stroke – who are nonetheless able to communicate quite effectively using nonlinguistic and nonverbal means such as body posture, gaze and gesture (e.g. Goodwin, 2000b). (Indeed, therapy often concentrates on these spared abilities as a means of compensating for linguistic disability (Carlomagno, 1994; Davis and Wilcox, 1985.)) At the same time, they are equally familiar with the converse situation – for example, individuals with autistic spectrum disorder who are unable to communicate effectively despite having reasonably good linguistic abilities (e.g. Blank, Gessner and Esposito, 1979). The key factor which differentiates such cases is the level of competence in a range of nonlinguistic cognitive capacities such as memory, attention and inferential reasoning, and clinicians have thus tended to be far more aware than linguists of the role of cognition in pragmatic functioning (Perkins, 1998c). A further motivation for a semiotic view of pragmatics comes from neurolinguistics, which suggests that much of what is commonly understood as pragmatic competence is controlled by the right cerebral hemisphere, as opposed to linguistic competence, which is subserved to a much greater extent by the left hemisphere (Paradis, 1998a). This apparent double dissociation between language and pragmatics evident in clinical research suggests that, rather than focusing so exclusively on linguistic pragmatics, as linguists and pragmaticists have tended to do so far, it might be more fruitful to consider in a more integrated fashion the role of nonlinguistic as well as linguistic, and of nonverbal as well as verbal, competencies in pragmatic functioning. Thus we might define pragmatics generally as (the study of) the use of linguistic and nonlinguistic capacities for the purpose of communication. Some progress in this direction has been made by theories of pragmatics such as Relevance Theory (Sperber and Wilson, 1995), which emphasizes that language is one communication 'aid' among many, albeit a uniquely complex and central one. Also, the pragmatic significance of the way in which communication may be distributed across both verbal and nonverbal modalities has started to be addressed in the psychological, sociological and anthropological study of language (Clark, 1996; Kendon, 2004; McNeill, 2000a) and in the study of language development (Kelly, 2001). What has not yet been fully appreciated, though, is the unique insight into the nature of such an extended view of pragmatics afforded by the study of communication disorders.

2.2.2   Normal vs abnormal pragmatic behaviour

Researchers who wish to study the nature of pragmatic impairment naturally look to mainstream pragmatics for their definitions, theoretical constructs, terminology and analytical methods. Rather than definitions of pragmatics itself, which are invariably the focus of pragmatics textbooks, their starting point has to be some account of what constitutes 'normal' pragmatic *ability* or 'typical' pragmatic *behaviour* in order thereby to be able to identify and characterize the pathologically abnormal and atypical. One difficulty with this is that, although it is generally assumed in mainstream pragmatics that we are attempting to describe what typically occurs in the normal population, definitions of what counts as normal are rarely made explicit, if they are considered at all. For example, Grice's Maxim of Quantity states: '1. Make your contribution as informative as is required (for the current purposes of the exchange). 2. Do not make your contribution more informative than is required' (Grice, 1975: 45), but there is no account of how informative or uninformative a contribution would need to be to count as an instance of abnormal or pathological behaviour. Quantifiable definitions of pragmatic ability – as opposed to disability – are rare (see, for example, Slugoski and Wilson's (1998) operational account of pragmatic competence). Quantifiable definitions of pragmatic *disability*, on the other hand, are far more common but typically vague. In most accounts, a range of supposedly normal (or abnormal) pragmatic behaviours are simply given, and individuals are described as being pragmatically impaired if either a sufficient number of behaviours are (or are not) observed or their performance of the behaviours meets (or fails to meet) specified criteria of acceptability or of frequency within a given time frame or situation.

A number of checklists, or 'profiles' (Crystal, 1992), of pragmatic behaviour have been devised for clinical use, and although they are largely unknown outside clinical circles, they are nevertheless a potentially useful resource in mainstream pragmatics in that they aim to provide an itemized and comprehensive account of pragmatic competence (albeit in terms of behaviours which are susceptible to impairment), and are often based on careful observation. Some incorporate an inventory of items derived from a particular theory of pragmatics (e.g. Damico (1985) and Bloom *et al.* (1999), based on Grice's maxims of conversation) or a particular analytical approach (e.g. Perkins, Whitworth and Lesser (1997), based on Conversation Analysis), though most are constructed around an eclectic set of items drawn from a range of sources where theoretical consistency is sacrificed for comprehensiveness. Table 2.1 lists the main section headings in three commonly used profiles.

In each of these profiles, the main categories are further subdivided into 30, 50 and 23 subcategories respectively. For example, *sociolinguistic sensitivity* in Penn (1985) includes 'polite forms; reference to interlocutor; placeholders; fillers, stereotypes, acknowledgments; self correction; comment clauses; sarcasm/humour; control of direct speech; indirect speech acts'; *turn taking* in Prutting and Kirchner (1983) includes 'initiation; response; repair/revision; pause time; interruption/overlap; feedback to speakers; adjacency; contingency; quantity/conciseness'; and *inappropriate initiation* in Bishop (1998) includes 'talks to anyone and everyone; talks too much; keeps telling people things that they know already; talks to himself; talks repetitively about things that no-one is interested in; asks questions although he knows the answers'. Some checklists target

Table 2.1 *Main category groups of three pragmatic impairment checklists*

Profile of communicative appropriateness (Penn, 1985)	The pragmatic protocol (Prutting and Kirchner, 1983)	Children's communicative checklist (pragmatics sections) (Bishop, 1998)
Response to interlocutor	Speech acts	Inappropriate initiation
Control of semantic content	Topic	Coherence
Cohesion	Turn taking	Stereotyped conversation
Fluency	Lexical selection/use across speech acts	Use of conversational context
Sociolinguistic sensitivity	Stylistic variation	Conversational rapport
	Intelligibility and prosodics	
	Kinesics and proxemics	

pragmatic competence in particular clinical conditions such as aphasia (Whitworth, Perkins and Lesser, 1997), right hemisphere damage (Bryan, 1989), traumatic brain injury (Benjamin *et al.*, 1989), cognitive impairments such as dementia and Parkinson's disease (Perkins *et al.*, 1997) and children with developmental language disorders (Bishop, 1998; Roth and Spekman, 1984a, 1984b), while others are more generic in nature and applicable to a range of conditions (Dewart and Summers, 1988, 1995; Prutting and Kirchner, 1983). Most checklists require direct observation of the individual(s) being described, though some are based either partially (Perkins *et al.*, 1997) or wholly (Bishop, 1998) on the report of others, such as carers or parents, who have experienced the individual's pragmatic behaviour at close quarters over an extended period of time. Finally, a number of checklists are available based on the observation of pragmatic behaviour in typically developing children over a given age range, and are therefore able to provide developmental norms for comparative purposes in the assessment of pragmatic impairment in children (e.g. Gutfreund, Harrison and Wells, 1989; Ninio *et al.*, 1991; Prinz and Weiner, 1987; Shulman, 1985).

Despite their undoubted value as a means of comparing various clinical and healthy populations, or individuals at different stages of treatment, and of characterizing normal pragmatic competence, checklists have clear limitations. Firstly, although they provide a description of pragmatic ability and disability, they typically afford little sense of explanation at a theoretical level or in terms of any underlying contributory factors. Secondly, as will be apparent from Table 2.1, there is considerable variation among different checklists both in terms of what items are included or left out, and also how individual items are described. In other words, there are as many implicit definitions of pragmatic ability and disability as there are checklists. Thirdly, because checklist items are typically selected on the basis of observation and impression, their capacity to characterize a specific type of pragmatic impairment uniquely and objectively must be viewed with caution. For example, in a survey of a wide range of checklists, case studies and group studies, all purporting to provide a description of a condition known as 'semantic-pragmatic disorder',[1] Taylor (2000) found so many variations and contradictions that, other than a shared focus on conversational difficulties, there was a relative lack of consistent common ground between them. The very existence of such a large number of pragmatic checklists (for further examples, see Conti-Ramsden and McTear (1995), Smith and Leinonen (1992) and Penn (1999)) is indicative of a need to accommodate a wide range of opinions on the precise nature of pragmatic impairment, and by implication a lack of agreement on how the term should be defined.

2.2.3   Neurological, cognitive and behavioural perspectives

We have noted above that language pathologists tend to be far more aware than linguists of the neurological and cognitive substrates of pragmatic behaviour. How important are these factors in understanding the nature of pragmatics, and are some more important than others?

In recent years, and particularly in the case of acquired communication disorders in adults, the neurological basis of pragmatics has increasingly become a major focus of study (Paradis, 1998b; Stemmer, 1999b), and the term 'neuropragmatics' is often used when impaired pragmatic functioning is being described (Stemmer, forthcoming). Sometimes there may appear to be an assumption that pragmatic impairment can *only* be described in neurological terms (e.g. 'A few ... theories ... do not even consider possible relations between pragmatics and the brain and therefore cannot accommodate clinical data' (Bara, Bosco and Bucciarelli, 1999: 523)). However, despite the fact that pragmatics – like all capacities and behaviours pertaining to the human organism – must involve neural mechanisms at some level (an uncontroversial view as pointed out by

---

[1] Semantic-pragmatic disorder was originally identified and named by Rapin and Allen (1983). Its status has been somewhat controversial, being seen by some as a mild form of autism (Brook and Bowler, 1992) and by others as a distinct condition in its own right (Bishop, 1987). Many clinicians have now abandoned the term in favour of 'pragmatic language impairment' (PLI), which is used to refer to children with pragmatic difficulties in the absence of impairments found in autism and specific language impairment (Bishop, 2000; Bishop *et al.*, 2000).

Chomsky (Stemmer, 1999a: 400–1)), pragmatic impairment is also and simultaneously a cognitive/linguistic and a social/behavioural phenomenon, and may be validly described at these levels whether linked to neural activity or not. Discussions of neuropragmatics are invariably couched in terms of communication, language and cognition, yet the distinctions between these levels are not always made clear. Bara (2000), for example, moves between terms involving 'neuro' and 'cognitive' as though the two were effectively synonymous. The title of his article is 'Neuropragmatics: brain and communication', yet the opening sentence states, 'Our field of research is *cognitive* [my emphasis] pragmatics, that is, the theoretical and empirical study of the mental events involved in human communication' (p. 10). The problem is that, despite technological advances in areas such as functional magnetic resonance imaging, we are still a long way from being able to specify with any confidence the degree of coextensiveness between specific neural events, specific cognitive activities and specific behaviours such that we may use one to define, or posit the existence of, the others. For example, the existence of a particular class of neurons called 'mirror neurons', which appear to be involved in representing the mental states of others (sometimes referred to as having a 'theory of mind', and seen by many as crucially deficient in autism) (Gallese and Goldman, 1998) and the identification of activity in a particular locus of the brain during the performance of tasks seen as requiring a theory of mind (Fletcher *et al.*, 1995), does not necessarily entail the existence of some discrete cognitive entity called 'theory of mind', even though such a construct may be useful in theorizing at a cognitive or behavioural level. The issue of the relationship between neurological, cognitive and behavioural features of pragmatics and other related matters will be returned to in Chapter 3.

We have seen that the definitions and descriptions of pragmatic ability and disability in general use are extremely varied. In the next section I will examine the application of particular theoretical approaches to the study of pragmatic impairment to see whether they are able to lend more focus and rigour to this enterprise.

2.3   The clinical application of pragmatic theories and analytical methods

Not all theories of pragmatics have been applied in the clinical domain, and I shall restrict myself here to those which have. Bates' approach to pragmatics and communication impairment (e.g. Bates *et al.*, 1996) will be left until Chapter 3, and further theories which have not yet been clinically applied – such as Clark's 'joint action theory' (Clark, 1996) – will also be considered there.

2.3.1   Speech Act Theory

Speech Act Theory (Austin, 1962; Searle, 1969) focuses in essence on the communicative functions of utterances in terms of what the speaker aims to achieve by virtue of speaking (i.e. the illocutionary force or point of an utterance) and in terms of the resulting effect on the addressee (i.e. its perlocutionary effect). A wide range of possible speech acts have been identified and classificatory schemes have been devised for their analysis (e.g. Hancher, 1979; e.g. Searle, 1976). Much has been made of the distinction between direct and indirect speech acts. In direct speech acts, the illocutionary point is evident from the grammatical and semantic properties of the utterance – for example, *Raise your right hand* is a request by virtue of its imperative form. With indirect speech acts, on the other hand, the illocutionary force is not directly derivable from the formal properties of the utterance, but must be inferred – for example, *My foot hurts* could, in certain circumstances, be taken to mean 'get off my foot' and its illocutionary force would therefore be that of a request, rather than a statement, as its indicative syntax might initially suggest.

Speech Act Theory has been used to analyse communication disorders in a range of clinical populations, including adults with aphasia (Wilcox and Davis, 1977) and right hemisphere damage (Hirst, LeDoux and Stein, 1984), schizophrenia (Meilijson, Kasher and Elizur, 2004) and traumatic brain injury (Bara, Tirassa and Zettin, 1997; McDonald, 1992b), and children with Asperger's syndrome (Ziatas, Durkin and Pratt, 2003), autism (Loveland *et al.*, 1988), dysfluency (Ryan, 2000), focal brain injury, hydrocephalus (Bara *et al.*, 1999) and hearing impairment (Yont, Snow and Vernon-Feagans, 2003). It has been observed, for example, that people with aphasia (resulting from damage to the anterior left hemisphere) are in some circumstances able to interpret indirect speech acts even when they cannot understand their literal meaning, whereas right hemisphere damaged patients are able to understand the literal but not the intended meaning (Hirst *et al.*, 1984). Inventories of speech acts have been devised (e.g. Ninio *et al.*, 1991) which make it possible to determine whether children are able to produce the full range of speech acts expected for their age group.

Although Speech Act Theory has been widely used in experimental studies, where the ability to produce or understand particular types of speech act is targeted, it has well-known limitations (Allan, 1998; Levinson, 1983), some of which can cause problems for the analysis of clinical data. Firstly, Speech Act Theory has tended to focus on single, isolated utterances independently of discourse context (Geis, 1995). In Transcript 2.1, spoken by a man with traumatic brain injury, each utterance is well formed and has the illocutionary force of a statement. However, as a piece of discourse it lacks coherence because of its sudden inexplicable topic shifts. Speech Act Theory has little to say about this.

Transcript 2.1

I have got faults and . my biggest fault is . I do enjoy sport . it's something that I've always done . I've done it all my life . I've nothing but respect for my mother and father and . my sister . and basically sir . I've only come to this conclusion this last two months . and . as far as I'm concerned . my sister doesn't exist. (from Perkins, Body and Parker, 1995: 305)

A further assumption commonly made by speech act theorists is that each utterance has only one illocutionary point. The untenability of this assumption has been made clear particularly in studies of psychotherapeutic discourse (e.g. Labov and Fanshel, 1977; Stiles, 1992), and is also patently evident in interactions involving communication-impaired individuals. In Transcript 2.2, from a conversation between T, a speech and language therapist, and P, a 5-year-old boy with autistic spectrum disorder, there are several problematic exchanges as T tries to elicit the name of P's teacher.

Transcript 2.2

```
 1  T:  what's your teacher called?
 2  P:  Benton
 3  T:  that's your school . Benton
 4      and what are your teachers called?
 5  P:  oh . cos it's my friend
 6  T:  cos it's your friend?
 7  P:  yeah
 8  T:  you've got a teacher . Mrs ...
 9  P:  Allport
10  T:  Mrs Allport
11      any other teacher?
```

To label T's responses in lines 3, 6, 8 and 10 simply as 'assertives', as suggested by Searle (1979), tells us nothing about the subtle and varied ways in which these utterances indicate in addition the relative appropriateness of P's preceding utterance. In line 3, T both accepts yet supportively corrects P's utterance in line 2. Her utterance in line 6 is simultaneously an indication that P's preceding turn is not what T expected, a clarification request and an invitation to respond. T's utterance in line 8 reformulates her question from line 1, but as a statement frame with an empty slot which P is invited to fill. Finally, in line 10 she accepts P's preceding utterance by repeating it in an appropriate frame, and in line 11 implicitly indicates its correctness by moving on to a further question.

Viewed in this way, each utterance can be seen to have a range of distinguishable illocutionary purposes in accordance with the requirements of multiple agendas. As originally construed, Speech Act Theory is not well equipped to handle this.

2.3.2 Conversational Implicature

Grice's theory of Conversational Implicature proposes that all conversants follow a 'Cooperative Principle' according to which we generally assume that what is said to us is said in good faith, and is furthermore at some level truthful, relevant, and as clear and explicit as it needs to be as required by the situation (Grice, 1975). These latter conditions are described as 'Maxims of Conversation', which may be glossed as: 'Don't say any more or less than you need to' (Maxim of Quantity); 'Don't say anything you believe to be false or for which you lack adequate evidence' (Maxim of Quality); 'Be relevant' (Maxim of Relevance); and 'Don't be obscure or ambiguous, but be brief and orderly' (Maxim of Manner). Maxims may be broken in order to trigger 'implicatures'. For example, in the following exchange,

A: I love you.
B: And I'm the sugar plum fairy.

under certain circumstances, if B's utterance is taken literally it appears to break both the Maxim of Quality (i.e. it is untrue) and the Maxim of Relevance. However, if we assume that B is 'implicating' (i.e. intending A to understand) 'I don't believe you' by saying something he believes to be equally false, then we can derive an interpretation that is clearly not breaking these maxims at all.

Grice's theory has been widely used in research on communication impaired populations, including adults with aphasia and right hemisphere damage (Ahlsén, 1993; Bloom *et al.*, 1999; Foldi, 1987; Kasher *et al.*, 1999; Stemmer, Giroux and Joanette, 1994), traumatic brain injury (McDonald, 1992a, 1992b, 1993a), learning disability (Brinton and Fujiki, 1994) and schizophrenia (Tényi *et al.*, 2002), and children with autism (Surian, Baron-Cohen and van der Lely, 1996) and specific language impairment (Bishop and Adams, 1992). Kasher *et al.* (1999), for example, devised an 'implicatures battery' based on Grice's maxims to assess the ability of left and right brain damaged stroke patients to derive implicatures based on both verbal and nonverbal material. Both groups were significantly impaired compared to age-matched normal controls, leading the authors to conclude that both cerebral hemispheres contribute to the processing of implicatures.

Like Speech Act Theory, despite having served as an important conceptual framework for understanding pragmatic impairment, Grice's theory of Conversational Implicature is not always easy to apply in the analysis of clinical data. In Transcript 2.3, a speech and language therapist (T) and a young boy with autistic spectrum disorder (F) are looking at a picture.

Transcript 2.3

1 T: what are they eating?
2 F: cake
3 T: who's holding the cake?
4 F: a circle
5 T: who's eating the sandwich?
6 F: the bread

F's utterances in lines 4 and 6 are clearly anomalous in some way – and in Gricean terms one might say that they are breaking the Maxim of Relevance. However, they are perhaps not entirely irrelevant in that the cake has a circular shape and the sandwich is partly made of bread, and it is not clear, furthermore, that the child is being irrelevant intentionally and therefore trying to trigger implicatures (and, if so, what they might be). Transcript 2.4 is from a conversation between a therapist (T) and a similarly impaired child (G) also discussing a picture.

Transcript 2.4

1   T: why's that man got a bandage?
2   G: plaster
3   T: he's got a plaster. why's he got a plaster?
4   G: on the boy
5   T: on the boy?
6   G: he's hurt his knee
7   T: I wonder how he hurt his knee
8   G: yeah
9   T: I wonder what he did
10 G: sit on a chair
11 T: is it summertime?
12 G: er . yeah
13 T: is it? how do you know?
14 G: erm . they've got a pram

If this were a conversation between unimpaired individuals, one might assume that G was deliberately being irrelevant and/or obscure (i.e. breaking two maxims) in an attempt to trigger implicatures such as 'G doesn't want to answer T's question' or 'G is not interested in this topic'. However, in the case of this particular child we can be fairly certain that he is being as truthful, explicit, clear and to the point as he can and is not knowingly breaking any maxims. Judging by T's apparent acceptance of G's anomalous responses as valid, it is likely that her awareness of his pragmatic impairment leads her to discount such implicatures.

This point is often missed in clinical protocols based on Grice's maxims, where degree of pragmatic impairment is seen as a function of how many (and/or which) maxims are broken. Such judgements are invariably made from the perspective of an objective observer who makes implicit comparisons with 'normal' conversational behaviour. However, when seen from the perpective of the patient, things look quite different and more often than not there is no intention to break any maxims.

2.3.3   Relevance Theory

Relevance Theory takes a rather different approach from Speech Act Theory and Conversational Implicature in that it characterizes pragmatics in terms of cognitive processing rather than contextualized action or usage principles (Sperber and Wilson, 1995). It has been used to analyse the communication of adults with Asperger's syndrome (Happé, 1991), dementia (Garcia et al., 2001), frontal lobe deficits (McDonald and Pearce, 1996), right hemisphere damage (Dipper, Bryan and Tyson, 1997), schizophrenia (Mitchley et al., 1998) and traumatic brain injury (McDonald, 1999), and of children with autism (Frith, 1989) and various other pragmatic difficulties (Leinonen and Kerbel, 1999; Schelletter and Leinonen, 2003). According to Relevance Theory an utterance is seen as 'relevant' to the extent that it guarantees enough 'effects' to merit the hearer's attention while at the same time putting the hearer to no undue effort in order to achieve this goal. This is known as the 'principle of relevance'. What this effectively means is that we assume that any utterance addressed to us takes the form it does for a good reason, and that any extra effort required to process it (e.g. working out the punchline of a joke) guarantees some kind of pay-off (e.g. amusement). Dipper et al. (1997) found that the Principle of Relevance was evident in text processing by a group of adults with right hemisphere damage (RHD). Compared with normal controls, they derived limited linguistic information from texts – in particular, the procedural information provided by discourse connectives – and instead relied excessively on encyclopedic knowledge. The fact that the RHD patients could justify their wrong answer shows that the principle of relevance applies (i.e. there was a rationale that could be interpreted in terms of contextual effects and processing costs), but the different balance of inputs to its computation resulted in different outputs from what is found in the normal population.

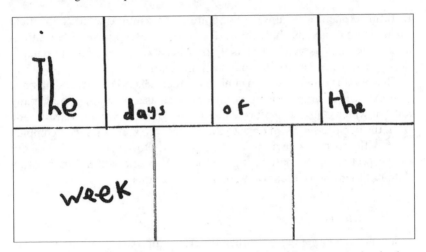

Fig. 2.1 The response of a child with autism to the request 'write the days of the week in these seven boxes'

Relevance Theory provides a useful means of characterizing the effortfulness often experienced in interactions with communication impaired individuals. For example, Figure 2.1 shows the response of a child with autism who was given a piece of paper with seven rectangles drawn on it and asked to 'write the days of the week in these seven boxes' (Perkins and Firth, 1991).

Although this might seem a wilful and deliberately obtuse misreading of the speaker's intention, this was certainly not the case and the child was clearly trying to do what he thought was required. Given the child's obvious inferential difficulties, with hindsight the speaker might have phrased the request far more explicitly – and laboriously – as: 'write Monday in the first box, Tuesday in the second box ...' and so on. In other words, once the speaker takes on board that in conversations with autistic people one effectively does not share the same 'cognitive environment', one can readjust the weighting of the equation between processing effort and communicative effects to compensate for this. In short, for effective communication to be achieved, the autistic person's inferential burden must be taken on by the interlocutor, who is required to expend greater effort in being more linguistically explicit and thus leave less to infer.

According to Sperber and Wilson (1995: 162), unlike Grice's Cooperative Principle and maxims which are norms that must be followed, or violated to achieve special effects, '[c]ommunicators do not "follow" the principle of relevance; and they could not violate it even if they wanted to' because human cognition is intrinsically relevance-oriented. This is so fundamental that it applies even in the case of individuals with a communication impairment (Wilson, personal communication). This sometimes appears to be misunderstood. Leinonen *et al.* (2000), for example, refer to cases of children not making appropriate inferences as instances where 'the principle of relevance is not working appropriately or is only working up to a point' (p. 178), and Leinonen and Kerbel (1999) state '[w]e would conclude that Sarah, and probably many other children with pragmatic impairments, fail to operate with the principle of relevance adequately' (p. 387). Presumably what they must mean by this is that these children have a problem with *computing* relevance, rather than with applying the principle. As noted above in the case of the autistic boy and the study by Dipper *et al.* (1997), judgements may vary regarding the nature of the different inputs into the computation of relevance and their relative weightings, but the principle itself cannot but apply.

Relevance Theory models communication from the perspective of the hearer, and some have criticized Sperber and Wilson for failing to take sufficient account of the collaborative and reciprocal nature of communication between individuals (e.g. Clark, 1987; Wilks, 1987). In Chapter 4, some of the insights provided by Relevance Theory will be incorporated into an interactive model, which specifies, for example, the role played by inferential/deductive processes in determining output as well as input.

2.3.4   Discourse Analysis

In clinical linguistics, discourse impairments are often treated as a diagnostic category in their own right, distinct from pragmatic impairments, though in many cases the difference is little more than terminological and depends on the theoretical background of the framework being used, the academic tradition from which it derives and the particular phenomenon which is the object of scrutiny. Pragmatics may be regarded as a component of discourse to the extent that factors such as inference generation and nonlinguistic context contribute to the coherence of spoken and written 'text'. At the same time, discourse may be seen as a component of pragmatics to the extent that text which either precedes or follows a given utterance forms part of the context which helps to determine the utterance's meaning. Collected works on pragmatic impairment are as likely to contain articles on discourse disability (e.g. Stemmer, 1999b) as edited books on discourse disability are likely to include chapters on pragmatic impairment (e.g. Bloom *et al.*, 1994). If the focus of one's research is phenomena such as coherence, cohesion, discourse markers, information structure, narrative or topic, it is more likely to be referred to as discourse. If it focuses on issues such as implicature, inference, reference, politeness or speech acts, it will usually be considered to come under the heading of pragmatics. Conversation is equally comfortable in both camps. As we shall see later, a clinical perspective makes it clear that discourse and pragmatic impairments – however one wishes to label them – are linked to the same range of underlying cognitive, linguistic and sensorimotor functions, and this may provide a useful means of addressing terminological inconsistency.

Discourse Analysis in various guises has been used to study a wide variety of communication impairments, as can be seen in Table 2.2.

Table 2.2 *Discourse analytic studies of communication impairment*

Type of impairment	Examples of studies using discourse analysis
amnesia	Caspari and Parkinson (2000)
aphasia	Armstrong (1987, 1991); Berko Gleason *et al.* (1980); Chapman, Highley and Thompson (1998); Christiansen (1995); Huber (1990); Kimelman (1999); Lemme, Hedberg and Bottenberg (1984); Lock and Armstrong (1997); Orange *et al.* (1998); Perkins *et al.* (1999); Simmons-Mackie and Damico (1996); Ulatowska and Chapman (1994)
Asperger's syndrome	Adams *et al.* (2002)
autism in adults	Dobbinson, Perkins and Boucher (1997, 1998, 2003)
autism in children	McCaleb and Prizant (1985); Loveland, Kehres and Sigman (1993); Loveland *et al.* (1990); Tager-Flusberg (1995); Thurber and Tager-Flusberg (1993)
dementia	Cherney and Canter (1990); Chenery and Murdoch (1994); de Santi *et al.* (1994); Ehrlich, Obler and Clark (1997); Guendouzi and Müller (2001, 2002); Mentis, Biggs-Whitaker and Gramigna (1995); Nicholas *et al.* (1985); Ripich and Terrell (1988); Ripich, Carpenter and Ziol (2000)
Down's syndrome	Loveland *et al.* (1990)
dyslexia	Snyder and Downey (1991)
fetal alcohol syndrome	Coggins, Friet and Morgan (1998)
focal brain injury	Dennis (1998); Reilly, Bates and Marchman (1998)
fragile X syndrome	Sudhalter and Belser (2001)
frontal lobe deficit	McDonald and Pearce (1996)
hearing impairment	Kretschmer and Kretschmer (1994)
hemidecorticate children	Lovett, Dennis and Newman (1986)
hydrocephalus	Barnes and Dennis (1998); Dennis, Jacennik and Barnes (1994)
learning disability	Donahue (1994); Griffith, Ripich and Dastoli (1986); Thurber and Tager-Flusberg (1993)
mania	Wykes and Leff (1982)
posterior fossa tumour	Hudson and Murdoch (1992)
psychosis	Chapman *et al.* (1998); Laine *et al.* (1998); Lock and Armstrong (1997); Ramanathan (1997); Ribeiro (1993, 1994)

Table 2.2 *(cont.)*

Type of impairment	Examples of studies using discourse analysis
right hemisphere damage	Brady *et al.* (2005, 2003); Brownell and Stringfellow (1999); Joanette and Goulet (1990, 1993); Molloy, Brownell and Gardner (1990); Sherratt and Penn (1990); Tompkins *et al.* (2001); Winner *et al.* (1998)
schizophrenia in adults	Rochester, Martin and Thurston (1977); Wykes and Leff (1982)
schizophrenia in children	Caplan (1996); Dennis *et al.* (1998); Ewing-Cobbs *et al.* (1998)
semantic pragmatic disorder	Adams and Bishop (1989)
traumatic brain injury in adults	Biddle, McCabe and Bliss (1996); Body and Perkins (1998); Coelho (1999); Coelho, Liles and Duffy (1991a, 1991b); Hartley and Jensen (1991, 1992); Liles *et al.* (1989); Mentis and Prutting (1987); Perkins, Body and Parker (1995); Snow and Douglas (1999); Snow, Douglas and Ponsford (1995); Togher, Hand and Code (1999)
traumatic brain injury in children	Biddle *et al.* (1996); Chapman *et al.* (1992, 1998); Dennis and Barnes (1990); Jordan, Murdoch and Buttsworth (1991); Van Leer and Turkstra (1999)
specific language impairment	Conti-Ramsden and Friel-Patti (1983); Miranda, McCabe and Bliss (1998); Stojanovik, Perkins and Howard (2002)
stuttering	Trautman *et al.* (1999)
Williams syndrome	Rossen *et al.* (1996); Stojanovik *et al.* (2002, 2004)

I shall restrict myself here to four examples of the way in which discourse may be impaired, together with some suggestions for clinical data analysis.

Individuals with autistic spectrum disorder (ASD) often have problems seeing the relationship between events in a narrative structure. When asked to tell the story in the picture sequence shown in Figure 2.2, one child with ASD said: 'he runs into the road and then the postman who's driving the ambulance knocks him down'.[2]

When presented with the pictures shown in Figure 2.3 in random order and asked to assemble them into a story sequence, he produced the arrangement shown. When this was corrected, as seen in Figure 2.4, he described the resulting story as follows: 'so – he puts them in the vase and then – he puts them back on and it's nice and then he puts them in the bin'.

---

[2] The pictures in Figures 2.2, 2.3 and 2.4 are from the LDA Language Cards (Sequential Thinking) and reproduced by kind permission of LDA, Abbeygate House, East Road, Cambridge CB1 1DB, UK.

Fig. 2.2 Narrative picture sequence

Fig. 2.3 A child's incorrect attempt to arrange a series of pictures to tell a story

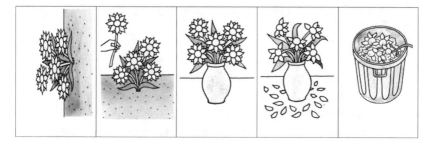

Fig. 2.4 Corrected picture sequence

Using the framework of story grammar (Mandler and Johnson, 1977; Thorndyke, 1977), one could say that the child demonstrates little notion of episodic and story constituent constructs such as setting, theme, plot, complication and resolution within a story schema. Alternatively, one might describe this as an inability to coordinate micropropositions within a superordinate macrostructure (Huber, 1990; Kintsch and van Dijk, 1978). A wide range of alternative analytical approaches is also available, but what should not be ignored in cases such as this are the possible underlying cognitive difficulties which some describe in terms of 'weak central coherence' (Happé, 1996). As we shall see later, although it may be appropriate to describe a particular behaviour as an instance of discourse or pragmatic disability, in order to treat it, it is helpful to have in addition some understanding of the cognitive or neurological dysfunction which underlies the symptoms.

In Transcript 2.5, the underlying cause of what may be seen as a discourse impairment appears to be at least partly linguistic. R is a woman in her sixties with a diagnosis of fluent receptive aphasia.

Transcript 2.5

T: do you wear them all the time or just for reading?
R: no I don't . if I want somebody to read them you see . and they go why . oh well they've seen the lady . and we've seen them . and they're going very nicely . but you see I know they're a bit awkward . because with it being a new erm . [meiz] you . things what I've got to gave them . and they're not too bad . but you see I've just got these . you see . I'm still on these

(from Perkins, 1985)

R has problems with lexical retrieval, and tends to substitute pronominal forms instead. The consequences of this for her discourse are that much of what she says is referentially opaque – i.e. a 'coherence' problem – and it is impossible to work out which pronominal forms are coreferential – i.e. a 'cohesion' problem (Halliday and Hasan, 1976).

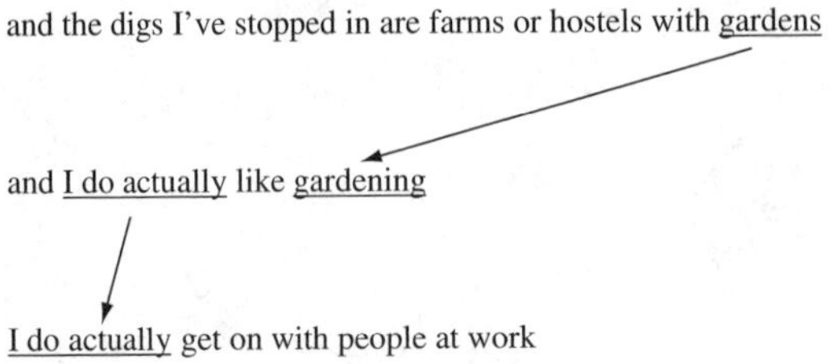

and the digs I've stopped in are farms or hostels with <u>gardens</u>

and <u>I do actually</u> like <u>gardening</u>

<u>I do actually</u> get on with people at work

Fig. 2.5 Cohesion without coherence in the conversation of a man with traumatic brain injury

Cohesion and coherence difficulties are not inevitably associated. In Figure 2.5, which shows an extract from the conversation of a man with traumatic brain injury (Perkins *et al.*, 1995: 300), there are two unexpected and incoherent topic shifts. Despite this, however, there is still lexical cohesion between each utterance as shown.

The final illustration of the application of discourse analysis to communication impairment focuses on a feature of conversational interaction. In Transcript 2.6, David, a speech and language therapist, and Pat, a woman with a sub-arachnoid haemorrhage, are looking at some photographs of Pat's family.

Transcript 2.6

```
 1  Pat:     that's Anne de la Haye my sister . and that's . Michael her youngest
             son
 2  David:   oh right yeah
 3  Pat:     and that's Jean-Baptiste de la Haye . her husband
 4  David:   good lord . that's a . [name and a half
 5  Pat:                           [big name.
 6           yes it *is* a name and a half. you're quite correct aren't you?
 7           it *is* a name and a half
 8  David:   I presume he's from France
 9  Pat:     Jean-Baptiste de la Haye *is* from France. yes
10  David:   it sounds like it
11  Pat:     it does sound like it to me actually
12           yes it does
```

A well-known feature of interactions between people of differing status such as teachers and pupils (Sinclair and Coulthard, 1975), doctors and patients (Lacoste, 1998) and therapists and clients (Letts, 1985) is the way in which the professional member of the dyad often provides evaluative feedback on the other party's contributions. In Transcript 2.6, however, it is the client Pat, rather than the therapist, who does so in lines 6–7, 9 and 11–12. This gives an impression of role reversal, though Pat appears quite unaware of this, and certainly did not behave in this way prior to her injury. The anomaly is only evident, however, if we are aware of the status and role of the speakers.

Discourse analytic approaches to conversation have sometimes been criticized for attempting to impose 'premature formalization' (Levinson, 1983: 287) in the shape of prespecified categories to analyse what is essentially an open-ended and dynamic negotiation between two or more individuals. Discourse analysis typically looks at textual patterns within a decontextualized transcript which focuses attention on what is really a *product* of the conversational interaction rather than the *process* itself (Penn, 2000). As Clark (1996: 337) puts it: 'The problem is that transcripts are like footprints in the sand. They are merely the inert traces of the activities that produced them, and impoverished traces at that.' As we shall see in later chapters, in order to understand the complex nature of phenomena such as compensatory adaptation in conversations involving individuals with a communication impairment, the interactive process itself cannot be ignored but must be given centre stage. One approach to the analysis of conversational discourse which does just this is covered in the next section.

2.3.5   Conversation Analysis

Although Conversation Analysis (CA) may be regarded as a type of discourse analysis (Schiffrin, 1994), it is being considered separately here in its own right because of the surge of interest in recent years in its application to communication disorders, particularly aphasia, and also because of its relevance to the model proposed in Chapter 4. The distinctness of CA from other approaches to discourse analysis comes from its roots in ethnomethodology (Garfinkel, 1967), its focus on conversation – or 'talk-in-interaction' – as an integral feature of social interaction, its eschewal of preconceived theoretical constructs or categories, its use of recordings of naturally occurring interactions as its primary data, and its fine-grained inductive approach to data analysis. It views conversation as being co-constructed between participants and examines the significance of sequential phenomena, and the way in which participants orient to each other and manage the interaction generally (Atkinson and Heritage, 1984). Rather than simply taking account of and reacting to context, conversation is also seen as continuously shaping and renewing the context. Features of conversation such as turn organization (Schegloff, 1996), conversational repair (Schegloff, Jefferson and Sacks, 1977), speaker overlap (Schegloff, 2000), repetition (Sorjonen, 1996) and prosody (Couper-Kuhlen and Selting, 1996) are seen as crucial in this process.

CA has been used to analyse the conversation of adults with aphasia (Beeke, Wilkinson and Maxim, 2003a, 2003b; Damico, Oelschlaeger and Simmons-Mackie, 1999; Ferguson, 1996, 1998; Goodwin, 2000b, 2003a; Heeschen and Schegloff, 1999, 2003; Klippi, 1996; Lesser and Milroy, 1993; Lind, 2002; Oelschlaeger and Damico, 1998, 2003; Perkins, 1995; Rhys, 2005; Simmons-Mackie and Damico, 1995, 1997; Springer, Miller and Bürk, 1998; Wilkinson, 1995; Wilkinson, Beeke and Maxim, 2003), autism (Dobbinson, Perkins and Boucher, 1998), commisurotomy (Schegloff, 1999, 2003), dementia (Friedland and Miller, 1999; Guendouzi and Müller, 2002; Kempler, Van Lancker and Hadler, 1984; Perkins, Whitworth and Lesser, 1998; Rhys, 2001), motor neurone disease (Bloch, 2005), psychosis (Ribeiro, 1994) and traumatic brain injury (Friedland and Miller, 1998), and of children with autism (Damico and Nelson, 2005; Dickerson *et al.*, 2005; Local and Wootton, 1995; Tarplee and Barrow, 1999; Wootton, 1999), Down's syndrome (Wootton, 1989), learning disability (Donahue, 1994), phonological impairment (Gardner, 1997), prosodic impairment (Wells and Local, 1993), psychosis (Audet and Ripich, 1994), pragmatic impairment (Radford and Tarplee, 2000), specific language impairment (Merrison and Merrison, 2005) and Williams syndrome (Tarling, Perkins and Stojanovik, 2006).

Simmons-Mackie and Damico (1996) used CA to examine discourse markers in the conversation of people with aphasia. They found that a range of verbal and nonverbal markers including neologisms, gesture, posture and eye gaze, and atypical use of repeated words such as *yes yes yes*, were used for a range of communicative functions such as reorientation towards a new topic, turn initiation and termination, participant role and propositional attitude. Despite the fact that the markers used were idiosyncratic, interlocutors appeared from their own conversational behaviour to orient towards and understand them quite quickly, and yet showed little conscious awareness of doing so. What might have easily been overlooked or simply dismissed as incidental symptoms of aphasia turned out to be the highly systematic and pragmatically skilled deployment of unusual means for usual purposes.

CA is useful for highlighting the strategies used by communicatively impaired individuals to compensate for their linguistic or cognitive problems. Transcripts 2.7 and 2.8 are from a conversation between K, a student, and B, a 12-year-old boy with Williams syndrome (Tarling *et al.*, 2006: 588). B has an IQ of 50, poor expressive and receptive syntax and word-finding problems, all of which can cause him difficulties when responding to questions. Nevertheless, although B is often unable to answer questions very well, he goes about *not* answering them in an entirely appropriate way. In Transcript 2.7 his response in lines 2–3 is hardly satisfactory in terms of its informativeness, and yet he is more than adept at the negotiation of conversational turns. Repetition of the same phrases – a common ostensible signal of 'thinking aloud' – enables him to take his turn, while at the same time indicating potential problems with completion (Clark, 2002) and therefore that K may take the floor again should she so wish.

Transcript 2.7

1 K: date of birth . when's your birthday?
2 B: mm d'oh . date of birth date of birth .
3   s s September the something September the something
4 K: September . and how old are you now?

In Transcript 2.8, when K declines the implicit offer to take the floor after a similar sequence of repetitions, B is able to self-repair in line 6 by explicitly relinquishing his turn and offering the floor to K. More informally, one might describe this as changing the topic to get himself out of a sticky situation.

Transcript 2.8

1 K: is that Rio Ferdinand? *(points at picture)*
2 B: yeah that's uh that's something something something
3   *(points at picture)*
4   . that's something Leonardinode that's something something
5   something .
6   okay then . shall we get on with that again?

Thus, despite his cognitive and linguistic difficulties, B shows considerable interactional skill and copes with difficult questions in much the same way as an unimpaired speaker might.

In its emphasis on the sequential progression of conversation, CA has contributed to a perspective shift in pragmatics away from the formal properties of decontextualized utterances and texts and towards a more dynamic view of interaction. This has been of particular value in clinical linguistics in that it has highlighted the fact that a communication disorder is not the sole problem of an individual, but just one factor which impacts on interpersonal communication and which may therefore be partially resolved through the mediation of others. CA has also contributed to a better understanding of compensatory adaptations through which this may be achieved and which may thus be targeted in intervention (e.g. Lesser and Milroy, 1998; Simmons-Mackie and Damico, 1997; Whitworth *et al.*, 1997). CA is nevertheless limited in that it is solely dependent on the inductive analysis of naturally occurring conversation. There has on the whole been little interest in factors which may contribute towards an explanation of this orderliness. As Duranti (1997: 278) puts it from an anthropological perspective: 'Are ... preferences ... such as the overall reluctance to correct others ... due to universals of human politeness or are they necessary features for the survival of the species?' It was noted earlier in this chapter that pragmatics is simultaneously a neurological, cognitive and behavioural phenomenon, and a comprehensive theory of pragmatics must ultimately incorporate all of these. Levinson (1983: 367) has observed that 'in the long run CA analyses may perhaps be found deficient as rather simple reconstructions of the no doubt immensely complicated cognitive processes involved in conducting conversations', but despite a growing body of work on cognitive pragmatics we still know very little about the cognitive mechanisms which underlie the behaviours described by CA. In subsequent chapters I will attempt to make some progress in this regard.

2.4   The need for a holistic approach

Terms such as 'pragmatic impairment/disability/disorder/dysfunction' have been used to refer to behaviours found in conditions as disparate as aphasia, Asperger's syndrome, autism, dementia, Down's syndrome, focal brain injury, frontal lobe damage, hearing impairment, hydrocephalus, learning disability, right hemisphere damage and schizophrenia (Perkins, 2003). As such, they lack discrimination and are hardly adequate as diagnostic descriptors. This might not be a problem if the behaviours thus referred to were the same across all of these conditions. Unfortunately, they are not. The waters are further muddied by inconsistencies in the way the terms are used. It is highly significant that neurolinguists and clinicians have apparently felt the need to embrace a broader, semiotic view of pragmatics than most pragmatic theorists, although this has gone largely unacknowledged. This suggests that the phenomenon of pragmatic disability – and by implication pragmatic ability – is not adequately accounted for by at least some mainstream pragmatic theories. We have seen above that the theoretical constructs and analytical apparatus from a range of approaches to pragmatics enable us to describe the behaviour of people with communicative impairments reasonably well, and are to some extent inter-translatable for descriptive purposes.[3] However, although theories of pragmatics provide a means of *describing* pragmatic impairments, the level of *explanation* they afford is rarely adequate for clinicians, in that it does not translate easily into clinical

[3] See Perkins (2003) for an analysis of a single dataset using different approaches.

intervention. For example, in Transcript 2.9 the child could be *described* as breaking Grice's Maxims of Quantity, Relevance and possibly Manner ('be brief'), but such descriptive labels do not get us very far when trying to design a remedial programme. One can hardly tell the child to 'stop breaking Grice's maxims'!

Transcript 2.9

Adult: and what's in this picture?
Child: it's a sheep . on a farm . and my uncle's farm
      and it has babies . baby lambs
      and tadpoles . frogs have baby tadpoles
      but tadpoles don't have any legs . do they?
      but frogs have legs . and it was in the pond . and mommy
      saw it . . .

(from Perkins, 2002: 2)

What is needed in order to move beyond mere description is some account of the underlying causes of pragmatic impairment. As an illustration of this, consider Transcripts 2.10 and 2.11.

Transcript 2.10

Prompt: the man who sits on the bench next to the oak tree is our mayor
Gary: amen

Transcript 2.11

Adult: can you think of any more?
Matthew: a remote-controlled cactus

Transcript 2.10 shows the response of Gary, an 8-year-old boy, to a prompt from the CELF sentence recall task (Semel, Wiig and Secord, 1987), where the subject is required to repeat the sentence heard. The exchange shown in Transcript 2.11 is from a conversation between Matthew, also aged 8, and an adult who has been eliciting names for pets. Several have been correctly named immediately prior to this. Gary's and Matthew's responses may be described in similar terms as instances of pragmatically anomalous behaviour in that they appear to be irrelevant both in a Gricean and Relevance Theory sense. However, the underlying causes in each case are quite different. Gary has problems with verbal memory and syntactic comprehension. The prompt sentence is both too syntactically complex and too long for him to internally represent and retain in short-term memory. He focuses instead on the final phrase 'our mayor', which he mishears and/or misunderstands and repeats as 'amen'. Matthew, on the other hand, has a diagnosis of autistic spectrum disorder, and problems with social cognition make it difficult for him to take proper account of prior and surrounding context during conversation. His syntax and verbal memory, in contrast to Gary, are normal for his age. Clearly, any assessment or intervention based solely on a superficial pragmatic description which failed to take account of these underlying differences would be less than adequate.

What I shall propose in the remainder of this book is a holistic approach to pragmatics which takes account not only of the behaviour of individuals involved in the communicative process, but also of the underlying factors which contribute to such behaviour. One motivation for this is to meet the needs of clinicians who require such an understanding of pragmatic impairments in order to treat them. But in addition, because these needs turn out to be more exacting than those of linguists in a number of respects, the provision of such an account can also inform pragmatics more generally by focusing attention on features of communicative interaction which are not adequately considered by current theories. Any theory which purports to throw light on the nature of the human mind should be able to encompass both the normal and the pathological, and it is reasonable to assume that a single account which can explain instances of normal and abnormal behaviour in terms of a common set of mechanisms and processes is to be preferred.

3 Pragmatics and modularity: components, dissociations and associations

3.1 Introduction

It was concluded in Chapter 2 that, in order for pragmatics to be a useful concept for clinicians, it needs to be specified at least in part in terms of its various underlying contributory factors. But what are these factors, and how should we conceptualize them? Can they be grouped in such a way as to constitute a single overarching entity, or are they so disparate and diverse that no coherent notion of pragmatics is possible? In this chapter I will focus on some of the cognitive and linguistic bases of pragmatics and will consider whether pragmatics itself can be construed as a discrete component of the mind, as has been intimated by some pragmatic theorists.[1] Drawing on language pathology research, I will then examine how far the individual cognitive and linguistic dysfunctions which are seen as giving rise to pragmatic impairment may themselves be regarded as distinct mental entities; and how they relate both to each other and to the pragmatic behaviours that they engender. This will involve an examination of what has become known as the 'modularity of mind' debate. Any account of human communication which sees the role of cognition as integral – whether it be in relation to pragmatics, semantics, syntax or some other feature – would appear obliged to take a view on whether or not some or all aspects of cognitive processing are inherently modular. In other words, does the human mind consist of a set of distinct components, each purpose-built (either through evolution or ontogenesis) for a specific task, or is it instead a general-purpose problem solver?

In the account of cognitive and linguistic processing I will eventually elaborate, I will try to resist taking a hard line on this issue as far as I can. This is for several reasons. Firstly, as we shall see, there is no consistent view of what the essential characteristics of modules are supposed to be.

---

[1] Although language is widely seen as a cognitive system, I will be using 'language' and 'cognition' as shorthand terms for 'linguistic cognitive systems/processess' and 'nonlinguistic cognitive systems/processes' respectively, as is common practice.

Secondly, the evidence for the existence of modules is sometimes contradictory. And thirdly, the emergentist approach that I will be proposing is in any case compatible with either view. Although I will end up using terms such as 'memory' and 'syntax', which might appear to suggest an implicitly modular approach, I will simply be using them as flags of descriptive convenience to refer to processes or entities which appear to be implicated in the workings of cognition and language, while remaining agnostic about their precise nature as modules or otherwise.

Why bother, then, to engage with the modularity debate in the first place? The primary reason is to be able to focus on the more general conceptual and methodological distinction between dissociations and associations (which will be considered in more detail below). Compared with the amount of effort expended in trying to identify cognitive and linguistic dissociations, relatively little attention has so far been paid to the co-dependency and interaction that exists between such entities and processes, however loosely or tightly we may define them, and I aim to show that such interactions are as important a feature of mental activity as the nature of the entities and processes themselves. In addition, a preliminary consideration of cognitive and linguistic capacities as modules or otherwise will provide a foundation for their more detailed treatment in later chapters as elements of pragmatic functioning.

3.2   Modularity

Although the concept has been around for centuries, it is the particular view of modularity proposed by Fodor (1983) that has stimulated debate in recent decades. Fodor argued that various aspects of human cognition may be 'modules' – i.e. distinct and autonomous cognitive systems which are genetically hard-wired, domain-specific, fast, automatic and informationally encapsulated (i.e. their inner mechanisms cannot influence, and are not influenced by, other workings of the mind – only their outputs are available). Perceptual input systems such as visual and linguistic processing, for example, are seen by many as modular, whereas psychological processes such as deductive reasoning (which appear to cut across a range of cognitive domains) are generally viewed as non-modular, and are subsumed by Fodor under 'central systems'.

Interestingly, from the point of view of this book, many of the arguments in support of the existence of mental modules are based on clinical research evidence of apparent dissociations between various linguistic and cognitive capacities in communication disordered populations (e.g. Bellugi *et al.*, 1988; Rondal, 1994; Smith and Tsimpli, 1995; Thomas and Karmiloff-Smith, 2002; Yamada, 1990). For example, it is argued that if, following a brain injury, a person can no longer perform a particular task A, and yet is still able to successfully perform task B, we may reasonably hypothesize that the mental processes underlying task A form a distinct and self-contained cognitive system. If, in addition, we find that another person after a stroke is still able to perform task B but can no longer perform task A (i.e. a case of 'double dissociation'), our hypothesis is further strengthened and may be extended to include the distinctness of the cognitive processes underlying task B. Fodor, one of the main proponents for the existence of such discrete, self-contained cognitive systems, points out that one would also expect such patterns of dysfunction to be linked with a specific underlying neural architecture.[2]

A whole range of variants on the Fodorean theme has been suggested, extending from Sperber's proposal for massive modularity including distinct modules for individual concepts (Sperber, 1996, 2002) to non-modular connectionist-based approaches (Elman *et al.*, 1996). Karmiloff-Smith (1992) has taken issue with Fodor's stipulation of the innate specification of modules, and provided evidence for the view that much of the modularity we see in the adult brain may well be a result of the developmental process with considerable input from the environment (i.e. the so-called 'neuroconstructivist' approach (Karmiloff-Smith, 1998) discussed later in this chapter). Other features of Fodor's original specification have also been queried. Tsimpli and Smith (1998) argue that theory of mind is not informationally encapsulated and therefore only a 'quasi module'. Coltheart (1999), in a reinterpretation of Fodor's proposal, claims that the only defining feature of cognitive modules is domain-specificity,[3] the other features being merely contingent; and Sperber and Wilson have adopted a similarly looser definition – namely 'a domain- or task-specific autonomous computational mechanism' (Sperber and Wilson, 2002: 9). Finally, Jackendoff, who is interested in the way that modules 'talk to' each other, argues that modularity is best seen as a continuum, measurable in degrees, rather than as a set of absolute, discrete entities. As he puts it: '[t]wo domains connected by a narrow "information bottleneck" will be relatively modular: not very many parts of each domain can affect the other. As the interface becomes richer, more parts can interact. If communication between the two domains is wide open, it is

---

[2] Fodor's caution over this link – cf. 'I don't, however, wish to overplay this point' (1983: 99) – is often overlooked.

[3] Coltheart's definition of domain-specificity is as follows: 'a cognitive system is domain-specific if it only responds to stimuli of a particular class: thus, to say that there is a domain-specific face recognition module is to say that there is a cognitive system that responds when its input is a face, but does not respond when its input is, say, a written word, or a visually-presented object, or someone's voice' (Coltheart, 1999: 118).

impossible to say where one leaves off and the other begins' (Jackendoff, 2002: 229).

3.3   Modularity and pragmatics

Diagrammatic representations in introductory textbooks showing how pragmatics fits into the discipline of linguistics frequently give the impression that pragmatics is a discrete component of the communication system, on a par with syntax and the lexicon. However, there have been very few attempts to construe pragmatics as some kind of cognitive module. Kasher (1991) hypothesizes that knowledge of basic speech act types such as assertions, questions and commands constitutes a module, as does knowledge governing basic aspects of conversation such as turn taking and repair. On the other hand, knowledge of 'non-basic' speech acts such as congratulations and proclamations, and of the processes involved in implicature, politeness and deixis, is seen as dependent on central systems. There are problems with Kasher's approach (for critical assessments, see Sinclair (1995) and Carston (1997)), which partly result from his attempt to fit pragmatics into a Chomskyan theory of competence. This commits him to the problematic view that pragmatics is concerned with *knowledge* and independent of communication. Furthermore, as Sinclair (1995: 531) points out, Kasher's view of the modularity of pragmatics applies 'only to basic speech acts, which represent but a small fraction of the domain covered by his theory'. Another cognitively based theory which directly addresses the issue of modularity is Relevance Theory (Sperber and Wilson, 1995). For a number of years Sperber and Wilson held that pragmatics is not a cognitive module at all, but rather 'the domain in which grammar, logic and memory interact' (Wilson and Sperber, 1991: 583), though more recently they have argued to the contrary that 'pragmatics ... is a distinct modular system with its own proprietary concepts and procedures' (Carston, Guttenplan and Wilson, 2002: 1) dedicated to attributing intentions to others. It should be noted, though, that their definition of module here is far looser than Fodor's (as noted above) and that they equate pragmatics primarily with comprehension (Sperber and Wilson, 2002).

Both Kasher's and Sperber and Wilson's accounts have their origins in pragmatic theories which are very selective in their coverage of cognitive processes. For a more comprehensive and explicit coverage of the role played by specific cognitive capacities (modular or otherwise) in pragmatic functioning, we must once again turn our attention away from mainstream theoretical pragmatics to the language pathology research literature. Here we find that a wide range of cognitive systems has been implicated in pragmatic impairment. These include nonlinguistic capacities such as inference generation (Dipper *et al.*, 1997), social cognition (Cohen *et al.*, 1998), theory of mind (Volden, Mulcahy and Holdgrafter, 1997), executive function (Tannock and Schachar, 1996), memory (Almor *et al.*, 1999), affect (Lorch, Borod and Koff, 1998) and conceptual knowledge (Rein and Kernan, 1989), as well as linguistic capacities such as phonology (Campbell and Shriberg, 1982), prosody (Wertz *et al.*, 1998), morphology (Tesak, 1994), syntax (Niemi and Hägg, 1999) and lexis (Chobor and Schweiger, 1998). What evidence is there that these pragmatically significant capacities are modular in nature?

3.4 Modular dysfunction vs central capacity overload

Many types of communication impairment are attributed to dysfunction in a specific cognitive or linguistic system. This is particularly so in cases of acquired brain damage resulting in aphasia. There are other instances, though, such as developmental and degenerative disorders, where it is harder to identify a specific system dysfunction as the cause of the problem, and explanations in terms of 'cognitive central capacity overload' are sometimes proposed. The distinction between these two types of explanation depends to some extent on which model of the mind one is using. If one adopts a modular approach and distinguishes between a small set of dedicated modules such as language, vision, auditory perception, etc. on the one hand and some kind of central executive system on the other which is unable to penetrate the dedicated encapsulated modules, one is left with a general cognitive overload explanation for any communicative impairment which is not directly attributable to an impairment within one of the specialized modules. It is not always clear, though, whether the overload is attributed to central cognitive functions in Fodor's sense, or to some more general and unspecified form of cognitive disruption.

Another difficulty with the cognitive overload vs system dysfunction dichotomy is that the former is a processing or 'performance' account, whereas the latter is often expressed in terms of 'competence'. Performance explanations of communicative capacity, whether construed in terms of connectionism (Elman *et al.*, 1996), dynamic systems theory (Thelen and Smith, 1994) or the Competition Model (Bates and MacWhinney, 1989), do not presuppose an innately specified language module, whereas 'competence' explanations (Chomsky, 2002) typically do. Competence and performance approaches are not necessarily incompatible, however. Notions such as cognitive overload, adaptation and compensation are necessarily couched in processing/performance terms, but the systems they access may be regarded either as competences or processing states, and competence can be seen as being prewired to a greater or lesser extent. At any rate, much of the research into communication disorders discussed below rarely considers such issues and therefore encompasses a theoretically eclectic range of views by default.

3.5   Impairments attributed to modular dysfunction

I will now consider three communication impairments, all of which impact on pragmatic functioning and which have been widely regarded as paradigm cases for the modularity of mind, and for which one would therefore expect to see direct evidence of the nature of the modules themselves. We will see, however, that in each case the evidence is not straightforward.

One frequently mentioned contender for modular status based on selective impairment is syntax. Agrammatism, a term commonly used to describe disturbances of sentence planning and production and linked to damage in Broca's area of the left hemisphere, has long seemed a prime candidate for impairment to a specifically linguistic module. Indeed, agrammatism was described by Kean (1977) as being 'symptomatic of a syntactic deficit'. However, evidence has gradually accumulated to suggest a far more complex picture implicating a range of cognitive systems, as acknowledged by Kean in a later article (Kean, 1995). Caplan (1987) has suggested that in some cases agrammatism may be a compensatory adaptation to poor articulatory ability. Others have argued that structural and procedural knowledge is actually intact in aphasic agrammatism and that the deficit is in fact a compensatory adaptation to limitations in working memory capacity (Martin and Feher, 1990). As Kolk (1995: 294) puts it: 'structural simplicity results from message simplification on the part of the aphasic speaker in an attempt to prevent computational overload'. Several studies have shown that aphasic-like comprehension errors may be induced in normal adults by increasing computational demands in other areas such as working memory, and thus suggesting that apparent damage to a syntax module may instead be an artefact of constraints on processing capacity (Bates, Dick and Wulfeck, 1999; Blackwell and Bates, 1995; Dick et al., 2001; Miyake, Carpenter and Just, 1994, 1995; Silkes, McNeil and Drton, 2004). Caplan and Hildebrandt (1988) also suggest an explanation for agrammatism in terms of compensation in the face of reduced computational resources, though they use instead the notion of a limited 'parsing workspace'. They suggest that one common compensatory heuristic used by agrammatic aphasics in sentence comprehension is to assign thematic roles in the order Agent, Theme and Goal to sequential noun phrases regardless of the actual syntactic structure. Other explanations of agrammatism (Butterworth and Howard, 1987; Schwartz, 1987) also assume use of compensatory strategies to conserve processing resources, and some go as far as to suggest that agrammatism itself is no more than an 'interactional artifact' (Heeschen and Schegloff, 2003). Such evidence, however, does not preclude the possibility that certain elements of syntactic competence *are* modular in nature. In an extensive review of the research on agrammatism, Grodzinsky (2000) suggests that the only syntactic process that can be conclusively linked with Broca's area is 'trace deletion' – 'the copying of a constituent to another position in a sentence and the substitution of the material in the original position by a trace' (p. 5) – with other syntactic abilities being more widely distributed throughout the left hemisphere than was previously thought. Nevertheless, he still feels able to conclude that language is 'a distinct, modularly organized neurological entity' (p. 1) on the basis of its distinctness from other cognitive abilities. This does not mean, though, that the *production* and *comprehension* of syntax are not both constrained and facilitated by other cognitive systems. Although the question of whether agrammatism is evidence for modularity still provokes fierce debate (see, for example, van Lancker's review article on this topic and the variety of peer commentaries it attracted (van Lancker, 2001)) the evidence against a straightforward modular account continues to accumulate.

Specific language impairment (SLI) in children is another example of a communication disorder which has been used to argue for the existence of a grammar module. By definition, the term 'SLI' implies a specific dysfunction of the language system and is applied to 'children who show significant deficits on language learning ability but age-appropriate scores on non-verbal tests of intelligence, normal hearing, and no clear evidence of neurological impairment' (Leonard, 2000b: 1). There are three major but distinct explanations of SLI: (1) as a (modular) deficit in linguistic knowledge (i.e. a competence problem), (2) as a processing deficit in specific mechanisms (i.e. a performance problem) and (3) as a limitation in general processing capacity (Leonard, 1998). Several groups of researchers see SLI as an inherent deficit in a Chomskyan language module – for example, as an inability to mark tense in main clauses (the so-called 'optional infinitive' account) (Rice, Wexler and Cleave, 1995) or to apply Binding Theory (van der Lely and Stollwerk, 1997). With regard to the role of specific processing mechanisms, as in the case of agrammatism in adults, memory limitations have been implicated as a possible causative factor in SLI. For example, there is evidence that sequential verbal memory is deficient in SLI children compared with their normally developing peers and younger language-matched children (Gathercole and Baddeley, 1990), and Ullman and Pierpont (2005) in their 'procedural deficit' hypothesis propose problems with procedural memory as the single underlying cause of SLI. Auditory perception may also play a key contributory role in SLI as argued by Tallal and colleagues (e.g. Tallal, Stark and Mellits, 1985). Explanatory accounts in terms of limited processing capacity argue that children with SLI have insufficient resources to cope with the full range of linguistic processing demands and therefore are both slower and selective in the features to which they attend (Deevy and Leonard, 2004; Hanson and Montgomery, 2002; Leonard, 1998; Montgomery, 2002; Norbury and Bishop, 2002a). The causes of this resource limitation are not always specified. Locke (1994, 1997), however, proposes that SLI and other developmental language disorders arise as a result of maturational asynchronies between various neural mechanisms. These result in the compensatory reallocation of resources to areas of the brain which may not be ideally equipped to carry them out. This ultimately leads to an overall reduction in processing capacity. As with agrammatism, therefore, the evidence from SLI for the existence of one or more language modules is equivocal.

Finally, Williams syndrome has been held by some to provide the most clear-cut case of a dissociation between language and cognition, and therefore justification for the modularity hypothesis. It has frequently been reported that the grammatical ability of individuals with Williams syndrome (WS) is unimpaired relative to their comparatively low intelligence and poor performance in other cognitive domains such as spatial ability and planning (Bellugi et al., 1988). In this respect it has been seen as the 'opposite' of SLI (Pinker, 1999), and SLI and WS together have been claimed to provide strong evidence for a modular double dissociation. However, just as evidence has gradually accumulated, suggesting that SLI may rarely – if ever – be a unitary and discrete condition, research in the last few years has shown that both expressive and receptive grammatical ability in WS is actually far from intact and that language learning in this condition may be more like second language acquisition than normal first language acquisition (Karmiloff-Smith et al., 1997, 1998). For example, in a comparative study of children with WS and children with SLI, Stojanovik et al. (2004) found that children with WS can show a constellation of difficulties across formal domains of language functioning which is often in line with their general cognitive ability, and that on certain linguistic tasks they may even perform as poorly as children with SLI. In a related study (Stojanovik, Perkins and Howard, 2006), they also found that WS does not present with a consistent profile, and that, although in some children with WS verbal ability may be in advance of non-verbal ability, there are also cases where they are at an equivalent level. Finally, Phillips et al. (2004) have shown that problems with spatial cognition in WS constrain comprehension of spatial expressions. Thus the stark dissociation of language and cognition so confidently asserted by Pinker (1999), Clahsen and Almazan (1998) and others on the basis of evidence from WS may need to be tempered.

Agrammatism, SLI and Williams syndrome all have an impact on pragmatic functioning (Perkins, 2003), but the evidence for the linguistic and cognitive impairments which underly them being modular, and therefore being underlying contributory factors in pragmatic impairment, is equivocal. Empirical investigations of language pathologies have shown that the original conception of modularity is oversimplistic and that dissociations between various linguistic and nonlinguistic cognitive capacities may not be as clear cut as has often been claimed. None of the alternative explanations of agrammatism, SLI and WS are necessarily incompatible with a modular account. Independently of whether or not one considers there to be a specific language module, and, if so, what its properties are and how they are specified, interactions across a range of cognitive processes are invariably involved in language processing, and in some cases at least it seems likely that impairments which might once have been considered as dysfunctions within a specific module may in fact be a consequence of interactions elsewhere in the overall organism. As noted by Karmiloff-Smith (1999: 559): 'in almost every case of islets of so-called intact modular functioning, serious impairments within the "intact" domain have subsequently been identified ... and in cases of purported singular modular deficits, more general impairments have frequently been brought to light'.

What alternative explanations are there? As we have seen above, some have argued that SLI and agrammatism may be accounted for in terms of limited processing capacity which affects the way different areas of the language system interact, and is predicated upon the existence of varying degrees of co-dependency between such subsystems. I will now consider whether this may prove a potential contender for an underlying cognitive explanation of pragmatics.

3.6   Impairments attributed to central capacity limitations

The cognitive overload approach to communication impairment assumes that individual systems are intact but that dysfunction occurs within the organism as a whole due to inadequate central processing capacity. Earlier studies of linguistic deficits assumed that language was hierarchically organized such that syntactic problems, for example, were likely to affect phonology and articulatory accuracy (i.e. a 'top–down' effect) (Menyuk and Looney, 1972; Shriner, Holloway and Daniloff, 1969) and/or vice versa (i.e. a 'bottom–up' effect) (Panagos and Prelock, 1982). It soon became apparent, though, from work in psycholinguistics (Bock, 1982), that a more complex set of interactions was involved. One of the clearest expositions of this view is that of Crystal (1987), who likens breakdown in language processing capacity to a bucket in which 'an extra "drop" of phonology (syntax, semantics, etc.) may cause the overflow of a "drop" of syntax (semantics, phonology, etc.)' (p. 20). Others describe the same phenomenon in terms of a 'resource allocation' or 'demands–capacities' model whereby fluency breakdown, for example, is attributed to external and/or internal demands which exceed the speaker's cognitive and/or motoric capacities (Adams, 1990; Karniol, 1992). Crystal's (1987) model allows for one-way, two-way and multiple interactions between distinct linguistic 'levels' of phonetics, phonology, morphology, syntax, semantics and discourse. He provides illustrations from the spontaneous speech of a language impaired boy whose fluency, intelligibility and semantic specificity decreased as he attempted more complex syntactic structures. Others have noted similar 'trade-offs' in language impaired children between syntax and phonology (Fey et al., 1994; Masterson and Kamhi, 1992; Paul and Shriberg, 1982), between syntax and articulatory accuracy (Haynes, Haynes and Jackson, 1982), between semantics and pragmatics (Sahlén and Nettelbladt, 1993), between syntax, morphology and phonology (Panagos and Prelock, 1982), between syntax, phonology and articulatory accuracy (Panagos, Quine and Klich, 1979), between syntax, phonology and lexis (Prelock and Panagos, 1989) and between phonology, prosody and pragmatics (Campbell and Shriberg, 1982). Trade-offs have also been reported in aphasic adults between phonology and lexis (Kohn, Melvold and Smith, 1995), between lexis and discourse (Christiansen, 1995), between syntax, lexis and memory (Martin and Feher, 1990), and between syntax, morphology, semantics and pragmatics (Tesak, 1994). Numerous specific examples of such trade-offs will be discussed in Chapters 4 to 8.

What is as interesting as the trade-offs themselves is whether there is a pecking order of vulnerability among different areas of the linguistic system. Some have found evidence for a recency effect – i.e. systems which are less firmly established are more prone to disruption under pressure. Masterson and Kamhi (1992), in a study of normal and language disabled school-age children found a trade-off between syntactic and phonological complexity but not between syntactic and phonological accuracy. They speculate that this may be due to the latter skills 'being more firmly established and requiring less processing capacity in primary-aged children' (p. 1073). The link between syntax and phonology is one which appears to be particularly strong. Bishop and Edmundson (1987) report that 79 per cent of their subjects with SLI who had deficits in syntax also exhibited impairments in phonology. Fey et al. (1994), on the other hand, found no evidence that an intervention programme to improve grammar (and which did so successfully) led to spontaneous improvement of phonological output in SLI children impaired in both areas, so the relationship may not be a straightforward one.

Studies of trade-offs in language performance often implicitly assume some kind of modular view of various subcomponents of language, but it is not always apparent what exactly is meant by 'pragmatics', 'phonology', 'syntax', 'morphology' and so on. For example, phonological performance has been characterized variously in terms of 'final consonant deletion, stopping, palatal fronting and velar fronting' (Campbell and Shriberg, 1982), mean number of phonemes per utterance (Fey et al., 1994) and mean number of syllables per utterance (Panagos and Prelock, 1982). Syntactic performance has likewise been measured variously in terms of number of grammatical morphemes produced correctly (Masterson and Kamhi, 1992) and a range of standard grammatical performance assessment procedures which are operationally, rather than theoretically, defined (Crystal, 1987; Fey et al., 1994; Prelock and Panagos, 1989). Some have restricted pragmatic performance to appreciation of metaphor and non-literal meaning (Champagne, Desautels and Joanette, 2003), excluding capacities such as theory of mind, whereas others see pragmatic ability as being exclusively a function of theory of mind (Sperber and Wilson, 2002). In other words, communicative competence is variously represented as a subset of any number of performance features which happen to be easy to measure. Another difficulty is that some of the findings reported in such studies are based on sentence imitation rather than on spontaneous speech, and one of the few studies to compare both modes found that trade-offs are more frequent in imitated than spontaneous speech (Masterson and Kamhi, 1992). It is important to ask how successfully one may extrapolate from a specific behavioural task to a discrete underlying modular system. It is rather like trying to characterize the nature of a car by means of a single feature, such as the time it takes to accelerate from 0 to 60 miles per hour, while ignoring everything else.

The studies referred to above focus on operational dependencies between systems and only implicitly on the modular status of the systems themselves. Rather than focusing attention so exclusively on dissociation, it may be at least as important to consider the extent to which seemingly discrete capacities and behaviours may be associated. While not wishing to deny the evidence for various degrees of compartmentalization, specialization and 'modularity', it is important to be aware that this view of things is driven by a particular methodology – i.e. that of positing particular types of discrete entities and searching for dissociations of behaviours attributed to them as evidence for their existence. Despite the widespread use of this approach in cognitive psychology and neuropsychology, we should be extremely cautious about what we conclude from its findings (Dunn and Kirsner, 2003; Karmiloff-Smith, Scerif and Ansari, 2003). An alternative and at least equally valid stance, with a psychological pedigree dating back to Piaget, Vygotsky and beyond, is to focus instead on association, interaction and adaptation and on how apparently discrete and self-contained entities may simply be a secondary consequence of these. At one level, the choice between dissociation and association is that of which metaphor (and concomitant theory and methodology) one finds most illuminating. In what follows, I will adopt an approach which puts co-dependency and interaction at centre stage rather than dissociation, and which sees pragmatics as a secondary 'emergent' phenomenon, rather than a primary one. Ultimately I will argue that a focus on associations rather than dissociations provides a particularly illuminating account of pragmatics.

3.7   Background to an interactive emergentist pragmatics

The reader may be forgiven for wondering how an excursus into the modular status of impairments such as aphasia, SLI and Williams syndrome – hardly primary contenders for pragmatic impairments – is relevant to the key theme of pragmatics. Recall that in the concluding section of Chapter 2 it was noted that certain behaviours engendered by most, if not all, communication impairments may be described in pragmatic (albeit broadly defined) terms, and that pragmatic impairment thus appears to be an inescapable concomitant of communication impairment.[4] What this suggests is that, rather than viewing pragmatic ability as a relatively discrete system on a par with syntax, phonology or working memory, it may be more accurate to see it as a by-product of the way such systems interact. There is strong evidence, as we have seen above, that communication impairments whose symptoms are most readily described in terms of, say, syntax involve far more than this, and that the syntactic impairment may well be merely the tip of an iceberg constituted by a complex chain of interactions and adaptations involving both linguistic and cognitive processes. What I will propose is that such interactions and

---

[4] As noted above, the few attempts to characterize pragmatics as a discrete modular entity adopt a much narrower perspective and focus exclusively on specific sub-areas of pragmatics such as basic speech act types (Kasher, 1991) or the role of theory of mind in comprehension (Sperber and Wilson, 2002).

adaptations – rather than the entities involved in the interactions – are the essence of pragmatics. Pragmatic ability and disability are thus 'epipheno-menal' (Perkins, 1998a) and 'emergent' (Perkins, 2005a). In order to explain what I mean by this, let us first consider how such terms are used more generally within the linguistic and cognitive sciences.

3.7.1   Emergence

'Emergence' is the term applied to a process whereby a complex entity results from a set of simple interactions between 'lower-level' entities. For example, anthills result from the aggregate effects of millions of local, minor acts by ants, rather than from a grand design in the mind of some ant-architect (Johnson, 2001), and the time-telling properties of a watch depend on local interactions between a set of individually simple cogs and springs. As Clark (1997: 107) puts it: 'emergent patterns ... are largely explained by the collective behavior ... of a large ensemble of simple components ..., none of which is playing a special or leading role in controlling or orchestrating the process of pattern formation.' Similarly, minds may be seen as 'emergent properties of brains ... produced by principles that control interactions between lower level events' (Chomsky, 2002: 63, quoting Mountfield). Emergent processes can unfold across a range of time frames including those of evolution, embryology, the human lifespan and history, as well as during ephemeral events such as online cognitive processing and conversational interaction (MacWhinney, 1999). The study of emergence in cognitive science has led to a reappraisal of the discreteness and autonomy of a range of phenomena including individuals and the human mind. For example, Hutchins (1995) has shown that the cognitive characteristics of teamwork are not attributable to any single individual member of the team, and Clark (1999: 14) describes the human cognitive profile as '*essentially* the profile of an embodied and situated organism'.

In the language sciences, emergence has been invoked as a way of explaining a wide range of phenomena, including language development (Locke, 1993), developmental and acquired language disorders (Christman, 2002; Locke, 1994), the role of discourse in determining grammatical form (Hopper, 1998), diachronic language change (Givón, 1999) and language evolution (Knight, Studdert-Kennedy and Hurford, 2000). Although it may be modelled particularly effectively using connectionist networks (Allen and Seidenberg, 1999), and is often linked to functionalist approaches to language (Bates and MacWhinney, 1989), emergence, as MacWhinney (1999) points out, is also compatible with generative approaches to language, which are typically opposed to functionalism and connectionism.[5] In his Minimalist Program for syntax, for example, Chomsky regards 'the traditional constructions – verb phrase, relative clause, passive, etc. – [as] taxonomic artifacts, their properties resulting from the interaction of far more general principles' (Chomsky, 1995b: 17–18) and feels that 'the apparent richness and diversity of linguistic phenomena is illusory and epiphenomenal, the result of fixed principles under slightly varying conditions' (Chomsky, 1995a: 389). To take such a view is not to deny the heuristic value of such epiphenomenal constructs for observers in describing behavioural processes, but it does not necessarily follow that such constructs play any direct role for those participating in the process.

I will briefly consider three emergentist accounts of human communication which are compatible in different ways with the approach to pragmatics proposed in Chapter 4. These are: Bates and MacWhinney's Competition Model, Karmiloff-Smith's neuroconstructivist model and Clark's 'joint action theory'.[6]

3.7.2   The Competition Model

The Competition Model (Bates and MacWhinney, 1987) provides an account of language processing in terms of a complex interplay between the information value of a particular form or pattern (i.e. its *cue validity*) and the amount of effort involved in processing it (i.e. its *cue cost*).[7] For example, in a study comparing grammaticality judgements of American and Italian college students (Wulfeck, Bates and Capasso, 1991), Americans were significantly faster at detecting word order errors, whereas Italians were significantly faster on agreement errors. This is attributed to the fact that in English, word order has high cue validity whereas agreement has low cue validity, but the opposite is the case for Italian. As well as online processing tasks, the Competition Model has been used to account for patterns of language development and language impairment, such that items of high cue validity are acquired earlier in typically developing

---

[5] 'It is remarkable that approaches as apparently divergent as functionalist linguistics and principles-and-parameters theory share some common ground in terms of a mutual interest in emergentist accounts of both learning and processing' (MacWhinney, 1999: xii).

[6] The term 'joint action theory' is my own, not Clark's. Clark, in fact, proposes no one label for the theory expounded in his book *Using Language* (Clark, 1996), though he has no objection to the use of 'joint action theory' to describe it (Clark, personal communication).

[7] In this respect, it is not dissimilar from Sperber and Wilson's (1995) Principle of Relevance, expressed as the balance between cognitive effects and processing effort (see Chapter 2). Both may have been influenced by the notion of 'ecological validity' in Gibson's approach to perception (Gibson, 1969), though Gibson has criticized several features of the Competition Model (Gibson, 1992).

children, are more likely to be present in children with developmental language disorders and are more resistant to loss in individuals with aphasia (Bates *et al.*, 1996). This accounts for the variable developmental and impairment profiles found in speakers of different languages. The accessibility of a linguistic item in terms of its ease of articulation, perceivability and degree of confusability with other items is not absolute, but needs to be offset against the level of processing resources available – in other words, its cue cost will vary across and within individuals depending on the robustness of cognitive capacities such as attention and memory and the level of demand they are subject to on any given occasion. The constant competition between items and resources will be construed below as a continuous set of choices that need to be made. The apparently simple choice involved in, say, retrieving a particular lexical item is in reality an emergent function of a complex of choices, and 'what might be thought of as single events or behaviors can often be produced by multiple interacting mechanisms' (Elman *et al.*, 1996: 363).

3.7.3   Neuroconstructivism

'Neuroconstructivism' is a term coined by Karmiloff-Smith (1998) for an emergentist view of child development which places development itself at centre stage. She argues that, although the adult mind may be modular, it didn't start out that way. She criticizes accounts of language and cognitive development which implicitly take as their starting point the highly specialized adult brain and look for similarly specific constructs in the child. Such approaches run the risk of tipping the balance too far towards innatism, and do not sit comfortably with what is known about the massive plasticity of the infant brain. As she puts it:

a mechanism starts out as somewhat more relevant to one kind of input over others, but is useable – albeit in a less efficient way – for other types of processing too. This allows for compensatory processing and makes development channelled but far less predetermined than the nativist view. Once a domain-relevant mechanism is repeatedly used to process a certain type of input, it becomes domain-specific as a result of its developmental history ... Then, in adulthood, it can be differentially impaired. (Karmiloff-Smith, 1998: 390)

Much of the evidence for the neuroconstructivist view comes from the study of developmental disorders. Here, too, the assumption of adult-like dissociations between a range of linguistic and cognitive functions in children with impairments leads to the commonly (but mistakenly, according to Karmiloff-Smith) held view that specific areas of language or cognition may be impaired in children without there being any noticeable consequences for other aspects of functioning – as suggested, for example, by terms such as *specific* language impairment. This is referred to as the assumption of 'residual normality' – i.e. 'that, in the face of a selective developmental deficit, the rest of the system can nevertheless develop normally and independently of the deficit' (Thomas and Karmiloff-Smith, 2002: 729). Much of Karmiloff-Smith's research output over the last decade or so has been devoted to showing that, when one examines the evidence in sufficient detail, there is little to support the view that specific deficits occur in isolation, leaving the rest of the system intact. Compensatory adaptation, which plays a central role in neuroconstructivism, is a similarly key feature of the emergentist model of pragmatics proposed in Chapter 4.

3.7.4   Joint Action Theory

The Competition Model and the neuroconstructivist account are processing models in which factors such as social context and the communicative acts of others are seen essentially in terms of the way they constrain or facilitate the cognitive and linguistic processing of individuals. In other words, they are one set of factors among many others – e.g. the relative functional load of a particular phonological contrast or the balance between syntax and morphology in a specific language – rather than having any kind of privileged status. Such approaches may be contrasted with that of Conversation Analysis (as discussed in Chapter 2) in which communication involving language is seen exclusively in terms of the way interacting individuals orient towards each other to co-construct 'talk-in-interaction'. The significance, nature, and even the existence of any underlying cognitive mechanisms which might give rise to such events, are typically ignored. One attempt to integrate both cognitive and social aspects of interpersonal communication is Clark's Joint Action Theory.

Clark sees communication as a type of joint activity in which one person signals to another and the second recognizes what the first one means (Clark, 1996: 130). These are not two autonomous actions – as one might be led to believe from the accounts provided by some theorists (e.g. Searle, Grice, Sperber and Wilson): to be communicative, signalling and the recognition of the signal's significance cannot occur without each other. Phenomena such as turn taking and the structure of conversation more generally are not primary, but emerge from the coordination of a number of more basic acts which contribute to what Clark calls 'joint projects' – a type of joint action projected by one of its participants and taken up by the other(s). In fact, joint actions are actually seen as solutions to the problems posed by the need for coordination between participants. For example, in an 'adjacency pair' such as lines 1–2 in

1	Proposal	A: when do we leave?
2	Uptake/Proposal	B: in five minutes?
3	Uptake	A: if you say so

A projects a joint action in line 1 – in this case, a proposal by A for B to transfer information to her – which is not completed until B does exactly as requested in line 2, thus demonstrating uptake of the proposal.[8] Longer conversations may be created as a result of 'chaining'[9] such adjacency pairs together – thus utterance 2 additionally constitutes a proposal for further transfer of information, this time from A to B, to which evidence of uptake is provided in line 3. Such an account will hold few surprises for anyone familiar with Conversation Analysis, though, whereas CA is an analytical method, Clark's approach offers a coherent theoretical explanation for the phenomena described by CA. For example, the rules for turn allocation proposed by Sacks, Schegloff and Jefferson (1974) fall out quite naturally in Joint Action Theory as an emergent consequence of the requirements of joint projects, without the need to be spelled out explicitly (Clark, 1996: 329). In addition, as Clark points out, turn allocation rules do not provide a satisfactory account of phenomena such as 'back-channel' utterances (e.g. 'uhuh', 'mhm'), which overlap other speakers' turns, or of co-occurring, parallel nonverbal behaviours. The often unwitting tendency found in many theories of pragmatics to see language as the primary, if not the sole, vehicle of information transfer has been noted earlier (Chapter 2). While it may certainly be largely true – as proposed by the Competition Model – that the low dimensional nature of the linear speech signal may reduce the range of choices available for communicative expression, and indeed lead to phenomena such as 'blends', 'paragrammatisms' and 'cluttering' which result from errors in converting parallel into serial representations, Clark shows that the degree of reduction is not as extreme as many assume, and that considerable parallelism remains in the form of co-occurring gestural, postural and other nonverbal expression. Clark's notion of 'signalling' refers to a composite activity, distributed across modalities. The limitations of overly language-centred theories of pragmatics for explaining the nature of communication impairments have already been noted, and Clark's more fully semiotic approach will be taken up in Chapter 4.

---

[8] Proposals and uptakes are further deconstructed by Clark into four levels of action where each level is a prerequisite for the one above it.

[9] Other basic ways of creating extended joint projects are 'embedding' and 'pre-sequencing'.

3.8 Conclusion

Based on the evidence reviewed in this chapter, it seems clear that, rather than viewing pragmatics as a set of mentally instantiated functions (Kasher, 1991), as probabilistic reasoning processes (Paradis, 2003), or as a 'comprehension module' that enables us to interpret others' intentions (Sperber and Wilson, 2002) – each of these being seen as some kind of discrete entity that exists independently of other entities with which it interacts (e.g. language, memory, attention, intention, etc.) – there are good grounds for characterizing pragmatics instead as an epiphenomenal or emergent property of interactions between such entities. Pragmatics is what you get when entities such as language, social cognition, memory, intention and inferential reasoning collide in socioculturally situated human interaction, rather than its being instantiated or uniquely grounded in any single one of these. I will now proceed to flesh out this view as a coherent model of pragmatics which encompasses both typical and atypical manifestations of communicative behaviour.

4 Pragmatic ability and disability: an emergentist model

4.1 Introduction

In this chapter I will present an account of pragmatics which incorporates all the features identified in Chapter 2 as being required to account for pragmatic impairment, and which at the same time covers normal pragmatic processing. The approach used is an emergentist one and draws on interactional processing accounts as outlined in Chapter 3. Pragmatic competence is not a unitary phenomenon (McTear and Conti-Ramsden, 1992; Penn, 1999). It requires the integration of a range of cognitive, semiotic and sensorimotor abilities, and impairment of any of these can result in pragmatic impairment. Nevertheless, the term 'pragmatic impairment' tends to be used rather more narrowly to refer to the type of socio-cognitive impairment found in autism and right hemisphere brain damage. What I argue in this chapter is that pragmatic impairment results when there is a restriction on the *choices* available for encoding or decoding meaning, whatever they might be. These choices are characterized in terms of the semiotic, cognitive and sensorimotor capacities which underlie communicative behaviour. Pragmatic impairment is seen in terms of an imbalance within and/or between interacting cognitive, semiotic and sensorimotor systems, and also in terms of compensatory adaptation. As well as taking into account interactions within the individual, the proposed model also extends into the interpersonal domain such that a communicative dyad can also be seen as an integral cognitive, semiotic and sensorimotor processing system in its own right.

The approach is motivated by the following five principles which will be further elaborated in this chapter and in later chapters:
1. Pragmatics involves the range of choices open to us when we communicate.
2. Such choices are involved at all 'levels' of language processing, from discourse down to phonetics.
3. The choices are not exclusively linguistic, but involve other semiotic systems and the way communication is distributed across verbal and nonverbal channels.

4. In order to qualify as 'pragmatic', such choices must be motivated by the requirements of interpersonal communication.

5. There is frequently no direct link between an underlying deficit and a resulting pragmatic impairment. Rather, the latter may be the consequence of one or more compensatory adaptations.

Subsequently, a model will be outlined which comprises the following three key notions:

1. **Elements**. These are the entities between which interactions take place, and are of three kinds: (a) cognitive systems, (b) semiotic systems and (c) sensorimotor systems, and may be construed either as competences or as processes.

2. **Interactions**. These are the dynamic relations that occur between elements, and are motivated by the need to maintain a state of equilibrium within a given domain.

3. **Domains**. Interactions take place both within individuals – i.e. the *intra*personal domain – and between individuals – i.e. the *inter*personal domain.

Before considering these in more detail, I will briefly present three cases of communication impairment, none of which would typically be described as involving a primarily pragmatic disability, but which nevertheless manifest features which are undeniably pragmatic in nature and would therefore need to be accounted for within any pragmatic theory or approach which aimed to be comprehensive. We shall see that to successfully incorporate such cases within a systematic pragmatic account will require a reinterpretation of the nature of pragmatic ability and disability as emergent phenomena.

4.2   Three atypical cases of pragmatic impairment

4.2.1   Len

Len is a man in his sixties who has had most of his tongue removed as a result of oral cancer, leaving only the tongue root and a small part of the tongue dorsum. Consequently, the only English consonants he is able to articulate normally are /p/, /b/, /f/, /v/, /h/ and /w/, and his vowel production is similarly restricted. Amazingly, after a few minutes talking to him and 'tuning in', one finds that he is not particularly difficult to understand. This is partly because, although his phonological system is considerably reduced, it is still coherent and consistent. Furthermore, he is able to make use of glottal plosion, friction, nasalization, voice onset time and lip, cheek and jaw movement in various combinations to produce a range of sounds which, although unorthodox, map consistently on to much of the normal

English phonological system. An additional interesting feature of Len's speech is the interaction between his prosody and syntax. He pauses frequently, breaking up his speech into short, intonationally coherent chunks, and each pause is used to signal a syntactic phrase boundary.[1] In Transcript 4.1, a dash indicates a longer pause and a dot a shorter pause:

Transcript 4.1

I get up – to make sure – that my legs – will take me – where . I want . to go

Despite their restructuring, both Len's articulatory and phonological systems have regained their homeostatic integrity. In addition, his prosodic and syntactic systems have developed a slightly novel but fruitful relationship. A new state of homeostasis is likewise achieved between Len and uninitiated interlocutors after a few minutes' readjustment. All of these reorganizations appear to be quite unconscious. The radical choices that Len has made in restructuring his verbal output are clearly motivated by the need to make himself understood by his interlocutor, and are therefore pragmatically determined to the same extent that choosing to use a pronominal form such as 'it' instead of 'book' is pragmatically determined when the referent is contextually evident.

4.2.2   Lucy

Lucy, aged 4;10, has a diagnosis of specific language impairment (SLI). Although she is of normal intelligence, her phonology and syntax are very primitive for her age and she often has problems in making herself understood. In conversation, she makes noticeable use of gesture in two distinct ways. Firstly, when referring to objects and actions she typically accompanies her utterances with iconic signs, as in Transcript 4.2, which shows her in conversation with Sara, an adult whom she knows slightly:

Transcript 4.2

Sara: wellies'd be good for the snow wouldn't they? yeah I agree . anything else?
Lucy: [jɔ . glʊb] (*your . gloves*)   (*waggles fingers gesturing gloves*)
Sara: you'd need gloves for the snow
Lucy: [æn . hæ?] (*and . hat*)   (*gestures pulling on a hat*)

This is an extension of the iconic way gesture is sometimes used in conversation, and, given Lucy's impaired phonology and grammar, it

---

[1]   Interestingly, it has been noted that mothers segment their speech to infants in a similar way (the so-called 'bracketed input hypothesis') (Morgan, 1986), and that infants 7–10 months old have a preference for this kind of speech even before they know any syntax (Hirsh-Pasek et al., 1987).

provides the interlocutor with extra evidence to help her infer what Lucy means by what she is saying. The second use of gesture is more atypical, and it seems to play a role for Lucy rather than the interlocutor. Lucy's speech is mostly syllable-timed and sounds rather staccato. Sometimes when she is speaking she taps out the rhythm of her utterance with her hand, as in Transcript 4.3.

Transcript 4.3

Sara: what would you use a bucket for?
Lucy: p'put . 'something . 'in . 'the . 'bu'cket   *(tapping on the table in rhythm with her speech)*

This would seem to be of little benefit to the listener, and appears rather to provide for Lucy a kind of prosodic and tactile scaffolding for her utterance, distributing it, as it were, across two modalities. Sometimes the two different uses of gesture appear to be conflated, as in Transcript 4.4.

Transcript 4.4

Sara: what's he wearing a bucket on his head for?
Lucy: 'bu'cket . 'on . 'his . 'head   *(taps her head in rhythm with her speech)*

Lucy has not overtly been taught either of these uses of gesture.

4.2.3   Peter

Peter is 9 ½ years old and has word-finding problems.[2] He is a willing and engaging conversational partner, but his language problems sometimes make it difficult to follow him. In Transcript 4.5 he is talking to Sara about a recent holiday.

Transcript 4.5

Peter: last year we went to Bulgaria and it wasn't (.) er
Sara: .hhh
Peter: it was horrible
Sara: it was horrible?
Peter: but (0.8) .hh [wɪʔ] (.) [æɡɪ] we did like the dinner and (.) that (0.6) but erm (1.6) there were (.) [ʔæ] (.) there was (.) one called Mike (1.5) one called (2.1) oh (.) erm (3.4) erm (2.5) I don't know his name now
Sara: right
Peter: other one
Sara: right

---

[2] A brief case study of Peter can be found in Perkins (2001). We will revisit Peter in more detail in Chapter 8.

Peter: but there was (2.0) ff oh (.) and one was called John (1.6) I don't know the
        (0.5) other one
Sara: and who were they?
Peter: (1.4) they was do you know (.) erm (.) when you (.) do you know when (1.6)
        it's a servant (0.5) [and]
Sara: [right] (0.8) yeah
Peter: and (.) and they bring the dinner in for you
Sara: a waiter?
Peter: waiter (.) yeah

Peter possibly intends to say that, although the food was good, the service
in the hotel restaurant left something to be desired. Unfortunately, though,
his inability to access the word 'waiter' sends him off on a circumlocutory
tangent, and the ultimately successful outcome is the joint achievement of
both Peter and Sara. Because of his limited linguistic resources, conversational success with Peter typically requires considerable effort on the part
of his interlocutor. In pragmatic terms, one might say that Peter's reduced
linguistic encoding ability creates an excessive inferential burden for the
hearer. Put another way, one could say that conversations with Peter tend
to be unbalanced or asymmetrical.

4.2.4   Summary and preview

Although these three cases are very different, what they have in common
is that they illustrate an attempt to restore balance to a dysfunctional
system through a process of compensation. Len's compensation involves
the simplification and reorganization of his articulatory and phonological systems, and a modified interaction between his prosody and syntax. Lucy compensates by increasing her use of the gestural and tactile
communication channels. In Peter's case the compensatory behaviour is
carried out by his interlocutor, who retrieves the elusive word for him.
All three cases, though, require interlocutor input in order to succeed.
Although we are dealing in each case with the cognitive, semiotic and
sensorimotor processing of individuals, and it makes sense to talk of
compensation in an 'intrapersonal' context, in addition there are compensatory interactions *between* individuals. Indeed, I will be arguing
that the ways in which semiotic, cognitive and sensorimotor equilibrium
are achieved both within and between individuals are essentially
the same.

The rest of the chapter provides a means of systematically accounting
for cases such as those presented above as well as cases seen as more typical
instances of pragmatic impairment, and also encompasses pragmatic ability and disability more generally.

4.3   The scope of pragmatic ability and disability

How much should be included in pragmatics? Or, put another way, what can we afford to exclude? The underlying deficits which give rise to the atypical communication of Len, Lucy and Peter have little in common with the types of cognitive deficit commonly purported to contribute to conditions such as autism (impaired theory of mind, executive function or central coherence) and traumatic brain injury (impaired executive function) – both of which are seen as more prototypical examples of pragmatic impairment. And yet, as we have seen, the different ways in which Len, Lucy and Peter compensate for their various deficits are motivated by interlocutor needs and have clear pragmatic consequences. It would appear that these individuals are pragmatically compromised in terms of the additional inferential burden which is imposed on their interlocutor, and yet at the same time they show considerable pragmatic sophistication with regard to the appreciation of their interlocutor's communicative needs and the subtle adjustments they make to accommodate them. A similar point has been made by Schegloff (2003) in a case study of a 'split-brain' patient who, despite having been diagnosed as pragmatically impaired according to a range of psychometric tests, nevertheless demonstrated remarkable subtlety in the way he co-constructed conversational turn taking and sequence organization with the tester. How is it possible to be pragmatically competent and incompetent at the same time? In order to resolve this conundrum without falling into contradiction, it will be necessary to take a much broader view of pragmatics than is typically the case, while at the same time not losing sight of the subtlety and range of its various manifestations.

Mey (2001: 8–9) distinguishes between a 'component' view of pragmatics – for example, the modular account outlined in Chapter 3, according to which pragmatics is a self-contained component of the human mind on a par with syntax or lexis – and a 'perspective' view, according to which pragmatics is different in kind from theoretical and/or cognitive entities like syntax and lexis, exists at a higher level of abstraction than linguistic phenomena and effectively constitutes a metacognitive stance. As an example of the perspectivist view, Mey cites Verschueren's (1999: 7) definition of pragmatics as 'a general cognitive, social, and cultural perspective on linguistic phenomena in relation to their usage in forms of behaviour'. The emergentist account of pragmatics below is certainly not explicitly a component view – for reasons given in Chapter 3 – and yet neither is it a perspective view, although it does aim to incorporate most, if not all, of the aspects that Verschueren would wish to include. The difference lies in the fact that a perspective requires a perspective-taker or beholder, whereas an emergentist account does not. Who or what would the beholder be? If one interprets Verschueren's definition as being of the *study* of pragmatics, then the beholder is the student. If one sees it instead as a definition of pragmatics itself – i.e. pragmatics as competence, process or behaviour – then the beholder must be seen as some kind of latter-day 'ghost in the machine' or, as some psychologists have envisaged it, a metacognitive 'central executive' (Baddeley and Hitch, 1974) or 'supervisory attentional system' (Shallice, 1988). Emergentist explanations of cognition and behaviour have no need of such 'seductive bad idea[s]' (Dennett, 1998: 284). As Clark (1997: 220) concludes, after an extensive review of recent developments in cognitive science: 'Gone is the central executive in the brain.' The model presented here sees pragmatics as neither component nor perspective, but as an emergent property of human communication.

4.3.1   *Pragmatics as choices*

A not uncommon view of pragmatics is to see it as involving the range of choices open to us when we communicate (e.g. Crystal, 1997; Verschueren, 1999)[3] – for example, what is said, how it's said, why it's said, when it's said, where it's said, to whom it's said, who says it and even whether anything is said or not. Such choices are important not just for speakers but for all participants in an interaction. My decision to say to you, 'Would you mind moving your car?', rather than the less markedly polite 'Move your car', requires you to appreciate the implicit contrast between what I have and haven't said in order to choose an interpretation of politeness. (Furthermore, such choices may operate at any level of consciousness.) Len, Lucy and Peter may each be seen as pragmatically impaired, therefore, by virtue of the fact that the range of linguistic choices open to them is more restricted than those enjoyed by more typical speakers. Pragmatics is not limited only to linguistic choices, however, but as we shall see below also involves decisions about the division of labour across different communicative channels. Independently of whether or not one has at one's disposal the full range of coding forms to choose from, the ability to select the appropriate form is also crucial, and this relies on a range of cognitive capacities such as inferential reasoning and memory, which are discussed in detail in Chapter 5.

---

[3] '[Pragmatics refers to] the study of language from the point of view of the users, especially of the choices they make' (Crystal, 1997: 301). '[U]sing language must consist of *the continuous making of linguistic choices*, consciously or unconsciously, for language-internal (i.e. structural) and/or language-external reasons' (Verschueren, 1999: 55–6; author's italics). Sociolinguistics has been similarly conceptualized in terms of choices (Coulmas, 2005).

4.3.2   Pragmatics as choices at all levels of language

Pragmatic choices are not restricted to specific areas of the linguistic system but are involved at all levels of language processing from discourse down to phonetics (cf. Verschueren, 1999: 56). When you and I converse we have a range of options available for encoding what we want to say at each linguistic level. For example, our vocabulary can be formal or collo-quial; pedantic or poetic; polite or familiar. Our syntax can be complex ('the one just to the left of where your hand is') or simple ('that one'). We may use standard British English phonology (/bɑθ/) and morphology (*I've broken it*), or a different regional variant (/bæθ/ – *I've broke_ it*) if it turns out that we are both natives of Birmingham in the UK and wish to acknowledge it. You may signal a desire to end our conversation by explicitly using the discourse particle *anyway*, or omit it if you feel your intention is already contextually implicit. I may vary my intonation, tempo, pitch and loudness depending on my emotional state, communica-tive intent and a host of other factors. In addition, there is the potential for complex interplay between linguistic levels. For example, I may choose to request assent or dissent explicitly via syntax (Would you like a beer?) or prosody (Béer?) or purely implicitly (There's some beer in the fridge). Limited choice in any area of one's linguistic system, therefore – whether it be phonetics (e.g. Len), phonology, grammar (e.g. Lucy) or semantics (e.g. Peter) – has inevitable pragmatic consequences.

4.3.3   Pragmatics as choices across semiotic systems and modalities

It is widely assumed that communication is an essentially linguistic proc-ess, and the tendency within linguistics generally to rely so heavily on written transcripts of spoken language, and within semantics to focus on meanings which can be expressed as propositions, has only reinforced this impression. In spoken communication, however, we constantly make choices not only about what and how much to signal linguistically, but also about what and how much to encode using other signalling systems such as prosody, gesture, facial expression, gaze and body posture. Nonlinguistic signalling systems are seen as the poor relations of the communicative process because the meanings they are able to convey are inherently less complex, less extensive and less varied than those available to us through the code of language. Such an evaluation, however, is based on a comparative view of individual systems seen in isolation, whereas in reality they all constitute a conjoint, mutually dependent integrated system throughout which information is distributed more like a process of orchestration (Kendon, 2004). Signals are really composites of mutually dependent components. Because Lucy's grammar and phonology are relatively primitive, she 'chooses' to allocate more resources to her gestural system than you or I might. When she utters the word 'hat' – or, to be more precise, the phonologically ambiguous [hæ?] – she simultaneously produces an iconic gesture for hat. These two signals are mutually reinforcing and facilitate comprehension. A better developed phonological system would make such a gesture unnecessary and the result of Lucy's adjustment is thus perceived as atypical. Gestures are nonetheless a common companion of spoken language even when all linguistic resources are intact – a fact which is often ignored.

The view expressed here owes a great deal to that of Clark (1996), who sees face-to-face interaction as involving a composite signalling process which makes use not just of the voice but also the hands, arms, face, eyes and body. Nonverbal signals are frequently seen as a mere accompaniment to, or embellishment of, spoken language, whereas in fact both are integral. Kendon (2000), for example, shows that gesture is used not only to provide context for spoken language to assist in processes such as disambiguation, but also to contribute to the propositional content of an utterance, and McNeill (2000b) argues that the complex ways in which spoken language and gesture merge cast doubt on modular accounts of language.

In the language pathology and psycholinguistics literature various speech and language errors have been explained as resulting from the conversion of parallel into serial representations, constrained by the low dimensional nature of the linear speech signal. For example, an error such as 'first of-ly' may be seen as a 'blend' of the two distinct but semantically equivalent forms 'firstly' and 'first of all', which have accidentally fused into a single form during the utterance process (Fay, 1982). Such errors also occur in aphasic speech (where they are referred to as 'paragrammatisms') and have been described in similar terms by Butterworth and Howard (1987). In addition, though, a complementary strand of research has focused on the way in which compromised language systems compensate by taking advantage of the cross-modal parallelism inherent in the overall system, as noted above in the case of Lucy, where the informational load is distributed across both linguistic and gestural systems. Gestural compensation frequently occurs in both children and adults with language impairments, and in fact shares some features in common (e.g. Fex and Månsson, 1998). Goodwin (2003b) describes how a man with aphasia so severe that he is only able to speak the three words *yes*, *no* and *and* is nonetheless able to deploy these words in conjunction with a modified use of gesture and eye gaze to communicate surprisingly effectively. Thus, although speech involves converting parallel into serial representations, considerable parallelism remains within the communicative system as a whole and the degree of reduction overall is not as extreme as many have assumed. The choices involved in where and how communicative resources are deployed both within and across systems are the very essence of pragmatics. As Schegloff (2003: 26–7) observes,

surely in interaction things are continuously being done in words *and* in *other*-than-words, and the two are intermixed, and, most important, what is being done in words is partially *constituted* by what is being done in *other*-than-words. If the pragmatics is separated from 'the rest', can the rest issue in recognizable, coherent, and effective linguistic products? If there are such products, can the pragmatics possibly *be* cut off from the rest of the speech production process?

4.3.4   Pragmatics as choices motivated by interpersonal communication

Pragmatics is being characterized as involving the options which result from interactional possibilities available within a system. How, then, can pragmatic options be distinguished from those which exist in a wide variety of other systems, such as the engine of a car or the national economy? The difference is one of purpose and motivation. Pragmatic choices are those which are made by human beings because they wish or need to communicate with each other, and they involve the use of any resources which may help to do the job. Such resources (of which more below) typically include linguistic and cognitive systems, signalling systems such as voice, gesture and gaze, and perceptual systems such as vision, hearing and touch. In addition, they may also include tools such as writing implements and microphones or prosthetic devices such as hearing aids and glasses. The orchestrative choices implicit in a multimedia presentation using voice and gesture in conjunction with electronic text, sound and images delivered via Powerpoint[TM] are just as pragmatic as choosing a spoken noun phrase instead of a deictic pronoun in a telephone conversation, or choosing to speak more loudly in the presence of traffic noise. Although differing in obvious ways, resources such as lexis, body posture and mobile phones are alike in that they are all grist to the communicative mill.

Let us revisit for a moment Lucy's two different uses of gesture. Because her phonological system is rather basic and she is often misunderstood, she frequently supports her utterances with iconic gestures – for example, gesturing pulling on a hat at the same time as she says 'hat'. To the extent that her choice to do this is made in order to facilitate communication with her interlocutor, it can be described as pragmatic. In addition, Lucy sometimes taps on the table, or some other object, in time with her speech. The communicative significance of this activity is not at all apparent, and at times may even impede the interlocutor's comprehension. It is possible that its motivation is internal to Lucy and helps to trigger the motor programmes involved in speech production, although this is only conjecture. To the extent that her tapping movement is not motivated by the requirements of interpersonal communication, it may be seen as not pragmatic. If this is so, it would also be inaccurate to describe it as a 'gesture', which also implies communicative intent.[4] Likewise, using a mobile phone to send a text message rather than an email is a pragmatic choice. Choosing to use the phone as a paperweight is not.

4.3.5   Pragmatic impairment as compensatory adaptation

Lucy's atypical but communicatively helpful use of gesture is a way of compensating for a linguistic deficit. In the same manner, Len's use of prosody to signal syntactic boundaries and Peter's use of interlocutor support to effect word retrieval are also attempts to compensate for a specific deficit by making use of an alternative communicative resource. Communication is achieved by redistributing the message load within the overall system. In the cases of Len, Lucy and Peter there is no evidence to suggest that these compensatory adaptations are conscious and deliberate – the system, as it were, appears to have readjusted spontaneously.[5]

All communicative impairments have a pragmatic dimension in that they produce an interactional imbalance which results in a redistribution of resources and a concomitant reconfiguration of choices. It does not matter where in the system the original deficit occurs, or how it is compensated for. The deficit may be linguistic, cognitive, motor or perceptual, and compensation may be attempted by making adjustments to a similar or quite different system, or to a number of such systems simultaneously, either serially or in parallel. Because of this, there may be no apparent link between an underlying deficit and a resulting pragmatic impairment. Rather, the latter may be the consequence of one or more compensations. As we shall see later, compensatory adaptations may give rise to symptoms which may appear to be distinct impairments in

---

[4] Cf. Kendon's (2004: 15) definition of gestures as 'actions that have the features of manifest deliberate expressiveness'.

[5] In cases where compensatory adaptations are deliberately taught – as often occurs in therapeutic intervention – there is no guarantee that they will be effective, or even that they will be learnable. Consciously learned behaviours and spontaneous adaptive behaviours are quite different in kind. For further discussion, see Chapter 8.

their own right but are in fact merely an attempted solution to an underlying problem.

4.4   Elements, interactions and domains

4.4.1   Elements: semiotic, cognitive and sensorimotor systems

Notions such as compensation and adaptation have proved fruitful in the study of human cognition, particularly from a developmental perspective, and have played a notably central role in the work of Piaget (1952) and more recently in the application of dynamic systems theory to cognitive processing (Thelen and Smith, 1994). In such approaches, the human organism is seen as continuously adapting to environmental demands in order to maintain equilibrium. In language processing, however, such notions have been of more peripheral concern. In his monumental study of language production, for example, Levelt (1989) only discusses compensation in the context of the articulatory system. Instead, as was noted in Chapter 3, far more interest has been shown in the way in which cognitive and linguistic mechanisms may be dissociated from one another than in how they interact. In the study of communication impairment, on the other hand, the notion of compensation has attracted rather more interest because it is so apparent and common. This has led to the considerable body of research on trade-offs and compensatory adaptations reviewed in Chapter 3. As we saw there, however, there is little consistency in the way such components and their interrelations are characterized, and the distinction between the components themselves and how they are implicated in receptive and expressive language processing is often blurred.

In what follows I will refer to individual entities within an organism between or among which interactions may occur as *elements*. 'Element' is a deliberately neutral term which may be applied both to entities seen as systems and competences as well as processes or behaviours. As we saw in Chapter 3, terms such as 'language' and 'memory' reify for descriptive and heuristic convenience highly complex phenomena. Such phenomena may be seen either as a set of specific behaviours on the basis of which we may infer some general underlying competence system, or else as the full set of behaviours which the underlying system generates. Although my use of 'element' will be largely limited to semiotic, cognitive and sensorimotor systems and processes, assuming a neural substrate for each of these it is also possible to consider them in terms of their underlying neurological properties. Indeed, there is no need to stop at neurology: elements at all but the very lowest level may be seen as resulting from 'interactions all the way down' (Elman *et al.*, 1996: 319).

Table 4.1 *Some semiotic, cognitive and sensorimotor elements of pragmatics*

Elements of pragmatics

Semiotic	Cognitive	Motor	Sensory
Language:	Inference	Vocal tract	Hearing
phonology	Theory of mind	Hands	Vision
prosody	Executive function	Arms	
morphology	Memory	Face	
syntax	Emotion	Eyes	
semantics	Attitude	Body	
discourse			
Gesture			
Gaze			
Facial expression			
Posture			

Table 4.1 provides an outline of some of the elements whose interactions constitute pragmatics.[6] The semiotic elements shown provide us with the means of encoding and decoding meaning. The cognitive elements are instrumental in determining and interpreting what is communicated, and also whether, why, when, where and in what manner it is communicated. The sensory input and motor output elements allow for the reception and transmission of symbolically encoded information via different channels. These elements and their interactions will be explored in detail in Chapters 5 to 8. For present purposes, the list should be seen as simply illustrative and making no specific claims about the status of elements either as modules or processes other than that they represent aspects of symbolic, cognitive and input/output mechanisms which play a role in human communication. It also makes no claims about the distinctness or discreteness of elements. We know, for example, that the lexicon does not have the same kind of computational properties shared by the phonological, morphological and syntactic systems (Chomsky, 1995b), and overlaps to a large extent with conceptual knowledge which is not purely linguistically instantiated (Smith and Tsimpli, 1995). Similarly, prosody includes various subsystems including both the ability to convey emotional and attitudinal meaning via tone of voice and the ability to interact with various linguistic elements – for example, to mark focus within the sentence (e.g. it's ʼmy book vs it's my ʼbook) and to disambiguate word

[6] Variants of Table 4.1 have appeared in Perkins (1998a, 2000, 2002, 2005b).

meaning (e.g. 'contact vs con'tact). Among cognitive elements, theory of mind may be seen to overlap to some extent with executive functions in that deficiences in both have been implicated in alternative theoretical accounts of the key underlying deficit in autism (Hughes, Russell and Robbins, 1994). The discreteness and ontological distinctness of such elements may also be challenged, and in fact each may be seen as an emergent consequence of complex interactions in its own right (as has been noted, for example, by Snowling and Hulme (1994: 23) in the case of short-term memory).

4.4.2   Interactions: equilibrium, disequilibrium and compensatory adaptation

The essence of pragmatics lies in the ways in which elements such as those listed in Table 4.1 interact with one another. Interactions are evident in the way elements may *constrain* or *facilitate* one another (cf. Thomas (2005b: 33), who sees developmental disorders 'in terms of constraints on the developmental process – whether a given theory assumes the presence of domain-specific modular structure prior to language acquisition or assumes that such structure is the product of the developmental process itself'), and the way in which they may *compete* (cf. Bates and MacWhinney's (1996) Competition Model discussed in Chapter 3). For example, the syntactic complexity of our utterances is partly constrained by the limitations of our verbal short-term memory and the amount of attention we are able to allocate to sentence formulation (cf. O'Grady, 2005). The complexity of some of the written sentences found in the works of authors like Proust, for example, where a single sentence can run to a page or more, is quite beyond the productive capacity of most speakers because we are unable to keep track of what we have already said.[7] If, in addition, there are competing demands on our attention our syntactic output may be further simplified and we may even produce syntactic errors not unlike those found in agrammatic aphasia (Dick *et al.*, 2001). If, on the other hand, we choose instead to express ourselves in writing, we no longer need to rely on the limitations of short-term memory but instead can monitor what we have already written visually, and in this regard the effect

---

[7] Individual performance in this area varies considerably. The philosopher Isaiah Berlin was well known for his ability to deliver extremely long and syntactically complex sentences with great rapidity and panache. As noted in an obituary, 'American audiences often found him difficult to follow, both the rapidity and the number of syntactically perfect sentences, always exciting to follow – what would come next, could he possibly regain the main subject, spoken two minutes and 20 dependent clauses ago, with an object sufficient for climax not bathos? Yes, always – often to mass sighs of relief and admiration' (Crick, 1997).

on syntactic complexity of using a visual medium may be regarded as facilitative. Whether one interprets an interaction as constraint or facilitation is partly a matter of perspective. Len's use of prosody to highlight syntactic boundaries would appear to facilitate understanding, though his need to do so in the first place results from articulatory constraints on his phonological system, which in turn constrains his interlocutor's comprehension. Lucy's impaired phonology and grammar clearly constrain her communicative capacity as a whole, though her facilitative use of gesture helps to offset this. Peter's poor lexical retrieval – clearly a constraining factor within his own communicative system – is counterbalanced by Sara's carrying out the retrieval for him, such that the constraint is cancelled out by the facilitation. Alternatively, we could say that Sara has compensated for Peter's constraint or, if we see Peter and Sara as a self-regulating dynamic system, that there has been a compensatory adaptation within the system.

The key factor in all of this is equilibrium, and this is what counterbalances constraint and facilitation and motivates and accounts for interactions more generally. We might say that a domain achieves a state of *optimal equilibrium* where none of its elements or the relationships between them are impaired, and where impairment may consist of a developmental or degenerative abnormality, a lesion or some other intrusive damage, or an exceptionally low level of functioning in one or more elements relative to that of other elements. A domain will be in a state of *disequilibrium* to the extent that one or more elements or the relationships between them malfunction for whatever reason, but may achieve a state of *compensated equilibrium*, where compensation consists in the reallocation of functions from an impaired sub-element to one or more other sub-elements, and to a counterbalancing within the domain as a whole. Disequilibrium may or may not be fully compensatable, and a state of *optimal compensated equilibrium* is the best that can be achieved given a particular impairment. There are thus three possible states of a domain: equilibrium, disequilibrium and compensated equilibrium. Our perceptions of what constitutes normal or abnormal communicative behaviour do not map directly on to these states. Although such perceptions will typically be related to the relative seriousness of any impairments, the success of compensatory adaptations and a whole range of sociocultural constructs will also play a major role. Atypical communicators are seen as such because, although there may have been compensation for a specific dysfunction, the state of compensated equilibrium subsequently achieved is perceived as qualitatively different from that found in the interaction of typical populations. We will revisit the role of compensation in greater depth in Chapter 8.

4.4.3   Domains: the intrapersonal and interpersonal

All interactions occur within a specific organism or 'domain', which in turn may form part of a larger domain. The key domain for pragmatics is the 'interpersonal' domain, which involves interactions between two or more individuals, though insofar as interactions *within* individuals (i.e. the 'intrapersonal' domain) are interpersonally motivated, they also come within the scope of pragmatics.[8] To the extent that elements such as syntax or memory may also be seen as by-products of interactions, the term 'domain' might also be applied to them, and 'domain' and 'element' be seen as synonymous. However, I will for the most part be using 'domain' in a more restricted sense to refer to the scope of single-person and multi-person organisms only.

Impairment of an element in a domain can create a state of disequilibrium both within the domain itself and across domains. In Len's case, the impairment to his articulatory system has created a disequilibrium internal to the domain which is Len. This may be described as a state of intrapersonal disequilibrium. In addition, however, the main pressure for reorganization and compensation comes from the need to communicate with others. There is also, therefore, a state of equilibrium to be maintained in the interpersonal domain during the process of communication. The only motivation for Len to pause at syntactic boundaries is to facilitate his interlocutor's comprehension. There is a way, then, in which a communicative dyad or group may be regarded as an organism in the same way as an individual person, at least as far as equilibrium and compensation are concerned.[9] Let us consider some examples of this.

In the conversation between Peter and Sara shown above, because of Peter's linguistic impairment, there is greater pressure than normal on Sara to ensure conversational success. She compensates for Peter's word-finding problem by engaging with Peter in a search and guess exercise, doing

---

[8] One could extend the scale of domains both 'upward' – e.g. the sociocultural domain, and 'downward' – e.g. the neurological domain, though for the purposes of this book I will largely restrict myself to the cognitive, semiotic and sensorimotor interactions of the intrapersonal and interpersonal domains.

[9] Clark and Chalmers (1995) refer to such instances where the human organism is linked with an external entity in a two-way interaction as a 'coupled system', and regard such a system as a cognitive system in its own right, though this requires a conception of human cognition as 'a spatio-temporally extended process not limited by the tenuous envelope of skin and skull' (Clark, 1997: 221). A coupled system, though, is seen for example as person-plus-diary or person-plus-tractor rather than as person-plus-person. The view of person-plus-person as a coupled system – which is what I am referring to as an interpersonal domain – is more akin to that of Hutchins (1995), who sees a team of humans engaged in joint activity as an organism whose overall functionality exceeds that of its individual components.

extra inferential work and eventually producing the target word herself. In other words, equilibrium involving interactions between linguistic and cognitive elements can be regarded as a state that also extends across individuals. It is unlikely that Peter consciously and intentionally sets out to co-opt the resources of his interlocutor, nor should Sara's response be seen simply as a passive reaction or as a deliberate strategy. This is a joint project in the sense of Clark (1996) and is more than the sum of its parts. Although the source of the problem may be internal to Peter, its solution is no less a joint achievement than two people waltzing, wrestling or playing tennis.

Cognitive impairment can also create pressure for interpersonal compensation. Transcript 4.6 shows part of a conversation between a 4-year-old child (C) with autistic spectrum disorder and a speech and language therapist (T). C seems unable to infer that T's first utterance is intended as a request.

Transcript 4.6

T: can you turn the page over?
C: yes *(no sign of continuing)*
T: go on then *(points)*
C: *(turns the page over)*

T consequently encodes this fact explicitly by using an imperative and a pointing gesture. Adults with right hemisphere damage also have difficulties making appropriate inferences from spoken and written discourse (Brownell and Martino, 1998; Hirst *et al.*, 1984), which puts pressure on interlocutors to encode more information linguistically than they would normally.

In such cases, a cognitive impairment in one conversational partner has created a state of interpersonal disequilibrium, which is compensated for by the unimpaired interlocutor. Intrapersonal disequilibrium typically results in interpersonal disequilibrium, and unsuccessful intrapersonal compensation typically builds up pressure for interpersonal compensation. As regards the interpersonal balance between semiotic, cognitive and sensorimotor processing, impairment of any of these resources within a member of a conversational dyad typically brings about a concomitant readjustment of the interlocutor's resource allocation. Some examples are shown in Table 4.2.

One consequence of regarding the human dyad as a coupled cognitive system is that disorders of language and thought become common property, rather than solely the problem of an individual.

The distinctions and parallels drawn here between intrapersonal and interpersonal equilibrium are in some ways analogous to those drawn by

Table 4.2 *Interpersonal compensation for expressive and receptive communication impairments*

Impairment of expressive resources	Compensation by interlocutor
Semiotic – e.g. syntactic formulation problems	Greater reliance on inference based on contextual clues, shared knowledge, etc.
Cognitive – e.g. attention deficit	Greater reliance on gesture, eye contact, linguistic repetition
Sensorimotor – e.g. dysarthria, dyspraxia	Repetition of what hearer thinks has been said for verification by speaker
Impairment of receptive resources	Compensation by interlocutor
Semiotic – e.g. poor parsing, word recognition	Simplified syntax, use of gesture and visual clues
Cognitive – e.g. poor short-term memory	Frequent linguistic recapitulation and use of visual reminders
Sensorimotor – e.g. hearing impairment	Greater reliance on gesture, exaggerated articulation and other visual clues

Sperber and Wilson (1995) between the First Principle of Relevance (human cognition tends to be geared to the maximization of relevance) and the Second Principle of Relevance (every act of ostensive communication communicates a presumption of its own optimal relevance), where relevance is defined in terms of an efficiency balance between processing effort and contextual effects. Intrapersonal equilibrium may be seen as a property of the cognitive system of an individual which is governed by the First Principle of Relevance, whereas interpersonal equilibrium extends beyond the individual into the domain governed by the Second Principle of Relevance.

In order to count as pragmatic, interactions must be interpersonally motivated – i.e. by the exigences of human communication – though for analytical purposes their effects may be construed separately within either the intrapersonal or interpersonal domain, or in both simultaneously.

4.5   Conclusion

Most studies of pragmatic behaviour and pragmatic impairment focus on specific features such as speech acts, Gricean maxims, theory of mind or turn taking, which has sometimes given rise to the impression that pragmatics is a discrete, self-contained phenomenon. However, in its broadest semiotic sense, pragmatics is to do with the full range of choices (actual or potential) involved in communicative behaviour as a whole, and the breadth and complex nature of such choices becomes particularly apparent when we examine cases of communicative impairment, whether their primary underlying cause is semiotic, cognitive, perceptual or motoric.

According to this view, pragmatics is therefore an exclusive property of neither language (as many linguists seem to assume) nor cognition (as many language pathologists seem to assume), nor is it restricted to a specific semiotic system or a particular medium such as the vocal-auditory channel or the gestural-visual channel. The use of any cognitive, semiotic or sensorimotor system for communicative purposes is inherently pragmatic. The key systems in question are those of the individual – i.e. the intrapersonal domain – and the conjoint systems of pairs or groups of individuals – i.e. the interpersonal domain. These systems and their contributory subsystems comprise the elements of pragmatics. Pragmatic competence may be defined as the choices implicit in the relationships between elements, and pragmatic behaviour as the exercise of such choices.

The use of the term 'choice' should not be taken to imply that there is necessarily a conscious, superordinate 'chooser' in the sense of some central executive system. Rather, the occurrence (i.e. 'selection' or 'choice') of option A rather than option B will be an emergent consequence of states elsewhere in the intrapersonal or interpersonal domain. An individual, or a pair or group of communicating individuals, may each be seen as a single organism whose overall state of equilibrium is determined by the interactions among its elements. Pragmatic impairment may be defined as a state of disequilibrium within the interpersonal domain caused by a dysfunction in one or more elements which constrains or restricts the range of interactions within the domain as a whole. Dysfunctions may be compensated for, with varying degrees of success, by exploiting the considerable scope for 'trade-offs' among elements within one or more domains.

Pragmatics, whether seen as competence or performance, is therefore emergent. When characterized in this way, the burden of explanation shifts away from a consideration of pragmatics as a distinct conceptual or behavioural entity, and towards a consideration of the complex of underlying factors from which pragmatics emerges. This is the goal of Chapters 5 to 8.

5   Cognition and pragmatics

5.1   Introduction

In this and the next two chapters I will consider the way a wide range of elements contributes to pragmatic processing by examining the communicative consequences of breakdown in each one individually. As pointed out earlier, however, the relationship between a specific underlying deficit and its behavioural consequences is not straightforward, and the way each element interacts with others will also be a primary focus. In addition, Chapter 8 will be devoted to the pervasive role played by compensatory adaptation. Any cognitive, semiotic or sensorimotor deficit has pragmatic consequences in that it limits the range of choices available for communication. In this chapter we will consider the way this operates in the domain of cognition.

The fact that pragmatics involves cognition is widely recognized, though in mainstream pragmatics this role is rarely explicitly targeted. In cases where it is (for example in Relevance Theory, where human cognition is seen as inherently 'relevance-oriented' (Sperber and Wilson, 1995)), the tendency is to focus on one or a narrow range of cognitive processes such as theory of mind. In language pathology research, on the other hand, there has been increasing interest in recent years in the relationship between cognitive dysfunction and pragmatic impairment, particularly in conditions such as right hemisphere brain damage, traumatic brain injury and autism (Martin and McDonald, 2003). However, as we saw in Chapter 2, there is a great deal of inconsistency in the way terms such as 'pragmatic impairment' are used and understood, and the pragmatic theories most commonly used by clinicians – i.e. Speech Act Theory and Conversational Implicature – are not couched in cognitive terms,[1] which makes it difficult to establish clear links between specific cognitive deficits and specific pragmatic behaviours described using standard theoretical

---

[1] Relevance Theory is once again the exception.

approaches (see, for example, the discussion in Body, Perkins and McDonald, 1999). If instead we see pragmatic behaviour not as a distinct phenomenon in its own right but as an emergent function of interactions between cognitive (and other) processes, the characterization of pragmatic impairment becomes in principle more straightforward. In practice, we will still face difficulties tracing links between communicative behaviours and underlying deficits because of compensatory adaptations within the organism as a whole, but conceptually at least the task should be easier.

Cognition – the mental faculty which enables us to think and reason – has been characterized in a bewildering variety of ways. Gazzaniga (2000) sees attention, memory and language as primary cognitive functions, which are implicated in various 'higher' cognitive functions such as number processing and conceptual knowledge. Sternberg (1995), on the other hand, sees memory and language as already being higher functions, on a par with learning, thinking and intelligence. Carroll (1993) breaks cognitive ability down into language, reasoning, memory and learning, visual perception, auditory perception, psychomotor abilities, idea production, cognitive speed, and knowledge and achievement – each of which is seen as contributing to a higher order general intelligence. Rather than construing higher order cognition as intelligence, some neuropsychologists tend to think in terms of 'executive functions' (e.g. Shallice, 1988). Some see emotion as being separate from, though influenced by, cognition (Sternberg, 1995), whereas others see emotion as playing a crucial role in various aspects of cognitive processing such as decision making (Damasio, 1994). Some regard conceptual knowledge as a distinct cognitive entity, partly overlapping with the mental lexicon, whereas others think of it as a long-term memory store. The rationale for the particular selection of cognitive functions identified by separate section headings in this chapter is that they have all been singled out as having an impact on communicative behaviour in studies of pragmatic impairment. Having said that, one could clearly have cut the cake in a number of different ways. Some might choose to allocate more importance to attention, rather than subsume it under executive function. Others might feel uncertain about treating emotion and attitude as subcomponents of cognition, which has more to do with thought than with feeling. Ultimately, though, given our present state of knowledge, it probably matters less how the material is packaged than that the relevant issues are discussed. One important factor that will soon become apparent is the tremendous amount of overlap and cross-reference between the different sections of this chapter, which once again underlines the fact that pragmatics is more to do with interaction than compartmentalization, and that the salience and apparent individuation of any superordinate categories is ultimately a by-product of interactions between their subordinate elements.

In order to focus on those characteristics which are most significant for the emergentist model of pragmatics presented in Chapter 4, the discussion of each element will be guided by the following questions:

1. What are its essential characteristics?
2. In what communicative disorders is its impairment manifested?
3. How may it be impaired, and what are the pragmatic consequences in terms of restriction of communicative choice?
4. How does it interact with other elements within the intrapersonal domain, what impact does its impairment have on other cognitive, semiotic and sensorimotor elements, and what are the implications for resource allocation within the individual?
5. How does it interact with other elements within the interpersonal domain, how does its impairment affect expression and comprehension, and what are the implications for resource allocation between individuals?

5.2   Inference

5.2.1   Introduction

Inference is widely seen as the key cognitive process involved in pragmatics by linguists, psycholinguists and neurolinguists alike (cf. 'Every domain of pragmatics involves probabilistic inference' (Paradis, 2003)), and some use 'social inference theory' as an umbrella term for discussing theoretical accounts of pragmatic impairment such as theory of mind (Martin and McDonald, 2003). In the emergentist model the centrality of inference may be accounted for by the fact that the notion of *choice* is an inherent property of inference. Since pragmatic impairment is a function of disruption in communicative choice, and since inferential reasoning directly involves choosing between two or more alternative interpretations, problems with inferential processing are an inevitable concomitant of pragmatic impairment.

Inferential reasoning is not a single undifferentiated process. Three different types are commonly identified (Harley, 2001: 318): *logical inference*, which involves, for example, deducing that a rose is a flower; *bridging inference*, which enables us to link previous and current information – e.g. the fact that in 'The phone rang – he picked it up' 'it' is anaphorically coreferential with 'the phone'; and *elaborative inference*, which refers to the use of world knowledge to relate disparate items of information into a coherent whole – e.g. in order to make sense of the dialogue 'A: Children's hospital. B: One pound, please', we need to be aware that passengers who don't know the fare to a particular destination can elicit this information by stating their destination to the bus driver when getting on the bus.

McKoon and Ratcliff (1992) differentiate inferences on the basis of how much cognitive processing they involve. The logical and bridging inferences are seen as 'minimal' in this respect since they are relatively automatic and make minimal processing demands, whereas elaborative inferences such as identifying themes, predicting outcomes and attributing motivations and attitudes on the basis of behaviour make greater demands on processing resources. As Lehman and Tompkins (2000) point out, though, the distinction is not an absolute one; rather, the two types probably represent the ends of a continuum of processing demand. Furthermore, inferences which appear automatic in adults may require deliberate processing effort in children. For example, Milford (1989) (cited in McTear and Conti-Ramsden (1992: 110–11)) found a considerable difference in the ability of children and adults to distinguish between the presuppositions of factive and non-factive verbs.[2] The use of a factive verb like *forget* in 'I forgot that Peter phoned' enables us to infer that Peter actually did phone, whereas the use of a non-factive verb such as *believe* does not. Milford found that children aged between 4 and 7 years old were largely unable to distinguish between *forget* and *believe* in this way, and even 10-year-olds made the wrong inference in 60 per cent of cases.[3] Adults, on the other hand, made no errors at all. This suggests that the apparent automaticity of some types of inference generation may be the outcome of a long and gradual learning process.

Problems with inferential processing are not always easy to analyse. Because inference may draw on most, if not all, other cognitive, semiotic and perceptual processes – for example, memory and theory of mind, lexical and syntactic knowledge, and visual and auditory perception – it may be the case that an apparent breakdown in inferential reasoning is due not to a fault in the inferential process itself but to problems with one or more input processes. For example, an inability to read facial expressions accurately could lead one to mistake an ironical statement for a literal one. Although some have argued that inferential reasoning is verbally mediated, neuropsychological evidence suggests that it may well be an independent cognitive process (Johnson, 1995; Varley and Siegal, 2000). Bishop and Adams (1992), for example, showed that children with specific language impairment (SLI) were impaired in constructing an integrated representation from a sequence of propositions even when these were presented nonverbally, and Varley (2002) has shown that severe global

---

[2] With 'factive' verbs (e.g. *realize* and *agree*), the truth of the proposition expressed by the complement clause is presupposed, whereas this is not the case for 'non-factive' verbs (e.g. *think* and *assume*) (Kiparsky and Kiparsky, 1971).

[3] Eisele and Aram (1993) found that children with right hemisphere brain damage were less aware of the presuppositions of *forget* than their healthy peers.

aphasia does not necessarily affect the ability to carry out complex reasoning tasks. Inference is therefore a good example of a 'higher cognitive function' in that it relies on relatively large numbers of processes which may themselves have complex internal structures (Kosslyn and Smith, 2000: 961), and yet it may be conceptualized and characterized independently of them.

5.2.2   Impairment of inferential reasoning and its pragmatic consequences

Breakdown in the ability to draw inferences is evident in a wide range of communication impairments including autism (Minshew, Goldstein and Siegel, 1995), hydrocephalus (Barnes and Dennis, 1998), right hemisphere brain damage (RHD) (Lehman and Tompkins, 2000) and traumatic brain injury (TBI) (Martin and McDonald, 2005), and developmental language disorders of various kinds including autistic spectrum disorder, specific language impairment and pragmatic language impairment (Letts and Leinonen, 2001; Norbury and Bishop, 2002b).

The manifestations of poor inferential reasoning in communicative problems include difficulties in understanding sarcasm (McDonald, 1999), irony (Martin and McDonald, 2005), indirect requests and punchlines of jokes (Molloy et al. 1990), indirect replies (Holtgraves, 1999), lies (Winner et al., 1998), ambiguous utterances (Tompkins et al., 1994, 2001), stretches of text and discourse (Barnes and Dennis, 1998; Dipper et al., 1997), and others' mental states, attitudes and emotions (Bissett and Novak, 1995; Winner et al., 1998).

5.2.3   Inference: interactions in the intrapersonal domain

Within the intrapersonal domain, problems with inference are commonly characterized as difficulties in integrating different sources of information within a coherent framework and not being able to modify prior assumptions in the light of new information. In right hemisphere brain damage (RHD), such behaviours have been ascribed to limitations in overall processing capacity together with an inability to suppress inappropriate mental activations.[4] In developmental communication disorders such as autism, similar problems with inferential processing have been described as resulting from 'weak central coherence' (Norbury and Bishop, 2002b).

---

[4] Tompkins et al. (2002: 560) see problems with inference in RHD as 'a consequence of integration deficits, or difficulties constructing a coherent model by assimilating discourse elements into a conceptual whole'. For Brownell and Martino (1998: 315), 'the most pronounced deficit in patients with RHD can be characterized as a failure to revise the results of an initial inference to insure that the parts of a discourse all fit together'.

Inferential processing interacts with a range of cognitive systems and indeed, as noted above, is actually dependent on their input. This will be considered in more detail in the sections below devoted to specific cognitive systems, but for illustrative purposes I will briefly examine the way in which memory interacts with inference. Information retained in memory is of central importance in inferential reasoning. Norbury and Bishop (2002b) found a clear correlation between inferential ability and story recall in children with autism, SLI and PLI (pragmatic language impairment), and Dennis and Barnes (1990) found that, in children and adolescents with traumatic brain injury, inferential processing in discourse correlated with working memory capacity but not social knowledge. However, memory alone is clearly not sufficient for successful inference, and it is also important to distinguish between specific types of inference, memory and knowledge stored in memory. Jolliffe and Baron-Cohen (1999) observe, for example, that people with autism fail to make appropriate *elaborative* inferences despite having good *rote* memory, and Beeman (1998) suggests that adults with RHD may fail to activate information necessary to make appropriate *bridging* inferences (for example, in working out the punchlines of jokes) even when it is available in short-term memory. Dipper *et al.* (1997) also found that bridging inference errors made by a group of adults with RHD resulted from an excessive reliance on knowledge stored in their long-term encyclopedic memory over information available in short-term memory.

5.2.4   Inference: interactions in the interpersonal domain

In the interpersonal domain, inference plays a crucial role in determining what one's interlocutors mean by virtue of the information they convey via a range of signalling systems such as speech, writing, gesture, posture and facial expression. To these inputs into the inferential process must be added an ongoing assessment of the interlocutor's knowledge, intentions, beliefs, needs, desires, emotional state and a range of other factors derived via cognitive systems such as memory, knowledge and theory of mind. The counterbalancing and synthesis of these myriad competing inputs is the essence of the inferential process in pragmatics.

In Transcript 5.1, from a guessing game played by an adult and 6-year-old Jamel with ASD, the inability to infer the right answer in spite of the range of pertinent clues seems surprising:

Transcript 5.1

Adult: this is something to help you travel . to go places on . and it's got wheels
Jamel: car
Adult: and it's got a seat to sit on . and it's got a handlebar . and only one person can ride on it

Jamel: wheelchair
Adult: and . it's got pedals . it's got two wheels and pedals and a seat and a
         handlebar and one person can ride it
Jamel: a wheelchair
Adult: I don't think it's a wheelchair . can you think of anything else that has two
         wheels?
Jamel: bike

Potential contributory factors could be: a genuine ignorance of bicycles
(unlikely, given the eventual correct answer); executive rigidity in the form
of an inability to inhibit access to the lexeme 'wheelchair' or to focus on
more than one feature of an object at the same time; a misunderstanding of
the rules of the guessing game; a problem dealing with information
expressed only verbally; or general cognitive overload.

Inference plays a key role not only in comprehension but also in expression in that the form and content of what one chooses to convey must be
optimally tailored to the interlocutor's communicative requirements. In
Transcript 5.2, 5-year-old Sean, also with ASD, is describing a picture of a
man buying a Christmas tree. The man has a tree in his hands and there are
many more in the background. Emily is an adult he knows slightly.

Transcript 5.2

Sean: he's getting loads
Emily: what's he doing?
Sean: he's getting loads
Emily: getting loads of what?
Sean: these *(points to Christmas trees in picture)* – loads

Sean is not being linguistically explicit enough in what he says, presumably
because he has problems inferring what Emily already knows.[5] It may be that
he is unable to appreciate that her perspective could be different from his. As
we shall see in the section on theory of mind, speakers also need to be able to
infer whether their interlocutor can make the same inferences as them.

5.3   Theory of mind

5.3.1   Introduction

'Theory of mind' (ToM) – also referred to as 'mind-reading' – is a term used to
describe the ability to attribute mental states such as beliefs, intentions and
feelings to others, and to explain and predict the actions that derive from them
(Baron-Cohen, 1995; Carruthers and Smith, 1996b). Most definitions also

---

[5] We cannot, of course, rule out other possibilities, such as problems with lexical retrieval.

include one's own mental states. For example, others may entertain thoughts about our own thoughts, and thus in order to interpret their thoughts we need to be aware that our own may be the object of someone else's mind-reading. Like inference more generally, ToM is seen by many as a – if not *the* – key cognitive capacity involved in pragmatic understanding and a prime contender for modular status (e.g. Sperber and Wilson, 2002). Indeed, Wilson (2005) sees pragmatics as a specific subcomponent of the ToM module. However, rather than being viewed as a single, unitary entity, ToM is perhaps better construed as a continuum of abilities. Happé (1993) distinguishes between different levels of mind-reading ranging from a basic capacity to represent others' mental states (i.e. 'representational ability') to the potentially exponential representation of mental states about other mental states (i.e. 'metarepresentational ability'). For example, (a) entertaining the view that Jim intends to cheat me ('first-order' intention) is less complex than (b) entertaining the view that Jim doesn't intend me to understand that he's going to cheat me ('second-order' intention). Representational ability turns out to be sufficient to appreciate metaphor, though metarepresentational ability is required for an understanding of irony (Happé, 1993).

Two main theories of ToM have been proposed. According to the so-called 'theory-theory' account (Carruthers and Smith, 1996a), on the basis of someone's behaviour and its actual or imagined effects, we attribute to them the beliefs, desires, intentions, etc. that would make this behaviour rational. The 'simulation theory' (Stone and Davies, 1996), on the other hand, proposes that we simulate in our own minds the behaviour we observe, and infer what intentions, beliefs, desires, etc. we would have to have in order to behave in such a way ourselves. Both theories have wide support, though the simulation theory is favoured by recent research by Gallese and Goldman (1998), who have identified a class of neurons called 'mirror neurons', which appear to replicate in observers the same neural activity required to carry out behaviour observed in other agents.[6]

ToM ability is typically assessed by asking individuals to evaluate a story or role-play which requires metarepresentational ability in order to be properly understood. For example, if A sees B hide a ball under a cup, but doesn't see B subsequently remove the ball and put it in his pocket, we assume that A still thinks the ball is under the cup. However, children under the age of 4 and many people with autism will often intimate that A thinks the ball is in B's pocket, and are thus judged not to have developed a ToM.

[6] In the case of behaviour attributed to ToM, such activity would appear to be sited in the medial prefrontal cortex (Fletcher *et al.*, 1995; Gallagher *et al.*, 2000). Importantly, the functioning of mirror neurons appears to be impaired in people with autism (Dapretto *et al.*, 2006).

However, drawing conclusions about the existence of a putative cognitive entity called ToM on the basis of performance on such 'false belief' tasks is not always as straightforward as it might seem. Performance on ToM tasks can be variable and, in the case of autism, Boucher (1989) has suggested that some of this variability is consistent with the view that people with autism may have ToM skills but are not always clear about their appropriate use. The observation of behaviour in everyday situations raises similar difficulties. In Transcript 5.3, from MacLure and French (1981: 212), for example, one reading of Rosie's misinterpretation of the teacher's questions in lines 1 and 3, and the teacher's subsequent clarification of her meaning in lines 5–7, would be that Rosie is unable to appreciate that the teacher may have a different perspective from hers, because of an insufficiently developed ToM. However, an alternative explanation might be that Rosie (who is 5;2 and has only just started school) is not yet aware of the convention that teachers frequently ask questions, not because they don't know the answer but because they want to find out whether the children know the answer. This may be the first time that Rosie has the convention explained to her.

Transcript 5.3

Teacher and group are looking at slides

1	Teacher:	What can you see?
2	Rosie:	And they're going in the sand
3	Teacher:	Mm?
4	Rosie:	You have a look
5	Teacher:	Well you have a look and tell me
6		I've seen it already
7		I want to see if you can see

In Transcript 5.4, from Bishop and Adams (1989: 252), of a conversation between a speech therapist and a child with autistic spectrum disorder, a specific problem with being able to appreciate the therapist's separate perspective is perhaps more likely, though even here there may be a constellation of factors affecting the child's inferential abilities (see, for example, the discussion in section 5.2 on inference) rather than a specific ToM failure.

Transcript 5.4

Therapist:	what will happen if he doesn't get better?
Child:	he . get some medicine . and make . and make . my brother was feeling sick on Monday
Therapist:	right
Child:	. and I took my trouser off
Therapist:	uhuh .
	why did you take your trousers off?
Child:	he was sick on my trouser

In fact, the same behaviours which have been attributed to a ToM deficit have also been explained in terms of 'weak central coherence', which Frith (2003: 152) defines as 'the lack of an effect of context, and by implication, the lack of a drive for meaning', and which is exemplified in the fact that many people with autism will see a jigsaw puzzle as a set of interlocking fragments rather than as a coherent picture; and also in terms of 'executive dysfunction' (Ozonoff, Pennington and Rogers, 1991) (discussed in the next section), which provides an account in terms of various activities controlled by the frontal lobes such as flexibility and adaptability. The precise relationship between these three alternative conceptualizations in terms of overlap, perspective and precedence is not yet entirely clear (Martin and McDonald, 2003), which suggests that we should exercise considerable caution in seeing ToM as a discrete cognitive capacity.

5.3.2   Impairment of theory of mind and its pragmatic consequences

The condition most commonly associated with ToM deficit is autism, though, more recently, impaired performance on ToM tasks has also been identified in adults with right hemisphere damage (Champagne *et al.*, 2003; Happé, Brownell and Winner, 1999; Siegal, Carrington and Radel, 1996), schizophrenia (Langdon, Davies and Coltheart, 2002) and traumatic brain injury (Bibby and McDonald, 2005; Channon, Pellijeff and Rule, 2005; Levine, Van Horn and Curtis, 1993), and in children with developmental disorders and mental retardation (Capps, Kehres and Sigman, 1998), and with specific language impairment (Gillott, Furniss and Walter, 2004).

   The pragmatic consequences of an impaired ToM in terms of limitations in communicative choice are considerable. As Tager-Flusberg (1997: 155–6) notes, 'Impairments in a theory of mind lead to a highly restricted use of language that lacks the richness for which it has been designed.' One direct example of this in individuals with autism is the limited understanding, and sometimes infrequent use, of terms which refer to mental states such as emotions (Hobson and Lee, 1989), beliefs (Roth and Leslie, 1991; Wilson and McAnulty, 2000) and other propositional attitudes such as epistemic and deontic modality (Nuyts and Roeck, 1997; Perkins and Firth, 1991).[7] Insofar as an appreciation of others' intentions is necessary for an understanding of the concept of 'artefact', ToM has also been

---

[7] Epistemic modality concerns the extent to which we believe a proposition to be true (as in 'He may/must be right'), and deontic modality concerns the way in which an event which has not already occurred may be made to occur (as in 'You may/must leave now'). The 'strength' of an expression of epistemic modality is based on the nature of the evidence we have for something being true, whereas the strength of an expression of deontic modality is based on the degree of authority involved (Perkins, 1983).

deemed necessary to appreciate the meaning of artefact terms such as 'weapon' and 'toy' (Bloom, 1996, 2000).[8] An inability to appreciate and engage in communicative activities such as pretending (Leslie, 1988), joking (St James and Tager-Flusberg, 1994) and humour generally (Emerich *et al.*, 2003; Werth, Perkins and Boucher, 2001) has also been linked to ToM difficulties in autism. Winner *et al.* (1998: 90) found that, in adults with RHD too, the ability to distinguish lies from jokes was strongly correlated with the ability to attribute second-order beliefs, and Channon *et al.* (2005) found a similar link between poor comprehension of sarcasm and ToM ability in adults with TBI. In conversational interaction more generally, children with autism have been observed to respond less to comments and queries and make fewer relevant novel contributions than normally developing and language-delayed peers with an intact ToM (Capps *et al.*, 1998), and Volden *et al.* (1997) found that ToM ability seemed necessary for successful referential communication.

5.3.3   Theory of mind: interactions in the intrapersonal domain

Apparent interactions between ToM and other cognitive, linguistic and sensorimotor mechanisms in the intrapersonal domain have been reported, particularly in child development. Early language development has been found to be a good predictor of later ToM ability in typically developing children (Farrar and Maag, 2002), and, as noted above, some aspects of language performance may in turn be negatively affected by poor ToM ability. Tager-Flusberg (1997) reports a specific influence of the syntax of complementation on ToM performance in both typically developing preschool children and children with autism, though Miller (2004) suggests that the linguistic task demands of some false belief tests may be a key factor in preventing children with SLI from demonstrating their true level of understanding. Slade and Ruffman (2005) found that development of ToM correlated equally with syntactic and semantic ability, and Ruffman *et al.* (2003) argue that ToM is related to language ability generally rather than to individual aspects such as syntax and semantics. The link between ToM and linguistic ability thus appears to be particularly strong. Based on a study showing better performance in the same group of children on a false belief task involving word learning than in a standard false belief task, Happé and Loth (2002) have gone so far as to posit the

---

[8] The argument goes that, in order to be able to construe an object as a weapon, we need to be able to appreciate that the person who has made it, or is using it, *intends* it to have the function of a weapon.

existence of several distinct theories of mind, with that dedicated to linguistic communication being the most highly developed.

Sensorimotor mechanisms also appear to interact with ToM performance, though perhaps less directly. Peterson and Siegal (2000) report a series of studies which show that deaf children from hearing families tend to be delayed in acquiring ToM, and in fact perform no better than autistic children matched for mental age. Peterson and Siegal attribute this partly to the crucial role played by conversational interaction in ToM development, and to the restrictions on conversation imposed by hearing impairment.

5.3.4   Theory of mind: interactions in the interpersonal domain

Although ToM includes the attribution of mental states to oneself (as already noted above), and in addition interacts with other elements in the intrapersonal domain, it is in the interpersonal domain that problems attributed to ToM deficits generally become apparent. In fact, Woolfe, Want and Siegal (2002) argue on the basis of evidence from deaf children with ToM deficits that access to conversational interaction may be a prerequisite for development of ToM in the first place. However, although people who fail ToM tests typically have difficulties communicating with others, we should be cautious about assuming a straightforward causal link between the two. Transcript 5.5 is from a question and answer session between an adult, Lisa, and Frank, a boy aged 7;3 with a diagnosis of ASD. Not long before this interaction, Frank had failed a ToM test of the kind described earlier.

Transcript 5.5

Lisa: when do you open your Christmas presents?
Frank: in all the Christmas trees
Lisa: and who brings the presents Frank?
Frank: Santa Claus
Lisa: when do you get Easter eggs?
Frank: cracking the eggs
Lisa: that's right – when do you get Easter eggs?
Frank: from the chicken
Lisa: that's right
Frank: someone's got the chicken
Lisa: when is your birthday?
Frank: next day
Lisa: when do you have your lunch?
Frank: school dinners

Although most of Frank's responses to Lisa's questions are odd, and might potentially reflect an inability on Frank's part to infer her

communicative intent (cf. the explanation suggested by Blank *et al.*
(1979)), it is also noteworthy that children with ASD find wh- questions
in particular notoriously difficult, and it has been suggested that such
anomalous responses might instead result from language processing problems rather than being a direct consequence of a ToM deficit (Snow, 1996).
In a detailed analysis of interactions involving children with autism using
Conversation Analysis, Dickerson *et al.* (2005) found that their use of gaze
and pointing to achieve addressing and referring, and to initiate and
maintain bi-partite and tri-partite joint attention was actually considerably better than what one would have expected given their poor ToM
abilities.

In conclusion, whether or not one is prepared to infer the existence of a
dedicated ToM module on the basis of behaviour manifested in ToM
tasks, one would do well on the one hand to take careful note of the
complex range of interactions with other elements that are likely to be
co-related, and on the other to take account of the possibility that ToM
itself may be the outcome of lower level interactions in both intra- and
interpersonal domains.[9]

5.4   Executive function

5.4.1   Introduction

'Executive function(s)' (EF) is a term used to collectively describe a range
of higher cognitive processes such as planning, goal setting, monitoring,
evaluating, controlling, inhibiting, sustaining, sequencing, organizing, reasoning, synthesizing, abstracting, problem solving, decision making, multi-
tasking and overall cognitive flexibility. Other cognitive functions such as
memory and attention, and sensorimotor processes such as perception and
action, are also clearly implicated, and EF is seen as regulating, and mediating between, their various competing inputs and outputs. The notion of
choice implicit in such activities and the conception of EF as involving
interactions within and between cognitive and sensorimotor subsystems
directly implicates pragmatics. Indeed, executive dysfunction – like deficits
in inferential reasoning and ToM discussed above – is seen as a key contrib-
utor to pragmatic impairment (Martin and McDonald, 2003).

Transcript 5.6, from Allen (1983) (cited by Frith and Done, 1990: 248),
is a striking illustration of a particular manifestation of executive

---

[9] As Martin and McDonald (2003: 455) note: 'it is likely that the conceptions of TOM and
pragmatic understanding are highly related and possibly inextricably entwined, rendering it
unlikely that a clear causal direction exists between the two'.

dysfunction. An adult with schizophrenia is attempting to describe a picture but is unable to inhibit the perseverative intrusion of irrelevant (underlined) linguistic material.

Transcript 5.6

Some . farm houses . in a farm yard . <u>time</u> . with a horse and horseman . <u>time where</u> . going across the field as if they're ploughing the field . <u>time</u> . with ladies . or collecting crop . <u>time work is</u> . coming with another lady . <u>time work is</u> . <u>and where</u> . she's holding a book . <u>time</u> . thinking of things . <u>time work is</u> . <u>and time work is where</u> . you see her coming <u>time work is</u> on the field . <u>and where work is</u> looking towards other people <u>and time work is where</u> the lady . another lady is . looking across to the gentleman . thinking of <u>time with</u> him <u>and where work is</u> . <u>where</u> her <u>time is where working is and time</u> thinking of people <u>and where work is and where</u> you see the hills . going up . <u>and time work is</u> . <u>where</u> you see the . grass . <u>time work is</u> . <u>time work is and where</u> the fields are . <u>where</u> growing <u>is and where work is.</u>

If the intrusive sections are filtered out, the description makes perfect sense, but their presence constitutes a barrier to online comprehension which is clearly pragmatic, whether this be construed in terms of irrelevance, processing cost for the hearer or lack of control over language encoding choice on the part of the speaker.

EF has been conceptualized as a discrete (meta)cognitive system, incorporating a possibly modular 'central executive' (Baddeley and Hitch, 1974) or 'supervisory attentional system' (SAS) (Shallice, 1988). Others, though, see EF as constituting an emergent system, dependent as it is on the interactions of subordinate processes (Clark, 1997; Dennett, 1998) (see also discussion in Chapter 4).

5.4.1.1 Executive function and theory of mind Various authors have pointed to a potential overlap between EF and ToM, particularly as competing explanations of the major underlying deficit in autism (Russell, 1997). However, it has been hard to establish a convergence between the two. This is partly a result of the different research paradigms which gave rise to them, and also the fact that ToM explanations tend to focus on comprehension, whereas EF accounts focus more on output behaviour (Martin and McDonald, 2003:461). There is also some evidence that EF and ToM may be separate but complementary processes. Fine, Lumsden and Blair (2001) report a case of a patient with early left amygdala damage who showed significant ToM impairment based on a series of ToM tests but who performed normally on a range of EF tests. As the authors note, 'This clearly indicates, contrary to some suggestions, that performance on theory of mind tasks cannot be reduced to executive function ability' (Fine *et al.*, 2001: 295). With regard to a possible causal relationship between the two, Ozonoff *et al.* and Rogers (1991) have argued that, developmentally, EF is a necessary prerequisite for ToM. However, Fine, Lumsden and Blair's (2001) results suggest on the contrary that ToM is a prerequisite for EF, a position also supported by Perner (1998).

5.4.1.2 Executive function and central coherence Some have also suggested an overlap between EF and central coherence (see section 5.3) (Martin and McDonald, 2003). However, Frith and Happé (1994) argue that, in the case of autism, EF deficits and weak central coherence are not necessarily the same thing. For example, people with autism may exhibit poor inhibitory control of specific behaviours across a range of contexts, suggesting an EF deficit. On the other hand, this may simply reflect an inability to see the relevance of the differing contexts to the behaviour in question.[10]

5.4.1.3 Executive function and inference A third area of potential overlap is between EF and inferential reasoning. McDonald (1999: 501) sees inference generation and EF as similar processes, given that 'increasing degrees of impairment in the executive system correspond to greater and greater impairment of inferential reasoning'. She also notes that both EF and inference require simultaneous attention to be paid to multiple sources of information in parallel (as, in fact, does central coherence). Likewise, Tompkins *et al.* (2002) see poor inferential ability in RHD as resulting partly from an inability to suppress inappropriate mental activations (together with limited overall processing capacity), and Gernsbacher (1990) has attributed poor reading comprehension in adults to difficulties in suppressing irrelevant information.

5.4.1.4 Executive function and memory A fourth area of overlap has been suggested between EF and memory. McDowell, Whyte and D'Esposito (1997) explain the problems TBI patients have in carrying out two tasks simultaneously (e.g. pressing a space bar when they see a dot on the computer screen while counting aloud from one to ten repeatedly) in terms of a working memory deficit resulting from a dysfunction of the central executive system (of the type proposed by Baddeley (1986)). McDonald, Togher and Code (1999) also see poor EF performance on attentional tasks in TBI as a disruption of working memory, though they suggest that emotion and personality change following TBI also play a role

---

[10] As Frith notes, 'Of course it may be that some people with autism do have an additional impairment in inhibitory control, just as some have peripheral perceptual handicaps or specific language problems' (Frith & Happé, 1994: 127).

in executive dysfunction, and that working memory and EF are therefore not entirely coextensive.

The fact that EF has been closely linked, and sometimes even seen as identical, to four separate areas of cognitive functioning – i.e. ToM, central coherence, inference and memory – suggests firstly that our understanding of EF is still extremely rudimentary, and secondly that, whatever the best account of EF turns out to be, it will almost certainly be couched in terms of complex interactions between a range of cognitive, sensorimotor and behavioural elements, and therefore be pragmatic by default to the extent that it contributes to interpersonal communication.

5.4.2   Impairment of executive function and its pragmatic consequences

Executive dysfunction (ED) is most commonly associated with damage to the frontal lobes of the brain, and the term 'dysexecutive syndrome' (Baddeley and Wilson, 1988) has been used as a generic term for such impairment. However, in developmental disorders such as autism, it is not so easy to link ED to such a specific site. ED is seen as a major contributory factor in a wide range of communication disorders including attention deficit hyperactivity disorder (ADHD) (Barkley, 1997; Redmond, 2004; Tannock and Schachar, 1996), autism (Bishop and Norbury, 2005a, 2005b; Frith and Happé, 1994; Hughes, Plumet and Leboyer, 1999; Hughes, Russell and Robbins, 1994), fragile X syndrome (Cornish et al., 2004), obsessive-compulsive disorder (Spitznagel and Suhr, 2002), Parkinson's disease (Uekermann et al., 2003), schizophrenia (Morrison-Stewart et al., 1992), TBI (Godfrey and Shum, 2000; McDonald et al., 1999) and Tourette's syndrome (Pennington and Ozonoff, 1996). It has also been seen to play a role in communication problems following alcohol and stimulant abuse (Bechara et al., 2001), Alzheimer's disease (Hashimoto et al., 2004), aphasia (Beeson et al., 1993), depression (Alexopoulos et al., 2002), herpes simplex encephalitis (Alderman and Ward, 1991) and right hemisphere brain damage (McDonald, 2000).[11]

McDonald et al. (1999: 35) describe the behavioural consequences of ED as 'a disruption of the capacity to focus attention voluntarily and to deal with novel situations adaptively' (p. 35).[12] This leads more specifically to a loss of drive, resulting in 'uncontrolled apathy or inertia, rigidity,

---

[11] This is perhaps not all that surprising, given that frontal lobes form part of the right cerebral hemisphere as well as that of the left. Studies of right hemisphere disorder (RHD) are rarely as specific as those of the left hemisphere regarding site of lesion, and it may well be that those features of RHD that approximate to behaviours associated with ED are frontal in nature (McDonald, 1993b).

[12] Their account relates specifically to TBI, though it is applicable to executive dysfunction more generally.

inflexibility, and perseveration' (p. 35); a loss of control, leading to 'poor response inhibition' and behaviour which is 'impulsive, disinhibited, and distractible' (p. 36); and problem-solving behaviour which takes the form of an inability to 'anticipate a situation, or analyse it critically' (p. 36), a tendency to 'focus on concrete or superficial aspects of [the] environment', and an inability to evaluate one's progress critically and to modify it in the light of feedback (p. 36). When manifested in interpersonal communication, all these behaviours constitute a restriction of pragmatic choice.

Some of these behaviours are evident in the following Transcript 5.7, from Perkins *et al.* (1995: 304), in which C, a man in his late forties with TBI, is talking to T, a speech and language therapist, about trade unions:

Transcript 5.7

C: I admit this government we've got is not doing a good job but the unions are trying to make them sound worse than what they are
T: mm
C: they . they . cos I'm a Tory actually but I I do vote . if there's a . er . a communist bloke there I will vote communist but . it all depends what his principles are but I don't agree . with the Chinese communism . and the Russian communism
T: right
C: but I believe every . should be equal but . I'm not knocking the royal family because y . you need them
T: mm
C: and they they they bring people in to see take photos

C shows what has sometimes been called 'topic drift': despite the local sequential links between trade unions–government, government–Tory, Tory–communist, communism–Chinese/Russian communism, communism–equality, equality–Royal Family, Royal Family–tourist attraction, he is apparently unable to effectively monitor what has already been talked about or to relate each individual utterance to some overall coherent plan or goal.

A common manifestation of ED is repetitive and stereotyped language (cf. Transcript 5.6).[13] Alderman and Ward (1991) describe the case of a woman with dysexecutive syndrome following herpes simplex encephalitis who constantly repeated questions, instructions or demands for food, such as 'You will give me some chocolate won't you, you will be sure to give me some chocolate, won't you, won't you ...') (Alderman and Ward, 1991: 69). This made interaction with her so difficult that members of her treatment team became disinclined to work with her. In Transcript 5.8, from Bayles *et al.* (1985: 108), S, a person with dementia, is unable to inhibit

---

[13] See Perkins (1994) for a range of examples and wider discussion.

reference to an earlier stimulus (nail) even when it is no longer visible and a subsequent stimulus has been introduced. In other words, there is a lack of voluntary control over lexical selection:

Transcript 5.8

E: This is the first object. Tell me all you can about it. (NAIL)
S: It's a nail with a point on it, about two and a half inches from the three-fourths inch diameter head. It is a eighteen eighths penny. Long, its diameter, long, small point.
E: Can you tell me anything else about it?
S: It's about uh, two inches long?
E: Okay, that's fine. Here's the next object. Tell me all you can about that. (MARBLE)
S: It's a marble. <u>Doesn't look much like a nail</u>. It uh, two coloured. A dark colour of coral and white and you see through it. It's transparent at point and it's about (pause) three, no, two inches in diameter. No, that's too big. Two inches diameter I guess.
E: Two inch diameter.
S: <u>No, the-the-the nail is long.</u> It's so long that it-it it's long to here.

One of the key deficits in ED is the inability to direct, maintain and disengage one's attention, and this particular feature is highlighted in the name 'attention deficit hyperactivity disorder' (ADHD) applied to a particular condition typified by 'inattention, impulsiveness, and hyperactivity' (Tannock and Schachar, 1996: 128), which give rise to the following pragmatic deficits:

- excessive verbal output during spontaneous conversations, task transitions, and in play settings
- decreased verbal output and more dysfluencies when confronted with tasks which require planning and organization of verbal responses, as in story retelling and giving directions
- difficulties in introducing, maintaining, and changing topics appropriately and in negotiating smooth interchanges or turn taking during conversation
- problems in being specific, accurate and concise in the selection and use of words to convey information in an unambiguous manner
- difficulties in adjusting language to the listener and specific contexts.

(from Tannock & Schachar, 1996: 138–9).

5.4.3   Executive function: interactions in the interpersonal domain

As noted above, EF is by definition inextricably associated with the various cognitive, linguistic and sensorimotor elements in the intrapersonal domain over which it exercises control. How does its disruption affect communication in the interpersonal domain? Despite the tendency in the research literature to focus on the impact of ED on language production rather than comprehension, it has obvious consequences for both during interaction. This can be seen in Transcript 5.9, from Body *et al.* (1999: 99–100), where T, a speech and language therapist, is explaining part of the Rivermead Behavioural Memory Test (Wilson, Cockburn and Baddeley, 1985) to P, a 47-year-old woman with TBI. A range of tests showed her executive functioning to be impaired in the areas of focused attention, sustained attention, divided attention and information processing speed, and, in addition, her behaviour was typified by impulsiveness and perseveration.

Transcript 5.9

```
 1  T:  I'm going to set this alarm to go off in 20 minutes. When it rings I want
 2      you to ask me about your next appointment ...
 3  P:  It's on Wednesday.
 4  T:  Right. I want you to ask me when you're going to see me again.
 5  P:  On Wednesday probably.
 6  T:  OK. So when the alarm rings you need to ask me when you're going to
 7      see me again.
 8  P:  Will it be Wednesday? Will I see you on Wednesday?
 9  T:  Mmhm.
10  P:  Good, because I like you very much.
```

Despite reasonably good linguistic ability, P is apparently unable to give sufficient attention to the syntax of T's request in lines 2–3 (a receptive problem),[14] and perseverates with the same type of inappropriate response in lines 5 and 8 (an expressive problem). The impact of this on her interlocutor is that he reformulates the same request an additional two times (line 4 and lines 6–7) before finally conceding defeat and in line 9 answering the question she wishes to ask. Her comment in line 10 is overly familiar given the formal distance of the therapist–client relationship in this case, and this could be construed both as a lack of inhibition in her linguistic output (an expressive problem) and as a failure to attend to relevant features of the social context (a receptive problem). The negative interpersonal consequences of ED in TBI have also been described by McDonald and Pearce (1998: 102) who note that 'patients with executive impairments are less able to make nonconventional, socially effective requests that address possible obstacles to listener compliance than their non-brain-damaged counterparts'. In pragmatic terms, therefore, the typical range of receptive and expressive options available to people with TBI is clearly disrupted.

---

[14] Alternatively, she may simply be unable to inhibit the response 'Wednesday' on hearing 'your next appointment'.

We have seen above that ED may sometimes give rise to linguistic repetitiveness, though the role of the interlocutor in what is perceived as repetitive behaviour is usually overlooked. It is true that people with autism are often prone to repetitive activity such as rocking or hand-flapping whether others are present or not. However, careful studies of the type of repetitive verbal behaviour referred to as 'echolalia' – i.e. the 'repetition or "echoing" by a speaker of an utterance addressed to him' (Perkins, 1994: 325) – have shown that the repeated utterances often vary subtly according to their communicative function (Schuler and Prizant, 1985), and that interlocutors both orient to, and may even influence, the nature of the repetitions (Dobbinson *et al.*, 2003; Local and Wootton, 1995). For example, in a case study of a boy with autism, Damico and Nelson (2005) show that instances of repetitive verbal and nonverbal behaviour appear to be a compensatory adaptation both to interpersonal demands made by the interlocutor as well as to intrapersonal linguistic and cognitive deficits. Indeed, as argued by Body and Parker (2005: 383) 'people are not repetitive on their own'. By this, they mean that repetitive behaviour is repeated behaviour that is judged to be inappropriate within a specific social context. In an analysis of conversational interactions with Bernard, a man with TBI, they show that his topic repetitiveness was actually reinforced and compounded by his interlocutors through their use of information and clarification requests and backchannel behaviours. In other words, although his underlying tendency towards topic repetitiveness could be clearly attributed to ED and memory limitations, its problematic nature as an interpersonal phenomenon could partly be laid at the door of the conversational strategies used by his interlocutors. Although these strategies would not be out of place in typical polite conversation, their interaction with the repetitive behaviours arising from Bernard's executive dysfunction only served to exacerbate the problem. This has clear implications for intervention. As Body and Parker note: 'A key benefit of conceptualizing repetitiveness as a joint phenomenon is that by shifting the focus away from the verbal behaviour of the individual with TBI, some of the responsibility for changing the behaviour can also be reallocated' (Body and Parker, 2005: 389).

As a final example of the complex interplay between interlocutors and individuals with ED, Kegl and Poizner (1998: 137) report a study of deaf signers of American Sign Language who had Parkinson's disease (PD). Poor attention, sensorimotor planning and execution on the part of the patients eventually resulted in a redistribution of these processes between patient and conversational partner such that '[o]ver the course of the disease, unimpaired interlocutors gradually "became" the attentional system of signers with PD'.

To conclude, when considering the pragmatic effects of EF, one cannot avoid taking into account the complex range of interactions between cognitive, semiotic and sensorimotor elements, and rather than its being attributable to some unitary 'supervisory attentional system', there is good evidence for the view that EF may itself be the emergent outcome of lower level interactions in both the intra- and interpersonal domains, as argued by Dennett (1998), Clark (1997) and others.

5.5   Memory

5.5.1   Introduction

Memory plays a ubiquitous role in communication and some aspects of the way it is implicated in pragmatic functioning have already been reported above in the sections on inferential reasoning and executive function. Different types of memory that are commonly identified are (a) *sensory memory*, which is of very short duration and enables verbatim recall of – for example – immediately prior spoken or written language; (b) *short-term memory* (STM), which holds a limited number of items for processing; and (c) *long-term memory* (LTM), which is of long duration and virtually unlimited capacity. I will also use *medium-term memory* (MTM) as a broad umbrella term to refer to temporarily stored representations derived via STM and/or LTM.[15] Each of these plays a role in interpersonal communication, and STM, LTM and MTM in particular have been reported as having an effect on pragmatic performance.

5.5.1.1 Short-term memory STM is also often referred to as 'working memory' (WM) to underline the fact that it is active in cognitive operations rather than a static store.[16] The relationship between STM and executive function is seen as particularly strong (Baddeley, 1986), and is underlined by their common link to the frontal lobes (Shimamura, 1995). Gathercole and Baddeley's (1993) widely acknowledged and influential model of WM comprises a central executive which coordinates its activities generally including the amount of attention allocated, and transfer of input and output information. There are two subcomponents: the *visuo-spatial sketchpad* for nonverbal material in visual or spatial form, and the

---

[15] Kintsch (1998) uses the term 'long-term working memory' to refer to the activation of components of LTM by STM.

[16] Cf. Jackendoff's (2002: 207) description of working memory as 'not just a shelf where the brain stores material, but as a workbench where processing goes on, where structures are constructed'.

phonological loop for verbal information. Phonological WM is assessed by procedures such as digit span (recall of a series of numbers), word repetition and non-word repetition (Gathercole and Adams, 1993). The close link between WM and language processing more generally is evident in the fact that the ability of people with aphasia to comprehend language has been shown to correlate with their working memory capacities (Caspari *et al.*, 1998), and we will see below that poor WM is implicated in a wide range of communicative impairments.

5.5.1.2 Medium-term memory MTM, a kind of halfway house between STM and LTM and sometimes conflated with WM, contains representations stored temporarily as a result of repetition or rehearsal of a stimulus, or through particular attention being paid to it. It includes situational knowledge relating to the time, place, interlocutors and other features of the speaker's context of utterance, and a discourse record which keeps track of what has been said in the course of the interaction (Levelt, 1989). MTM incorporates what Baddeley (2000) refers to as an 'episodic buffer', capable of binding together different sources of information into episodes or chunks. This accounts for phenomena such as an amnesic bridge player with severely impaired LTM being able nonetheless to remember previous moves in a sequence of card games (Baddeley, 2003).

5.5.1.3 Long-term memory LTM incorporates *procedural knowledge* (knowing *how*) and *declarative knowledge* (knowing *that*), the latter consisting of *episodic memory* (i.e. knowledge of personally experienced items and events) and *semantic memory* (i.e. general world knowledge) (Levelt, 1989). The content of LTM is derived from representations in sensory memory and WM which have been consolidated via a process of 'rehearsal'. The more frequently an item from LTM is accessed by WM, the less likely it is to be forgotten.

Paradis (1994) uses the distinction between procedural (or implicit) and declarative (or explicit) memory to account for the linguistic abilities of bilingual aphasics who, following a stroke, may perform better in the language they acquired later. He argues that procedural memory is instrumental in learning a first language in conversational settings, whereas declarative memory subserves formal second language learning. Declarative memory provides metalinguistic knowledge which may still be available for careful, controlled language production of the second language, thus giving the impression that this language has been less damaged than the first. Similarly, Ullman and Pierpont (2005) hypothesize that SLI results from a procedural memory deficit which can be partly compensated for by declarative memory, such that some of the improvement seen in older children with SLI can be explained as a result of learning explicit rules in the same way that adult second language learners do.

LTM is necessary for successful communication in that access to relevant details of shared history and knowledge is crucial in deciding what to say and what to leave implicit in interactions with others. However, it is not sufficient by itself. For example, Jolliffe and Baron-Cohen (1999) report that people with autism fail to make appropriate elaborative inferences despite having good rote memory (as noted in section 5.2). Luria (1968) describes the case of an exceptional 'mnemonist' who was only able to interpret metaphors literally despite having total recall. Such feats of LTM in conjunction with pragmatic disability are also found in autistic savants.[17] As Sacks (1995: 190–1) notes, 'It is characteristic of the savant memory (in whatever sphere – visual, musical, lexical) that it is prodigiously retentive of particulars. The large and small, the trivial and momentous, may be indifferently mixed, without any sense of salience, of foreground versus background. There is little disposition to generalize from these particulars or to integrate them with each other, causally or historically, or with the self.' LTM must clearly be fully integrated with other intrapersonal elements for successful pragmatic functioning.

Communicative breakdown apparently resulting from impaired memory is not uncommon. In Transcript 5.10, Jim, a 39-year-old man with chronic paranoid schizophrenia, is at the end of a long meandering account of the importance of God as a positive influence in his life:

Transcript 5.10

Jim: so that's why I believe I was . introduced . to the Bible at a certain age . so that I wouldn't on the one hand panic . or erm go to the moon as it were you know cos it's so jus cos cos si su such a good thing er and and erm secondly erm (4.1 second pause) what was I saying?

But is this a failure of STM, MTM or LTM, or a more superordinate executive failure to monitor and coordinate elements of the mnemonic process together with other cognitive and linguistic elements? The complex interaction between memory and EF has already been noted. Indeed, as with other cognitive and linguistic elements, there are grounds for seeing processes such as memory not as discrete entities but as 'no more than a by-product of the mechanisms ... that exist primarily for the perception and production of speech' (Snowling and Hulme, 1994: 23). As with the other areas of cognition covered so far, it may be more accurate to construe memory as a nexus of interactions rather than a self-contained organism.

---

[17] In fact Luria's patient might well be described as having Asperger's syndrome if he were encountered today.

Table 5.1 *The effect of short-term memory problems on sentence repetition (1)*

Heard target	Stephen's repetition
Look at this.	Look at this.
What is that?	What is that?
I can carry it.	I can carry it.
I fell and hurt myself.	I hurt self.
Where did those come from?	Where from they come?

5.5.2 Memory impairment and its pragmatic consequences

Poor communicative interaction resulting from memory impairment has been reported in Alzheimer's disease (Almor *et al.*, 1999), amnesia (Caspari and Parkinson, 2000), aphasia (Caplan, 1995; Miyake *et al.*, 1995), autism (Ben Shalom, 2003; Boucher, 1989; Boucher *et al.*, 2005), Down's syndrome (Seung and Chapman, 2003), multiple sclerosis (Laakso, Brunnegård and Hartelius, 2000), RHD (Tompkins *et al.*, 1994), schizophrenia (Maher and Spitzer, 1993), SLI (Haynes and Naidoo, 1991) and TBI (Baddeley *et al.*, 1987; McDowell *et al.*, 1997). The pragmatic consequences of STM, MTM and LTM are rather different, however.

5.5.2.1 Short-term memory STM impairment imposes limitations on the amount of linguistic (or other) material that may be processed at any given time, which means that only a part of what one hears, for example, can be attended to, and one's utterances will typically be short or not fully formulated. Table 5.1 shows how Stephen, a boy aged 5;9 with a diagnosis of SLI, was able to repeat correctly sentences of up to four words in length,[18] but consistently failed at sentences of five words or more.

The same phenomenon has been noted in younger typically developing children. Harris (1975: 420) found that children unable to hold long and/or complex sentences in STM 'tended to make pragmatic inferences and excessively depend on knowledge about the world, as opposed to linguistic information' – i.e. LTM may be used to partially compensate STM limitations.

---

[18] From the 'Recalling Sentences in Context' subtest of the Clinical Evaluation of Language Fundamentals (CELF) – Preschool (Semel *et al.*, 1987).

Table 5.2 *The effect of short-term memory problems on sentence repetition (2)*

Heard target	Gary's repetition
Did the boy kick the ball?	ball kicked the ball
Was the car followed by the police?	car followed the policeman
Didn't the rabbit eat the carrot?	rabbit eat a carrot
Wasn't the ice cream bought by the girl?	ice cream bought [e] girl
The girl did not like the boy who lived down the street.	the boy not the street down
The big, brown dog chased the red ball.	dog brown dog chased red ball
The woman has read the twelve big, heavy, brown books.	heavy (unintelligible) books
The man who sits on the bench next to the oak tree is our mayor.	amen[a]
The postman sorted, labelled, bundled and delivered the magazines.	bundled magazine

[a] This item has already been reported as Transcript 2.10 in Chapter 2. Gary focuses on the final phrase 'our mayor', which he mishears and/or misunderstands and repeats as 'amen'.

Table 5.2 shows the repetition of more complex sentences on the same test as that shown in Table 5.1 by Gary, aged 8;0, who has poor verbal STM and consequent problems with syntactic comprehension and production.

A plausible explanation for these particular inaccurate repetitions is that the earlier part of the sentence may have been overwritten in Gary's STM by the latter part. A similar explanation would account for Gary's variable accuracy in syntactic formulation. Transcript 5.11 is typical of Gary's poor syntax in conversation:

Transcript 5.11

Student: and which room of the house do we have beds in?
Gary: beds are people to go in to they sleep . bed . in the night

However, on occasions, Gary is capable of producing less fragmentary utterances, as in Transcript 5.12:

Transcript 5.12

Student: what's in your bedroom?
Gary: um . let me see now . I got jumper shirt trousers shoes socks jeans I think that's it *(looking at what he is currently wearing)*

Here, apart from the formulaic 'let me see now' and 'I think that's it', Gary's conversational turn is essentially a list of nouns. The simple syntax, together with the visual prompts from looking at what he is currently wearing, considerably reduce the processing burden on his STM. This putative coping strategy is used successfully by Gary on a number of occasions. In this particular instance, however, it diverts him away from providing an accurate – and pragmatically appropriate – answer to the question.[19]

As noted in Chapter 4, sentence formulation problems in nonfluent aphasia have likewise been attributed by some to a deficit in verbal WM (alternatively called 'limited parsing workspace' (Caplan and Hildebrandt, 1988) and 'computational overload' (Kolk, 1995)), rather than to a primary linguistic deficit per se. It has also been found that by reducing the working memory capacity of unimpaired adults, their language comprehension can be made to resemble that of receptive aphasics (Miyake et al., 1994).

5.5.2.2 Medium-term memory MTM difficulties are closely linked to executive dysfunction in that sufficient attention to a representation (whether derived from STM or LTM) is required in order to keep it temporarily active. Wilson, Baddeley and Kapur (1995) describe the case of a professional musician with severe chronic amnesia who could remember events prior to the onset of his amnesia following herpes simplex encephalitis, but was unable to recall events occurring more than a few minutes prior to the present moment. Because his window of recall was so restricted, his conversation was extremely repetitive, often going over ground already talked about just a few minutes previously, and causing his interlocutors considerable frustration. Poor MTM also meant that it was no longer possible for new information to be transferred to LTM.

A less extreme – but similarly pragmatically disruptive – form of topic repetitiveness related to MTM problems is described by Perkins et al. (1995) in a case study of Colin, a man with TBI and with poor verbal and nonverbal recall.[20] Prior to the conversation shown in Transcript 5.13 (from Perkins et al., 1995: 311–12) between Colin (C) and his clinician (R), Colin has failed to answer a question posed by R and instead diverted the conversation to the topics of Caernarvon Castle, farming, gardening and religion. R attempts to get Colin to reflect on how he has managed to wander off the topic.

---

[19] A similar case is described in more detail in Chapter 8.

[20] On the Rivermead Behavioural Memory Test (Wilson et al., 1985), Colin's performance was poor both for free recall of information such as from a short story and on a verbal learning task. Recognition memory for both verbal and nonverbal information was at chance level.

Transcript 5.13[21]

R: right . can you remember what the original question was the . the subject I asked you to talk about?

C: no (– –) . forgotten *(spoken very softly)*

R: have a think

C: . I dont know . it's gone *(spoken very softly)*

R: what em . as you've just been talking there what what do you think you've been talking about . what what subjects have you covered – what have you just been telling me about?

C: . about religion

R: that was . one of them

C: . I like gardening . I wanted to be a farmer . but . I don't know now

R: right . you did say you wanted to be a farmer . how did you get on to farming?

C: cos I like gardening

R: . could be

C: . and .

R: what . what possible . er . no . well let me tell you that wasn't how you got onto farming about gardening . it was a it was another way . what other . what other links might be . what else might you have been talking about?

C: oh

R: to get onto farming

C: I wanted to be a farmer when I left school and I wanted my apprenticeship . so [(unintelligible)

R: [yeah . but why did you . why did you tell me . that you wanted to be a farmer what brought the idea of farming into your head?

C: well . that's . I like to be outside . and I like to see things growing . and it is nice . that when d you do enough food for people . you either eat them straight away or put them in the freezer

R: OK I'm going to give you one of the subjects that you talked about before you got onto farming . and I want you to see if you can tell me how you then got onto farming . you told me a bit about Caernarvon Castle – how did you get from there to farming?

C: . Caernarvon Castle? . and farming?

R: yeah

C: well it might be . oh I think it were digs . I had some lodging allowance . there were people who . woman put me up I did t' job on Caernarvon Castle . then she says do you . stop here and do these three jobs . and . I got digs for nowt

R: mhm

(Colin subsequently goes over the Caernarvon Castle episode again, and related issues. When asked again how he got on to the topic of Caernarvon Castle, he proceeds to get involved in the episode again and goes off on a different tangent.)

Because he is unable to remember what topics have been covered, when asked directly about them Colin either attempts to improvise an answer or

---

[21] Reproduced with permission from Perkins *et al.* (1995: 311–12), copyright John Wiley & Sons Limited.

else moves directly back into the topic he is being asked about. He continues to get totally caught up in the topic of the moment, which seriously disrupts the interaction.

5.5.2.3 Long-term memory The pragmatic consequences of LTM impairment vary according to the types of knowledge involved. Low intelligence or mental handicap can often lead to limited interests and therefore to a circumscribed semantic and episodic memory. This in turn can contribute to conversational repetitiveness, a limited conversational range and topic bias (Rein and Kernan, 1989). A similarly circumscribed knowledge base is also typical in autism as a result of obsessive interests (Baron-Cohen, 1989). Because of their socio-cognitive limitations, many aspects of social interaction are a closed book to people with autism, which further restricts what they are able to know. As Temple Grandin, a very able autistic person, writes: 'My interests are factual and my recreational reading consists mostly of science and livestock publications. I have little interest in novels with complicated interpersonal relationships' (quoted in Sacks, 1995: 249).

Pragmatic disruption arising from problems with retrieving specifically lexical semantic knowledge will be covered in section 6.4 on Semantics.

5.5.3   Memory: interactions in the intrapersonal domain

There are clearly complex interactions between sensory memory, STM, MTM and LTM, both in a developmental and online processing sense, in that one's conceptual knowledge is built up from representations attended to via WM/MTM, and which in turn derive from sensory impressions which have been held temporarily in STM.

STM has been seen to play a contributory role in various areas of language development such as lexis (Gathercole and Baddeley, 1993), morphology (Weismer, 1996) and language comprehension (Smith, Mann and Shankweiler, 1986). For example, if a child has difficulties accessing and storing the phonological forms of words because of limited WM capacity, this can result in systemic poor vocabulary knowledge (Gathercole and Baddeley, 1993). Children with better short-term memory (as assessed via non-word repetition skills) have been shown to have more advanced language development in terms of a wider lexical repertoire, longer utterances and a greater range of syntactic constructions (Adams and Gathercole, 2000). In Williams syndrome, where phonological STM is relatively good despite a range of other cognitive limitations, vocabulary development is typically robust (Grant *et al.*, 1997).

Interactions have been observed between STM and inferential processing in children and adolescents with TBI (Dennis and Barnes, 1990), between STM and syntactic comprehension and story recall in children and adults with Down's syndrome (Seung and Chapman, 2003), and between STM and lexical comprehension and retrieval in adults with multiple sclerosis (Laakso *et al.*, 2000).

The way in which STM, MTM and LTM interact with inferential reasoning has already been reported in the second section of this chapter.

5.5.4   *Memory: interactions in the interpersonal domain*

All aspects of memory processing reviewed above have interpersonal consequences. The relationship between memory and social interaction has been explicitly targeted in studies such as that by Donlan and Masters (2000), who found that the factor most strongly linked to social interaction skills in a group of children aged 5–10 with communication difficulties was STM ability as indicated by a measure of serial word span. This is particularly interesting in view of the fact that language comprehension appeared to have no influence at all on social skills.

As an example of how MTM problems may impact on conversational interaction, Perkins *et al.* (1995) suggest that excessive repetitiveness and topic bias in Colin (the man with TBI in Transcript 5.13) may be seen as a compensatory conversational strategy used to conceal the fact that he has forgotten what has been, and is being, talked about by either switching to a favourite default topic or by providing a general statement of opinion. In their case study, they describe various interpersonal management strategies used by family members and clinicians to help to counteract this behaviour.

The interpersonal pragmatic effects of impaired memory can also be seen in Almor *et al.*'s (1999) study of Alzheimer's disease (AD) in which poor comprehension of pronominal forms, and referential deficits in the form of excessive pronoun use at the expense of more explicit nominals, appeared to be a result of problems with WM, rather than lexical semantics per se. These findings are explained in terms of an 'information load hypothesis' defined as a relationship between 'cost' and 'function' according to which 'working memory impairment in AD leads to an overall decrease in the activation of referents, therefore enabling costly referring expressions (full NPs vs. pronouns) to attain more functionality for AD patients than NCs [normal controls]' (p. 222). Almor *et al.* report studies which show that communication with AD patients can be improved by reducing the use of pronominals and increasing lexical redundancy. This appears to occur spontaneously as an unconscious compensatory adaptation on the part of caregivers of AD patients.

5.6   Emotion and attitude

5.6.1   Introduction

Our ability to entertain, display and recognize emotions and attitudes is a crucial part of pragmatics, and has been closely linked with inference (Bissett and Novak, 1995), executive function (Bar-On *et al.*, 2003) and ToM (Baron-Cohen, 1991) in cases of communication breakdown. People with autism, for example, who find it difficult to read the emotions and attitudes in others' facial expressions, sometimes have recourse to explicitly learned rules such as:

literally false or puzzling speech + smile = joke
literally false or puzzling speech + frown = sarcasm

(Happé, 1991: 234). Emotion, or affect, has often been seen as separate from cognition per se, as it relates to feeling rather than thought, whereas mental attitudes such as hope and uncertainty more obviously involve thought in addition to feelings. In recent years, however, interaction between emotion and cognition has been found to be far more extensive than was previously thought, and both 'emotional intelligence' and 'cognitive intelligence' are now widely seen as complementary components of general intelligence (Goleman, 1995). The relationship between emotion and social cognition is also commonly recognized, to the extent that some psychologists conflate social intelligence and emotional intelligence into a single construct referred to as 'emotional and social intelligence' (Bar-On *et al.*, 2003).

As evidence of the close relationship between cognition and emotion, in recent years emotional and social intelligence has been shown to play an important part in the way we make decisions. Damasio's (1994) 'somatic marker hypothesis' proposes that particular feelings become associated with the events we experience, and that these feelings – or 'somatic markers' – are automatically brought into play when we envisage future scenarios which incorporate such a memorized event. Thus, although the process of making decisions is a mainly rational one, it is also directly influenced by previously experienced emotions. Somatic markers are seen as a high level type of bioregulatory response – i.e. 'those responses that are aimed at maintaining homeostasis and ensuring survival' (Tranel, Bechara and Damasio, 2000: 1047). The interrelatedness of cognition and emotion is also evident in the fact that both may be impaired through damage to a single cortical area (van Lancker and Pachana, 1998).

The processing of emotion has been strongly – though not uniquely – linked to the right cerebral hemisphere, particularly when realized through the medium of prosody and facial expression, but also lexically (Borod, Bloom and Haywood, 1998). In contrast with cognitive intelligence, which is 'more cortically strategic in nature ... emotional and social intelligence is more limbically tactical for immediate behaviour suited more for survival and adaptation' (Bar-On *et al.*, 2003: 1792). Van Lancker (1991: 64) sees emotional processing as a key feature of what she regards as a primary function of the right hemisphere – i.e. 'establishing, maintaining, and processing personally relevant aspects of the individual's world'.

5.6.1.1 The emotion–attitude continuum The nature of emotion and its contribution to communication is reasonably well known, though attitude has been much less explored. Van Lancker and Pachana (1998: 304) define 'attitude' as 'a stable mental position consistently held by a person toward some idea, or object, or another person, involving both affect and cognition'. However, their implied distinction between emotion and attitude – i.e. that the latter involves reasoning to some degree and is consistently held – is not always easy to draw. For example, they give 'dislike' as an example of an attitude, but dislike can be as irrational and inconsistent as fear or anger, which they describe as emotions. Indeed, a notion such as 'disgust' may be construed both as an emotion, when referring to affective experience, and as an attitude when expressed lexically in a locution such as 'I'm disgusted with your behaviour'. It may be more helpful to see emotions and attitudes as occupying specific points along a continuum determined by the relative degree of cognitive and/or emotional processing involved, as shown in Table 5.3.

Thus a mental state might be construed as an attitude as opposed to an emotion to the extent that it involved cognitive processing (however that were determined). This would enable us to include attitudes such as approval and impatience, which are associated with positive and negative emotion respectively, as well as so-called 'propositional attitudes' such as belief, which arguably may be held independently of a particular emotional state.

In some linguistic and philosophical discussions of propositional attitudes, sometimes referred to as 'modalities', 'evaluative' predicates such as *wonderful* and *awful* have been distinguished from 'epistemic' predicates such as *think* and *believe* on the grounds that the former involve emotion whereas the

Table 5.3 *The emotion–attitude continuum*

Emotion <----------> Emotion + Cognition <----------> Cognition		
e.g. joy, fear	*e.g. approval, hope*	*e.g. belief, prediction*

latter do not (Perkins, 1983).[22] This has been linked to the fact that evaluative predicates express an attitude towards a state of affairs which is presumed to exist (e.g. 'It's wonderful that they're alive'), whereas epistemic predicates are non-committal about whether the state of affairs expressed by the complement clause is true or not (cf. 'I believe that they're alive'). The rationale is that '[p]eople react emotionally to states and events that exist (rather than to non-existent, fictitious or hypothetical ones)' (Rosenberg, 1975: 478). Attitudes such as desire (sometimes referred to as 'boulomaic' modalities (Rescher, 1968)) might then be seen as part way between evaluative and epistemic attitudes in that they involve emotion in the same way as evaluatives, but are non-factive like epistemics (e.g. 'I want them to be alive').[23] Nespoulous et al. (1998) distinguish between what they call 'referential' or 'propositional' language, on the one hand, and 'modalizing' language on the other – i.e. the expression of an attitude towards the proposition. They suggest that, whereas the former is processed in the left hemisphere, modalization may be processed by right or left (1998: 327). They report cases of both fluent and nonfluent aphasia in which patients retain the ability to express propositional attitudes, even when they are unable to formulate the proposition to which the attitude applies, as in Transcript 5.14:

Transcript 5.14

I am very happy to . . . very happy . . . – oh, my God! – I am very . . . very well. I must admit that . . . hmm – my God! – I have . . . I have . . . I enjoy . . . because – how can I tell you? – hmm . . . I /trevo/ . . . I will put – won't I? – . . . it is silly, really. I will start to /berobi/ . . . hmm. It is stupid that . . . Then I told him: well, hand it! . . . I . . . I said, Maître, . . . and I preferred straightforwardly, . . . I am happy to have . . . (from Nespoulous et al., 1998: 312)

This suggests that the linguistic expression of propositions and propositional attitudes may be subserved by different neuroanatomical functions, and provides a further link between attitudes and emotions in that verbal expressions of emotion such as cursing are also thought to be processed outside the classic language areas of the left hemisphere (Jay, 2000).

5.6.1.2 Emotion, attitude and communication We communicate our emotions and attitudes to others through facial expression, gesture and other body language; through prosody and voice quality; and through

[22] Epistemic modality is defined and discussed earlier in this chapter in section 5.3 on theory of mind.
[23] Interestingly, Tsimpli and Smith (1998) report that Christopher, a polyglot savant with many autistic symptoms, was able to understand boulomaic predicates such as 'want' but not epistemic predicates such as 'suppose' or 'may'. They attribute this to an impaired theory of mind.

language itself; and impairment in any of these areas or an inability to make proper use of the visual and vocal-auditory channels in either direction will restrict the use of emotion and attitude in the communicative process. The effects of this should not be underestimated. As van Lancker and Pachana (1998: 311) observe, '[a]lthough emotion can proceed without language, verbal communication is ordinarily and normally imbued with affective and attitudinal nuances'.

The following summary by Bar-On *et al.* (2003) of the nature of emotional and social intelligence underlines its key role in the communicative process, and its particular relevance to pragmatics as conceived in this book:

(i) the ability to be aware of and express emotions
(ii) the ability to be aware of others' feelings and to establish interpersonal relationships
(iii) the ability to manage and regulate emotions
(iv) the ability to realistically and flexibly cope with the immediate situation and solve problems of a personal and interpersonal nature as they arise
(v) the ability to generate positive affect in order to be sufficiently self-motivated to achieve personal goals

(from Bar-On *et al.*, 2003: 1791)

5.6.2   Impairment of emotion and attitude and its pragmatic consequences

Communication difficulties resulting from problems with the expression and/or recognition of emotion have been reported in alcoholism (Townshend and Duka, 2003), Alzheimer's disease (Hamann, Monarch and Goldstein, 2002), autism (Fine *et al.*, 1991; Hobson, 1993), bipolar disorder (Murphy *et al.*, 1999), depression (Scherer, 1986), Down's syndrome (Kasari, Mundy *et al.*, 1990), Parkinson's disease (Dujardin *et al.*, 2004), RHD (Brownell and Martino, 1998), schizophrenia (Cohen and Docherty, 2004), TBI (Croker and McDonald, 2005; Green, Turner and Thompson, 2004; McDonald and Flanagan, 2004), Tourette's syndrome (Jay, 2000) and Turner syndrome (Lawrence *et al.*, 2003). Problems with the expression or comprehension of propositional attitudes have been noted in autism (Nuyts and Roeck, 1997; Perkins and Firth, 1991; Tager-Flusberg, 1997) and a polyglot savant (Tsimpli and Smith, 1998), and communication problems resulting from the sparing of modalizing language in conjunction with impaired propositional language have been reported in aphasia (Nespoulous *et al.*, 1998) and a case of callosal disconnection (Poncet *et al.*, 1984).

A distinction should be made between (a) disordered emotional state, such as emotional lability or flat affect; (b) problems with emotional or attitudinal expression; and (c) problems with reading others' emotions and attitudes. All three may be simultaneously present in a condition such as schizophrenia, with concomitantly severe consequences for communicative interaction. Phillips *et al.* (2003: 517), for example, report poor social performance in schizophrenia as being due to 'specific abnormalities in the identification of emotionally salient information, together with misinterpretation of the intentions of others and impaired evaluation or regulation of the resulting belief systems and emotional behavior'. However, most research on communicative impairment focuses on problems with reading others' emotions and attitudes, and occasionally on its consequences for emotional or attitudinal expression.

People with autism (which Hobson (1989: 22) describes as 'a disorder of affective and social relations') find it difficult to interpret others' emotions via their facial expression (Hobson, Ouston and Lee, 1988) and prosody (van Lancker, Cornelius and Kreiman, 1989), as do people with RHD (van Lancker and Sidtis, 1992). This severely constrains the ability to understand communicative intent, and there are concomitant constraints on language use. For example, atypical prosodic expression of emotion disturbance is commonly reported in autism (Baltaxe and Simmons, 1985) and RHD (Wertz *et al.*, 1998). In addition, expressive language in autism is limited in terms of the under-representation of words referring to emotion (Hobson and Lee, 1989) and lack of emotional awareness is also implicated in the impoverished nature of autistic narrative discourse (cf. '[a]mong children with autism ... the ability to identify and define a range of simple and complex emotions was associated with nearly every measure of narrative performance, including story length and the frequency and diversity of complex syntax and evaluation in both ... personal and storybook narratives' (Losh and Capps, 2003: 249)).

In TBI, although there does not appear to be a primary deficit in understanding emotion per se, the coordination of emotional processing with other cognitive functions may be restricted. For example, Dennis *et al.* (1998) report that a group of children with TBI were unable to interpret the affective significance of deceptive facial expressions despite understanding the emotions expressed. People with TBI may also show an inability to inhibit the expression of inappropriate emotions and attitudes. Recall, for example, the conversation in Transcript 5.9 between a woman with TBI (P) and a speech and language therapist (T), the last part of which is repeated as Transcript 5.15:

Transcript 5.15

T: OK. So when the alarm rings you need to ask me when you're going to see me again.
P: Will it be Wednesday? Will I see you on Wednesday?

T: Mmhm.
P: Good, because I like you very much.

P's final utterance, addressed to someone she does not know very well and who is acting in a formal professional capacity, is inappropriate and overfamiliar. Similarly inappropriate expressions of affect have also been reported in people with ASD – for example, in Transcript 5.16, from a conversation between a speech and language therapist (T) and a child with ASD (from Bishop and Adams (1989: 256)).

Transcript 5.16

T: Who is your best friend?
P: I haven't got one. Will you be my best friend?

In addition to their emotional and social processing deficits, people with autism also have problems at the more cognitive end of the emotion–attitude continuum. A study by Roth and Leslie (1991) showed that a group of adolescents with autism were unable to interpret modal expressions such as *think* and *pretend* correctly, and other studies have reported similar limitations both in the comprehension (Nuyts and Roeck, 1997) and expression (Tager-Flusberg, 1997) of epistemic modal predicates. This has been linked to problems with ToM, and reflects similar performance in typically developing children below the age of 4 (Leslie, 1988; Leslie and Frith, 1988). Although modal expressions such as *believe* appear to be devoid of emotional involvement, emotional and non-emotional propositional attitudes may be linked. Baron-Cohen (1991), in fact, has argued that the concept of *belief* may play a mediating role in the comprehension of emotions experienced by others. In a study comparing the understanding of causes of happiness and sadness, he showed that, compared with normal and mentally handicapped subjects of equivalent mental age, children with autism were unable to understand these emotions when resulting from beliefs, despite showing normal comprehension when they resulted from situations or desires.

5.6.3   Emotion and attitude: interactions in the intrapersonal domain

We have already noted intrapersonal interactions between emotion/attitude and prosody, facial processing, receptive and expressive vocabulary, syntax, narrative discourse and cognitive processing more generally, and via both auditory and visual modalities. In addition it is also worth noting that, from a developmental perspective, emotional and social intelligence has been seen as an essential prerequisite for the development of spoken language (Locke, 1993). Furthermore, if language fails to develop normally, for whatever reason, there are often negative emotional inter-personal consequences. Children with language impairments, for example, have often been found to have socio-emotional behaviour problems. A study by Redmond and Rice (1998) suggested that such behaviours in a group of children with SLI were a consequence of their communication difficulties, rather than resulting from a primary socio-emotional deficit. Similar findings have been reported by Goodyer (2000).

5.6.4 *Emotion and attitude: interactions in the interpersonal domain*

We have also seen above how crucial emotion and attitude are in the interpersonal domain, as evidenced, for example, in the characterization by some of social and emotional intelligence as a single psychobiological construct. Lack of awareness of the interpersonal significance of emotion is particularly telling in people with autism. Kasari Sigman, *et al.* (1990) found that, compared with typically developing and mentally handicapped children, children with autism showed relatively low levels of positive affect when sharing the experience of an event or toy.

In those impaired populations who retain their emotional and social ability to some degree, it can help to counteract their linguistic or cognitive deficits during communication. For example, in adults with restricted linguistic ability following a stroke, recognition of emotion in speech and facial expression has been shown to play a facilitatory role in their com-munication and to help compensate for impaired language comprehension (Lorch *et al.*, 1998). Social and emotional awareness is also a relative strength in individuals with Williams syndrome (WS). Reilly, Klima and Bellugi (1990) have shown that the narratives of children with WS are rich in the use of affective linguistic and paralinguistic devices such as lively prosody, exclamations and other 'audience hookers' compared with those of children with Down's syndrome matched for mental age. The overall effect of such devices is to engage the interlocutor, and recognition of others' affective state is also a relative strength in WS. In Transcript 5.17 (from Tarling *et al.*, 2006: 586), Brendan, a 12-year-old boy with WS, is talking to K, an adult whom he knows slightly. Brendan has an IQ of only 50 and a significant deficit in his receptive and expressive language skills, but is nevertheless able to draw on his considerable socio-emotional skills to partially compensate for this.

Transcript 5.17

1   B: and I and I can I can <u>growl</u> quite a lot (.) when I'm at <u>school</u> (1.3)
2   (*makes growling noise*)
3   K: (*makes growling noise*)

```
 4   B:   like like a werewolf
 5   K:   a[h::: ]
 6   B:    ["↑ooooo]oo↑" (growls)
 7   K:   I don't think I'd want to be near you at midnight then (1.7)
 8   K:   [°it would b]e a bit scary°
 9   B:   [be alright ]
10   B:   would be alright
11   K:   °would it be okay°
12   B:   I'll be your (.) I'll be your (.) um (.) d'you know (.) like baby bear
13        um (.) hhh (.) you know and the and the um (.) and the um the
14        big beast [(.) and] you're and you're tha- (points at K) that that
15   K:             [right ]
16   B:   princess
17   K:   oh like beauty and the beast
18   B:   yes
```

In lines 1–6, Brendan pretends to be a werewolf and K in turn pretends to be scared by his growling. Brendan's reaction to K's expression of concern (prosodically in line 5 and linguistically in line 7) is to try to reassure and to switch persona from werewolf to the protective beast from the film *Beauty and the Beast*. His voice quality and prosody also change to reflect his new persona. Brendan's behaviour appears to be a direct reaction and adaptation to his interlocutor's apparent affective state.

5.7   Conclusion

The link between cognition and pragmatics has been widely acknowledged, but is typically seen in terms of a single cognitive process such as inference, theory of mind or executive function. What we have seen in this chapter is that:

a) In any instance of communicative behaviour many different cognitive processes are engaged simultaneously and interactively.
b) Pragmatics is not the product of any single cognitive process.
c) There is a remarkable amount of overlap between different cognitive systems – and particularly between inference, ToM and executive function – to the extent that they may arguably be seen as representing different conceptual construals of a common set of processes but from different perspectives and with different emphases.
d) Each cognitive process which merits a single individuating label is itself the complex product of subsidiary interactions.

A central aim of this chapter has been to illustrate the heterogeneity of pragmatic behaviour by focusing in detail on the complex of cognitive processes on which it draws. We now turn our attention in Chapter 6 to the role that language plays in pragmatics, where a similar picture will emerge.

6   Language and pragmatics

6.1   Introduction

When asked to identify typical manifestations of pragmatic impairment, clinicians will invariably choose autistic spectrum disorder, right hemisphere brain damage and traumatic brain injury. The underlying causes of these disorders are usually seen as cognitive rather than linguistic, and their pragmatic nature as the effect they have on language use and comprehension or communication more generally. Although language and speech disorders are also regarded as potential contributory factors in pragmatic impairment in both children (McTear and Conti-Ramsden, 1992) and adults (Menn *et al.*, 1995) they are not usually seen as being so central. In order to reflect this general perception, I have in earlier work (e.g. Perkins, 2000) proposed a classification scheme in which pragmatic impairments with a cognitive basis are described as primary, whereas those with a linguistic or sensorimotor basis are seen as secondary (see Table 6.1). In addition, impairments with multiple underlying causes (e.g. both cognitive and linguistic) would be labelled as complex.

Although such a classificatory framework may provide a convenient way of differentiating pragmatic impairments based on their aetiology, it is admittedly only a first step, in that it takes little account of the emergent nature of pragmatic impairment as described in Chapters 3 and 4 according to which *any* underlying dysfunction will have pragmatic consequences by virtue of disrupting the process of communicative choice. Furthermore, since any single underlying dysfunction is merely the start of a complex chain of events brought about by the need for compensatory adaptation in both intrapersonal and interpersonal domains, all instances of pragmatic impairment turn out to be complex (rather than merely primary or secondary) to at least some degree. Hence the distinction between primary and secondary pragmatic impairment should be seen as nothing more than a reflection of a common perception of pragmatics

Table 6.1 *A classification scheme for pragmatic impairment*

Type of pragmatic impairment	Underlying cause
Primary pragmatic impairment	***Cognitive dysfunction*** – inference – theory of mind – executive function – memory – emotion and attitude
Secondary pragmatic impairment	***a) Linguistic dysfunction*** – phonology – morphology – syntax – lexis – prosody – discourse ***b) Sensorimotor dysfunction*** – auditory perception – visual perception – motor/articulatory ability
Complex pragmatic impairment Based on Perkins (2000: 22)	***Multiple sources***

which (as discussed in previous chapters) can be inconsistent and even self-contradictory.

In this chapter I will consider the pragmatic consequences of impairment within the domain of language in its various manifestations – i.e. those areas listed under 'Secondary pragmatic impairment a) Linguistic dysfunction' in Table 6.1. As was the case in Chapter 5, coverage of each linguistic element will be guided by the following questions, which are repeated here for convenience:

1. What are its essential characteristics?
2. In what communicative disorders is its impairment manifested?
3. How may it be impaired, and what are the pragmatic consequences in terms of restriction of communicative choice?
4. How does it interact with other elements within the intrapersonal domain, what impact does its impairment have on other cognitive, semiotic and sensorimotor elements, and what are the implications for resource allocation within the individual?
5. How does it interact with other elements within the interpersonal domain, how does its impairment affect expression and comprehension, and what are the implications for resource allocation between individuals?

6.2 Phonology and prosody

6.2.1 Introduction

Phonology and prosody are concerned with the way speech sounds vary systematically to convey meaning. Phonology focuses on the meaning contrasts between individual speech 'segments' – e.g. what distinguishes *pet* from *bet* – and prosody (sometimes called 'non-segmental' or 'supra-segmental' phonology) on the meanings conveyed by variations in pitch, loudness, speed, rhythm, silence – and sometimes voice quality – which typically extend over larger stretches of speech. Of the two, prosody has traditionally been more closely associated with pragmatics because of the way it can be used, for example, to express the speaker's emotion and attitude toward the propositional content of their utterance. Such a view, though, assumes the primacy of linguistically encoded information, and tends to dismiss as 'mere' pragmatics any information conveyed or derived through the use of nonlinguistic systems such as prosody and gesture. From the emergentist perspective, both phonology and prosody alike contribute to pragmatics by virtue of the range of communicative choices they incorporate. For example, in Table 6.2, which illustrates the pronunciation of a child aged 4;4 with a phonological disorder, all word-initial consonants and consonant clusters are realized as [d] and all word-final consonants as [s], and thus the range of lexical meaning contrasts it is possible to convey is severely curtailed. Words as distinct as *bed*, *dress* and *vest* are indistinguishable from one another, resulting in extensive

Table 6.2 *Example of a reduced phonological system*

Target	Child's realization
bed	[dɛs]
catch	[dats]
dress	[dɛs]
glass	[das]
chair	[dɛə]
jug	[dʌs]
pig	[dɪs]
roof	[dus]
shoe	[du]
teeth	[dis]
vest	[dɛs]

Source: (from Grunwell, 1987: 238)

ambiguity for the listener. Even familiar interlocutors with contextual support will have problems understanding some of what the child says.

The ability to signal meaning contrasts is likewise reduced in Transcript 6.1 (from Perkins (1985: 6–7)) which shows the stress and intonation patterns of a language-impaired 4-year-old-boy (P) talking to an adult (T).

Transcript 6.1

T: 'what's 'happening thère
P: 'that hórse
T: that's ríght
    have yôu 'been on a 'horse 'Christopher
P: 'been 'donkéy
T: hâve you
    was it gòod
P: 'been hórse
    'been 'donkéy
T: you've 'been on a dônkey
P: yéah
T: at the sêaside
P: yéah
T: ôh
P: 'seasíde
T: grêat   (from Perkins, 1985: 6–7)

In P's turns, every syllable is stressed and is spoken on a mid-level tone apart from utterance-final syllables which have a low to high rising tone. He is therefore unable – to give just two examples – to indicate contrastive stress (e.g. `she told him` vs ˇshe told`him) or to distinguish between utterance functions through contrastive use of falling and rising tones (e.g. She's`late (statement) vs She's'late (question)), which increases the inferential processing burden of the interlocutor.

Phonology and prosody have traditionally been treated separately. However, it has become increasingly clear that rigid distinctions between segmental phonology and prosody are unwarranted. Most phonologists now tend to adopt a 'nonlinear' perspective and describe phonological patterns in terms of hierarchically organized units such as features, syllables, feet, words and other categories (Goldsmith, 1990), which embraces much of what was once seen as the exclusive province of prosody.[1] In recent decades it has become clear that the way a particular sound segment is realized depends on its syllabic and lexical context and furthermore that

---

[1] Pitch patterns, however, are still generally regarded as being outside the scope of segmental phonology.

there is an interaction between phonological organization at segmental and sub-segmental levels and across larger organizational domains such as syllables and rhythm groups (Shockey, 2003). Such a perspective has considerable potential for the analysis of communication impairments. For example, Heselwood, Bray and Crookston (1995) found that apparent segmental errors in the conversational speech of a man with Down's syndrome appeared to be a secondary consequence of rhythmical simplification caused by problems with respiratory control. In the production of 'about a hospital' as [ə ˈbaːʔə ˈbɪɣʊ̆], for example, the truncation of the two rhythm groups 'about' and 'a hospital' effectively results in the loss of segmental phonological material – in this case, the first syllable of 'hospital'. However, most phonological assessments in clinical use continue to focus on segmental rather than non-segmental features,[2] and are phoneme-based (e.g. many would regard the pronunciation of 'dog' as [dɒ] as resulting from the deletion of the phoneme /g/), despite the fact that most phonologists now regard the phoneme as no more than a convenient descriptive label (Coleman, 2002).

As with other areas of language, approaches to phonology divide into those which focus primarily on phonology as a modular, self-contained system and those which characterize it as emergent. Advocates of the former approach see phonology as a cognitive phenomenon, quite distinct from phonetics (cf. Hale and Reiss (2000: 167): 'Phonology is not and should not be grounded in phonetics . . .'), while for advocates of the latter, phonology – at least ontogenetically – is no more (nor less) than a phonetic epiphenomenon (cf. Lindblom (1999: 13): 'For the child, phonology . . . represents an *emergent* patterning of phonetic substance' (cited in Vihman and Velleman (2000: 310; italics in original)). Modular accounts derive from generative phonology and include optimality theory (Hale and Reiss, 2000). Emergentist accounts of phonology, on the other hand, include 'gestural' or 'articulatory' phonology (Browman and Goldstein, 1992; Studdert-Kennedy and Goodell, 1995), according to which the phonological system derives ultimately from the child's articulatory movements, and exemplar theory (Coleman, 2003), which sees phonological contrasts as a function of the way multiple auditory traces (or 'exemplars') of words are laid down and organized in the memory.

Prosody has not been seen as modular because of the varied range of phenomena it includes, and such a view receives support from neurological studies which see prosodic processes as being 'made up of multiple skills

---

[2] Two notable exceptions being *The Prosody Profile* (Crystal, 1992) and *Profiling Elements of Prosodic Systems* (Wells and Peppé, 2003).

and functions distributed across cerebral systems' (van Lancker and Sidtis, 1992: 963). The fact that the boundaries between segmental phonology and prosody are becoming so blurred suggests that an integrated emergentist account may be particularly appropriate. This does not deny that different aspects of speech processing may be quite distinct, but simply shifts the focus to the interactions that operate between them. For example, Snow (2001: 583), who sees prosodic features such as intonation and final syllable lengthening as operating at a different hierarchical 'tier' from lexical phonological features, still allows for the fact that 'many children ... who have poor intelligibility can partly compensate for deficits in articulation by emphasizing their prosodic strengths'.

6.2.2 *Phonological and prosodic impairment and their pragmatic consequences*

Unintelligibility resulting from speech problems is the most common reason for referral for speech and language therapy in both paediatric and adult populations (e.g. Fox, Dodd and Howard, 2002). Phonological impairments may result from problems with sensory input, stored linguistic knowledge and/or motor output (Stackhouse and Wells, 1997). Disorders of prosody have been subdivided into *dysprosody*, which refers to an inability to control the physical parameters of pitch, loudness, duration, rhythm and silence, and *prosodic disability*, which refers to the use of such parameters as intonation, stress, tempo, rhythmicality and pause to convey meaning (Crystal, 1981). Brewster (1989) in addition highlights the interactive dimension of prosodic systems in the form of *prosodic disturbance* – i.e. the prosodic consequence of dysfunction elsewhere – and *prosodic deviation* – i.e. the use of prosody as a compensatory resource. The reduction in communicative choice resulting at least partly from phonological impairment is evident in a wide range of conditions, including adult degenerative disorders such as Parkinson's disease, motor neurone disease and multiple sclerosis (Miller and Docherty, 1995), ASD (Shriberg *et al.*, 2001), cerebral palsy (Whitehill and Ciocca, 2000), cleft palate (Grunwell, 1993), dysarthria (Kent *et al.*, 1999), dyspraxia (Shriberg, Aram and Kwiatkowski, 1997), glossectomy (Fletcher, 1988), hearing impairment (Lloyd, Lieven and Arnold, 2001) and SLI (Bishop, Bishop *et al.*, 1999). Pragmatic limitation resulting from prosodic impairment has been reported in aphasia (Kimelman, 1999), autism (Paul *et al.*, 2005), developmental speech and language disorders (Wells and Peppé, 2003), dysarthria (Bunton, Kent and Kent, 2000), Parkinson's disease (McNamara and Durso, 2003) and RHD (Walker, Pelletier and Reif, 2004).

6.2.3   Phonology and prosody: interactions in the intrapersonal domain

Interactions between phonology and prosody have been noted in atypical language processing. In a case study of a child aged 5;8 with speech problems, Chiat (1983) found that the accuracy of his production of velar plosives varied according to stress pattern. For example, /k/ was consistently produced as a velar plosive at the beginning of unstressed syllables – e.g. *monkey*: [ˈmʌŋgi], *Mikey*: [ˈmaɪgi], but as an alveolar plosive when the syllable was stressed – e.g. *man can*: [mæn ˈdæn], *my key*: [maɪ ˈdi].[3] Rate of speech can also affect segmental realization. Howard (2004) provides an analysis of utterance *A man taking a photo of a boy dressed up as a clown* produced by a 9-year-old child with developmental dysarthria. The first part [ə ˈmæñ teĩk̃xɪ ɔ̃ ˌfaˑtəˑ b̟βaɪ], produced at a rate of 5 syllables per second, was unintelligible because of excessive vowel reduction (e.g. the first diphthong in 'photo' produced as [a]), lenition of plosives (e.g. [b̟β] for the initial consonant of 'boy') and coda elision (e.g. omission of the consonant in 'of'). The second part [ˈdʋɛɬtː ˈʊpːʰ ɹɬː ə ˈkːl̥aʊn], in contrast, was produced at a rate of 2.5 syllables per second, showed little evidence of elision and was far more intelligible.

It is commonly noted that children with speech impairments often have problems with other aspects of language such as syntax, morphology and lexis (Leonard, 1995). In SLI, phonological impairment has been reported to co-occur with grammatical impairment in approximately 80 per cent of cases (Bishop and Edmundson, 1987), which some refer to as 'phonologic-syntactic syndrome' (Rapin and Allen, 1983).[4] Chiat's (2001) 'mapping theory' sees grammatical and lexical problems of children with SLI not just as concomitant problems, but as resulting from impaired phonological processing. One obvious example of the knock-on effect of phonological impairment for inflectional morphology is that if one is unable to produce fricatives in word-final position – e.g. *shoes* → [tu] – or word-final consonant clusters are reduced to a single stop – e.g. *gloves* → [dʌb][5] – then it will not be possible to distinguish between singular and plural regular nouns (as above) or between first and third person singular regular verbs in the present tense (e.g. *pay/pays, cut/cuts*). Interactions between phonology and morphology are also evident in acquired language disorders.

---

[3] In each of these cases, the velar plosive is also voiced ([g]) instead of voiceless ([k]).

[4] The co-occurrence of grammatical and phonological impairment was put much lower, at only 50 per cent, by Gardner *et al.* (2006) in a recent survey of a representative sample of 668 British children aged 3;4 to 6;6.

[5] These are actual examples from a language-delayed child described by Ingram (1976: 53), but such patterns are found extensively in both typically and atypically developing speech.

Janssen and Penke (2002) report an apparent effect of phonological environment on inflectional errors produced by German-speaking adults with Broca's aphasia. In a sentence completion task requiring the transformation of a first person singular present verb form into a participle, 91 per cent of participles were correctly inflected. In the remainder, most of the errors appeared to be phonologically conditioned. The suffix –*t* was correctly added to verb stems whose final segment was phonologically non-homorganic – e.g. *geleb-t* (bilabial + alveolar) – but in phonologically homorganic cases – e.g. *geheft-et* (alveolar + alveolar) – where an epenthetic schwa needs to be inserted between the two segments, the suffix tended to be omitted.

Interactions between phonology and semantics have been noted in both typical and atypically developing children. Donahue (1986) reports a case of a normally developing child whose lexical production between the ages of 1;6 and 1;10 was phonologically conditioned in that he would only name two-word items if they showed consonant harmony. For example, he was happy to say *big book* [bɪb bʊp] and *big bird* [bɪb bæb] where both initial consonants were identical, but refused to say – or even imitate – *big dog* or *big cooky*, whose initial consonants differed.[6] Word recognition deficits in children with SLI have been closely linked to problems with phonological representation and auditory perception (Dollaghan, 1998), and it has also been suggested that picture naming difficulties in dyslexic children are caused by poor phonological processing rather than being a lexical retrieval problem per se (Nation, Marshall and Snowling, 2001).

In addition to conveying emotion and speaker attitude as shown in Chapter 5, prosody, in the form of stress and intonation, interacts with both lexis (e.g. '*content* vs con'*tent*) and syntax (e.g. *visitors who they dislike* (= a restrictive relative clause) *are denied entry* vs *visitors, who they dislike* (= a non-restrictive relative clause), *are denied entry*). Paul *et al.* (2005) found that teenagers with ASD were impaired in both the grammatical and affective use of prosody in perception as well as production.

The most commonly reported interaction between phonology and cognition involves working memory. It has been argued that underlying problems with working memory are responsible for abnormal phonological development (Gathercole and Baddeley, 1993), and Marton and Schwartz (2003) report trade-offs between phonology, working memory

---

[6] Consonant harmony has also been reported as a compensatory mechanism used by individuals with fluent aphasia to produce words whose phonological specification is not fully accessible (Kohn *et al.*, 1995).

capacity and syntactic complexity in children with SLI. It has also been claimed that phonological short-term memory may underlie the good productive and receptive vocabulary found in Williams syndrome (Grant et al., 1997; Thomas, 2005b). Prosodic impairment, on the other hand, is most commonly linked to cognitive problems with affect and/or theory of mind in conditions such as ASD (McCann and Peppé, 2003), RHD (Wertz et al., 1998) and TBI (McDonald, 1999).

There are a number of ways in which phonology and prosody may interact with sensorimotor systems. For example, some phonological and prosodic consequences of glossectomy were outlined in the case of Len in Chapter 4. The reduction in his articulatory capacity led to a reorganization of his phonological system, and he made compensatory use of pausing and increased pitch range to signal the boundaries of syntactic constituents. Cleft palate is another organic condition which constrains motor output choice and affects the phonological system in various ways. An inability to build up sufficient air pressure to produce oral consonants at places of articulation anterior to the cleft opens up various compensatory options (Peterson-Falzone, Hardin-Jones and Karnell, 2001). For example, a speaker may react 'passively' and opt to articulate consonants at their normal place of articulation but with an overlay of nasality due to escape of air through the cleft into the nasal cavity. Alternatively, they may choose to compensate 'actively' and avoid nasal emission by restricting the place of articulation of their plosive and fricative consonants to the posterior part of the vocal tract. This results in a set of atypically 'glottalized' and 'backed' consonants. Such choices and their consequences are inherently pragmatic, and carry with them the additional interpersonal requirement of listener adaptation.

Speech disorders of neurogenic origin can also impact on motor systems. The unusual speech output features of 'foreign accent syndrome' (a condition in which speakers, following a stroke, are perceived as speaking with a foreign accent) are commonly attributed to prosodic disturbances in the form of difficulties with features such as rhythm and stress, which in turn can affect the motor output systems of articulation and phonation (Moen, 1990; Ryalls and Whiteside, 2006).

Impairments of sensory input also affect phonology. It has long been argued that problems with auditory perception – specifically with regard to processing brief, rapidly successive acoustic cues – contribute to phonological impairment in SLI (Tallal and Piercy, 1973) in conjunction with a range of other factors (Bishop, Carlyon et al., 1999). Because cleft palate is frequently accompanied by hearing impairment, an inability to perceive subtle phonological contrasts may be reflected in phonological output in addition to the adaptations to nasal emission mentioned above (Lennox, 2001).

6.2.4   *Phonology and prosody: interactions in the interpersonal domain*

Most research on the meaning conveyed by phonology and prosody focuses on lexical contrastiveness – e.g. what makes *flesh* distinct from *fresh* – and the local use of prosodic contrasts – e.g. what makes `*this man* distinct from *this `man*, or why *he's `coming* is more likely to be inter-preted as a statement than *he's 'coming*. However, an additional, and often overlooked, dimension of speech sound is the role it plays in more extended domains, and in particular its use in determining the course of conversational interaction. For example, in Tyneside English the aspira-tion of word-final plosives has been shown to signal the end of a con-versational turn (Local, 2003). Likewise, in a study of a prosodically impaired child very similar to P in Transcript 6.1 (i.e. he uses a rising tone on the last syllable of every utterance), Wells and Local (1993) argue that his final rise is also being used as a turn delimitation device. The use of, and orientation to, pitch height and movement has also been shown to play a critical role in joint turn management during play between young children and their mothers (Corrin, Tarplee and Wells, 2001).

In order for speech to be intelligible to others, accommodation is neces-sary on both sides. Most research on speech impairments, however, has focused on output without adequate consideration of the listener's con-tribution. Studies combining perceptual and instrumental analysis have shown that there is often a distinction between what the listener perceives and what the speaker may be intending to convey in terms of phonological contrasts (Hewlett, 1985). For example, in a study of a 6-year-old girl with a repaired cleft palate, Howard (1993) found that her realizations of /t, d, k, g/ were all produced as [ʔ] (glottal stop) with no difference in voice onset time or duration of preceding vowel, which are used to distinguish between voiced (/d,g/) and voiceless (/t,k)/ stops in normal speech. However, acoustic analysis showed that voicing contrasts were consistently signalled by means of closure duration and, despite the lack of additional distin-guishing phonetic features, this was evidently sufficient for intelligibility after a short period of familiarization on the part of the listener. Speech production and perception are clearly as much a joint activity as other levels of linguistic interaction, and the acoustic properties of the spoken language produced by impaired speakers are ultimately the result of nego-tiation and compromise between both interactants, and therefore inher-ently pragmatic.

6.3   Syntax and morphology

6.3.1   Introduction

Deficits in syntax (the internal structure of sentences) and morphology (the internal structure of words) – or, collectively, grammar – are widely seen as being implicated in pragmatic impairment, albeit indirectly. Transcript 6.2 shows an extract of conversation between a 51-year-old man with aphasia (P) and a researcher (R):

Transcript 6.2

R: you lived here with your mother before she was ill
P: and then yeah . well . waste of time . cos mother . here everyday . sit down you
     know . mm . go and . clean . forget about it . and then er . me said well rubbish
     that . rubbish . er . and er . doctor come for me . so
R: did they take you into hospital?

(from Perkins and Varley, 1996)

P's omission of obligatory clause and phrase elements (e.g. subjects and verbs) and problems with subject–verb agreement ('doctor come') and pronominal case marking ('me said') make it difficult to work out precisely what he is trying to convey. His inability to encode sufficient information using syntax and morphology places a considerable inferential burden on R, which is evident in her subsequent clarification request. His grammatical problems therefore have clear pragmatic consequences, whatever theory of pragmatics we may wish to use to describe them. Indeed, some aphasiologists see pragmatic impairment as an integral – rather than consequential – component of aphasia (Joanette and Ansaldo, 1999).

Do such syntactic and morphological problems result from a single underlying deficit? As noted in Chapter 3, views differ on whether syntax and morphology are discrete mental modules and therefore prone to specific impairment (e.g. van der Lely, 2005), the emergent outcome of more general cognitive processes (O'Grady, 2005)[7] and therefore likely to be concomitant with other impairments (Thomas and Karmiloff-Smith, 2002), or else a hybrid whereby, for example, regular morphological rules are subserved by a dedicated submodule but morphologically irregular words are rote-learned (Ullman *et al.*, 2005: 187). Evidence from communication disorders has led some researchers to posit several grammatical submodules. Thompson, Fix and Gitelman (2002) present a case study of a

---

[7] '[T]here is no grammar at all; an efficiency driven processor is responsible for everything' (O'Grady, 2005: 12).

neurologically impaired adult with an apparent specific impairment of inflectional morphology and intact syntax. The putative morphology sub-module may itself be seen as comprising further modular subcomponents. Tsapkini, Jarema and Kehayia (2002) describe a Greek-speaking non-fluent aphasic man with a selective deficit in the inflectional morphology of verbs but not nouns, and Wenzlaff and Clahsen (2004, 2005) found that a group of German-speaking agrammatic aphasics were selectively impaired in tense marking on verbs, while the marking of mood and subject–verb agreement was unaffected. Derivational and inflectional morphology have also been shown to be differentially impaired (Fix, Dickey and Thompson, 2005).

Descriptions of syntactic and morphological deficits are inevitably the-oretically loaded. Grammatical impairments are sometimes used as evi-dence for evaluating alternative theories of grammar (Gopnik and Crago, 1991; Ruigendijk, Vasic and Avrutin, 2006), but conversely, the character-ization of grammatical impairment in the first place will unavoidably be influenced by the particular theory one adopts. Penke (2003), for example, argues that agrammatism in German-speaking Broca's aphasics is the result of an underlying morphological deficit, which in turn affects syn-tactic representations. She goes on to point out, though, that how one construes this will partly depend on one's theoretical position: while Principles and Parameters theory regards verb inflections as syntactically determined, the Minimalist Program sees them instead as features of individual lexical items.

The manifestation of grammatical deficits is to some extent language-dependent. Languages vary with regard to the division of labour between morphological and syntactic encoding of meaning, and this has been shown to have a differential impact on the manifestation of both SLI (Leonard, 2000a) and aphasia (Kilborn, 1991) in different languages. For example, Leonard (1988) found that, whereas English-speaking Broca's aphasics often omit noun and verb inflections, Italian-speaking Broca's patients never seem to do so. Instead, they may substitute one inflection for another. Similarly, English-speaking children with SLI have difficulty acquiring English inflectional morphology, whereas their Italian-speaking counterparts show far greater proficiency (Loeb and Leonard, 1988). This has been explained in terms of the relative differences in 'functional load' or 'cue validity' (see Chapter 3) of this grammatical feature in English (a minimally inflected language) and Italian (a highly inflected one) (Bates and MacWhinney, 1989). This is pragmatically sig-nificant in that someone with limited grammatical resources will be influ-enced by the language they speak with regard to the elements of meaning they are likely to encode or leave implicit (Menn et al., 1995).

6.3.2　Grammatical impairment and its pragmatic consequences

Grammatical impairment is symptomatic of a large number of communication disorders, but most predominantly of SLI and agrammatic aphasia. Even communication impairments which are commonly assumed to have intact grammar – e.g. Williams syndrome – will typically show some sign of grammatical deficit if examined closely (Karmiloff-Smith *et al.*, 1997; Stojanovik *et al.*, 2004). The extent to which pragmatic abilities 'seem to rely on knowledge of some grammatical category, function, feature, or construction' (Leonard and Fey, 1991: 352) has been noted both in developmental (McTear and Conti-Ramsden, 1992) and acquired disorders (Menn *et al.*, 1995), and the pervasiveness of both grammatical and pragmatic impairment may not, therefore, be entirely unrelated. Commonly cited examples are the use of the definite article to indicate that a referent should be easily retrievable by a listener from memory or immediate context, the use of restrictive relative clauses to identify one of a set of possible referents (e.g. 'the man I mentioned earlier'), the use of particular constructions (e.g. interrogative) to signal speech act type (e.g. request) and the use of ellipsis to foreground new information and downplay old information (e.g. 'A: What colour are you going to paint it? B: Green'). More generally, though, any reduction in grammatical capacity will change the interactive dynamic between speaker and listener. A grammatically impaired speaker will require their audience to derive more information from context or via other semiotic systems (e.g. gesture), and a grammatically impaired hearer will typically require an interlocutor to simplify their grammatical output and/or make greater use of context and other communicative channels. In all cases, there will be an overall reduction in the range of communicative choice at both the individual and dyadic level.

As an illustration of this, consider Transcript 6.3 (from Stojanovik, 2002: 218–19), which is an extract of a conversation between V, a researcher, and M, an 11-year-old boy with SLI. M performed poorly on tests of expressive and receptive grammar and vocabulary (scoring between 1.5 and 3.0 standard deviations below the mean for his age group) but was normal for his age on tests of nonverbal cognitive ability. Using a range of measures focusing on exchange structure, turn taking and information transfer, Stojanovik identifed problems with expressive syntax and semantics as being the direct cause of conversational inadequacy in 60 per cent of M's utterances.

Transcript 6.3

1　M:　I'm gonna start Middle School in September
2　V:　oh brilliant

```
 3  M:  I want to in summer but I am start in September
 4       that's take very long long holidays
 5  V:  are you going anywhere for your holiday?
 6  M:  on Easter?
 7  V:  yeah
 8  M:  I am come round erm (.) some people's house come round Jonathan's
 9       house you know Jonathan
10  V:  oh yeah
11       are you a friend of Jonathan's?
12  M:  yes
13       I wanted to sleep somewhere else but at home but I can't
14       cause my mum says I (.) remember I told mum about Jonathan went to
15       Duncan's house for a weekend
16       so Jonathan went round my house on February
17  V:  right
18       now you want to go to Jonathan's house?
19  M:  yes
20       I come at Jonathan's house but it's not whole holidays but it's maybe
21       three or two
22       but he slept to his once Sunday once Monday
```

M's problems with the inflectional marking of number, person, tense and aspect, with the use of prepositions and subordinating conjunctions and with omissions and sentence formulation generally (possibly linked to lexical selection difficulties) mean that, although one can to some extent pick up the gist of what he is trying to say, there are too many information gaps and uncertainties to be entirely sure. This is particularly evident in V's clarification requests in lines 11 and 18.

6.3.3   Syntax and morphology: interactions in the intrapersonal domain

The extensive range of processing interactions in the intrapersonal domain between syntax, morphology and other linguistic elements was reviewed in Chapter 3, and we also saw in Chapter 5 that grammar was implicated in various cognitive processes too. A few further examples will be considered here.

An interaction between morphology and lexis is reported by Druks and Carroll (2005) in their single case study of DOR, a man with features of both Wernicke's and Broca's aphasia whose speech contained very few lexical verbs. He would either omit the verb completely (e.g. 'Joanna my wife just round the corner'), substitute the third person singular form of the copula (e.g. 'About a year ago he is all around the world') or use a nonfinite form of the verb (e.g. 'Very rare is to eat'). Druks and Carroll argue that the paucity of lexical verbs is not a primary deficit in itself but the result of a profound specific expressive and receptive deficit in tense marking. Because DOR's grammatical system was otherwise relatively intact, he was still aware that finite lexical verbs unmarked for tense were in some sense wrong, which effectively barred him from using them.

Grammatical processing ability can also both influence, and be influenced by, cognitive abilities. For example, it has been argued that grammatical problems in SLI result from an underlying deficit in procedural memory (Ullman and Pierpont, 2005). In turn, grammatical ability in SLI can directly influence performance on false belief tasks (Miller, 2004) and may therefore be implicated in theory of mind ability. Impairment in theory of mind itself has been linked to limited grammatical productivity in autism (Tager-Flusberg, 1997). Poor grammatical ability has been seen as a possible underlying cause of executive dysfunctions such as poor response inhibition in children with autism, SLI and PLI (Bishop and Norbury, 2005b), whereas poor response inhibition has itself been argued to be an underlying cause of limited grammatical productivity in children with fragile X syndrome (Sudhalter and Belser, 2001). The interactions between grammar and various cognitive elements may thus be multiple, iterative and reciprocal.

Interactions between grammar and sensorimotor elements are also common. Grammatical deficits have been linked to both visual and hearing impairments. Landau and Gleitman (1985) report a delay in the acquisition of auxiliary verbs by blind children, and grammatical errors are not uncommon in the language of hearing impaired children. Transcript 6.4 is taken from a piece of writing produced by a severely deaf 13-year-old girl (from Crystal, 1979: 297).

Transcript 6.4

On Friday I went home at twelty to four. My Mummy say Hello. I drink a cup of tea. Kim is play me. David is a read. I say's about at school. I watch the television. I go to bed at 9 o'clock. On Saturday I got up at 10 o'clock. I have a wash. I go down stair. I eat my breakfast. I go to up stair. I was Kim is sleep. My David is eat at breakfast.

There are a number of grammatical errors including omission of obligatory syntactic elements and noun and verb inflections, and particular problems with prepositions. A direct link between error and hearing impairment is likely in some cases (e.g. the confusion of [n] with [l] in 'twelty', and the omission of plural 's' on 'stair') though in other cases the relationship is more obscure.

As well as resulting from sensorimotor impairments, grammatical problems can themselves result in more extensive use of alternative motor resources, as has been noted in the compensatory use of gesture by individuals with aphasia (Ahlsén, 1991, 2005; Rhys, 2005) and SLI (e.g. the example of Lucy in Chapter 4).

6.3.4   Syntax and morphology: interactions in the interpersonal domain

Although grammar is traditionally seen as the province of the individual, there is a great deal of evidence to suggest that the development and use of grammar is mediated through interaction with others and is thus a joint enterprise.[8] It is now widely believed that an innate predisposition for social interaction plays a key role in the child's subsequent development of grammar (Locke, 1993), and Corrin et al. (2001) argue that the transition from single-word to multi-word utterances may well be achieved through interpersonal mediation. Indeed, where infants are unable to establish and manipulate joint attention, as frequently occurs in autism, productive grammar may develop inadequately, if at all (Rollins and Snow, 1998). Common practices such as ellipsis, where the grammatical integrity of a sentence may depend on a preceding sentence spoken by someone else, and anticipatory completions of an incomplete sentence by a conversational partner (Lerner, 1996) show that grammar may be seen as one component of turn construction in conversational interaction (Schegloff, 1996).

   Studies of interactions involving individuals with a grammatical impairment have highlighted this interpersonal dimension of grammar. Various researchers suggest that the so-called 'telegraphic' nature of agrammatic speech may well be the result of adapting to a specific type of interaction – i.e. ordinary conversation (Heeschen and Schegloff, 2003). Performance can vary considerably across situations, contexts and tasks such that the same individual with agrammatic aphasia may demonstrate greater grammatical ability in formally administered tests than in mundane conversation (Beeke et al., 2003a, 2003b; Wilkinson, 1995). Hofstede and Kolk (1994) found that omission and substitution of grammatical morphemes by a group of Dutch and German Broca's aphasics differed depending on whether they were describing a picture or engaging in free conversation, and Salis and Edwards (2004) found that the overuse of elliptical speech similarly varied acording to task. The same kind of effect has been observed in children. For example, a group of language impaired Swedish children were found to produce more phrasal expansions and grammatical morphemes per utterance in narrative production than in conversation (Wagner et al., 2000).

---

[8] An example of this is provided in the case study in Chapter 8 (section 8.5).

Grammatical performance may be affected in very specific ways by the interactional context. For example, in the study referred to above in which blind children were found to be delayed in their acquisition of auxiliary verbs, the apparent explanation was that the children's mothers tended to use more imperatives and ask fewer questions, thus providing fewer auxiliary exemplars in maternal input (Landau and Gleitman, 1985). At the other extreme, grammatical disability itself can have wide-ranging social consequences. Horowitz *et al.* (2005) describe how a group of language impaired children aged 4–7 were less successful than their peers at resolving conflicts in the playground.

6.4   Semantics

6.4.1   Introduction

Going on what has been published, language pathologists appear to have a rather circumscribed view of semantics, interpreting it primarily as word meaning and, to a lesser extent, thematic roles (i.e. such as Agent and Patient). Although semantic impairments have been studied fairly extensively within cognitive neuropsychology, semantics is still the poor relation of the language pathology family. As Crystal puts it, 'Semantics ... is a frontier which has still to be crossed in clinical linguistics' (2001: 682). Uncertainty over the boundaries of semantics in clinical contexts and its relation to pragmatics is evident in the once widespread use of the term 'semantic-pragmatic' disorder (see discussion in Chapter 2, footnote 1) to describe a wide range of communicative symptoms found in ASD which would appear to have rather more to do with pragmatics than semantics. Nonetheless, semantic impairment has a clear negative impact on interpersonal interaction, as is evident in Transcript 6.5, from a conversation between S, a student, and Tom, a 56-year-old man with severe word-finding difficulties following surgery on his left parietal lobe.

Transcript 6.5

1	S:	are you having problems finding the words?
2	Tom:	yeah . mm er finding t . er [dʊəz dʊəz] . er you know . I don't know what
3		you call it . I've been alright and er . I don't know it's [dɪs]. couple of
4		couple of .
5	S:	is it just certain words you're having difficulty with?
6	Tom:	neh not really . no I just not er . I just don't seem to be er . doing . I . I
7		shouldn't do . er . what I should be doing er . well I don't . I don't think
8		there is any way I think there should . should be a way er doing er better
9		doing . way I mean everything's right . she's done everything .

10		everything's been done in er . how can I *(looks up to the ceiling)* put this .
11		she's . she's [bɒn] me I'm alright . but I I don't seem to be er . I don't think
12		. I shouldn't do what I've been doing . er . with learner you know with
13		learner like you know
14	S:	with who?
15	Tom:	well I don't seem to be er . don't seem to be able to do it . I'm alright my
16		my . *(tuts)* I don't know *(laughs uncomfortably)* how can I . how can I
17		explain to my . er I'm alright in myself
18	S:	yeah
19	Tom:	I know . I'm doing in myself and I'm not doing nowt wrong . wrong in
20		my own . in my . she says . she seems to think . I think I think er the [dæɹɪt]
21		sh . should be be er . should be leaving er leaving it like and get it . get it
22		a bit better like you know . *(looks up)*
23	S:	who are you talking about? who's she?
24	Tom:	well . well our lass . she's not er . I don't think she's doing any nough .
25		she's not doing enough
26	S:	is this your daughter?
27	Tom:	no . not my daughter

Despite his apparently intact syntactic ability, most of Tom's words have minimal semantic content, with pronouns, grammatical function words and formulaic phrases (e.g. *I (don't) think*) predominating, and it is clear from S's responses in lines 14, 23 and 26 that the information encoded is insufficient for her to infer who Tom is talking about. Occasional higher content words such as *finding* (line 2) and *daughter* (line 27) are probably taken up from S's preceding turn. The semantic content of what Tom says is so minimal that it is difficult to see how his responses relate to the questions he is asked in lines 1, 5, 14 and 23, thus leaving open the possibility that his semantic comprehension may also be impaired.

The haziness of the perceived semantic–pragmatic interface is also reflected in neurological accounts of the lexicon where both right and left hemispheres are clearly involved but their precise relative roles are hard to specify (Joanette *et al.*, 1999). Beeman (1998) argues that in lexical comprehension the left hemisphere identifies a narrow range of specific semantic features, whereas the right hemisphere activates more distantly related features. As Zaidel (1999: 1028) puts it, 'The semantic "network" in the RH is apparently connotative rather than denotative; it is denser than in the LH, the arcs are longer (connect more distant concepts) and the semantic relationships among concepts are more loosely associative and dependent on experience.' The right hemisphere plays a significant role in processing formulaic language (van Lancker, 1987) and words with emotional content (Borod *et al.*, 1998), and may also play a key mediating role in lexical acquisition in children. Eisele and Aram (1993), for example, who found that children with RHD were less able than normal controls at recognizing the presuppositions of factive verbs like *forget*, have argued that the right hemisphere plays a mediating role in lexical development. The left hemisphere, on the other hand, is more involved with the syntactic and semantic co-occurrence of words. Its syntactic role is well known, but it also plays a part in semantic dependency. Kohn and Cragnolino (1998), for example, found that adults with left hemisphere lesions had significantly reduced access to semantic associations between words in their output. To reflect the right/left hemisphere functional divide, Wray (2002) has proposed a lexicon containing five categories of item ranging from most productive (e.g. grammatical function words – left hemisphere) to most formulaic (e.g. exclamations – right hemisphere) which map on to lexical and grammatical deficits found in LHD and RHD.

Lexical processing problems – both in expression and comprehension – are the most frequently cited examples of semantically caused pragmatic difficulties. Most output processing accounts derive from Garrett's (1980) model, which involves lexical selection, combination of words into grammatical structures, phonological encoding and articulation. Input processing involves segmenting the acoustic signal, phonological and grammatical parsing and mapping words on to items in one's mental lexicon. Interactions and potential sites of breakdown are therefore multiple and complex, as we shall see below, and this is recognized in various models devised to assess processing ability in adults (Kay, Lesser, and Coltheart, 1992) and children (Stackhouse and Wells, 1997). For example, two key questions to ask are: (a) Is a lexical deficit specific to spoken and/or written output or to auditory and/or visual input?; and (b) Is it a consequence of a problem with phonological representation and/or motor programming? Table 6.3 shows the performance of a 74-year-old man with aphasia on a

Table 6.3 *Performance of a man with aphasia on lexical production tasks*

	Naming	Reading aloud	Repetition
High frequency	9/20	19/20	20/20
Medium frequency	3/20	19/20	20/20
Low frequency	3/20	20/20	19/20

task comparing picture naming, reading aloud and repetition of words with varied frequency ratings (PALPA 54, (Kay *et al.*, 1992)).

His ability to access phonological representations of words from written and auditory input is clearly intact, and he is also able to make use of these representations to articulate the words. However, he clearly has problems making the link between a pictorial representation of a word and its phonological representation, and the frequency of the word is also a contributory factor in this.

Underlying conceptual deficits can play an important role in semantic problems, and it has been argued that in some cases difficulties in word finding and word comprehension are best seen as the result of loss of conceptual knowledge (Lambon Ralph and Howard, 2000). The inability of some individuals with aphasia to name members of semantic categories such as animals, body parts and fruit and vegetables suggests that conceptual knowledge is organized in highly specific semantic subsystems (Caramazza, 2000), and the mapping between conceptual and linguistic deficits can be quite precise. For example, Phillips *et al.* (2004) found that individuals with Williams syndrome, who have poor visuo-spatial abilities, have concomitant difficulties in understanding spatial prepositions, and Bird, Howard and Franklin (2000) have argued that problems with motoric and functional concepts result in verb deficits, whereas problems with sensory concepts result in noun deficits. However, underlying concepts do not necessarily map directly on to word classes. In a further study, Bird, Howard and Franklin (2003) found that a group of individuals with aphasia had problems with both nouns and verbs that had low imageability.

In Transcript 6.6, J, a 63-year-old man with fluent aphasia, is attempting to describe to S, a student, a picture of a man chopping down a tree.

Transcript 6.6

1	J:	first of all he is at the axe
2	S:	what's he doing with the axe?
3	J:	he is . he is the . er . the er . the axe . tree
4	S:	right . what's he doing to the wood . the tree
5	J:	he is axeing . the tree . he is axeing the tree
6	S:	nearly . what's he doing with the axe . it begins with *(writes 'C')*
7	J:	cutting
8	S:	yes you could say that . I was thinking of *(writes 'CH')*
9	J:	not chairing surely
10	S:	no
11	J:	ch . ch . chopping
12	S:	right . excellent . so why is he chopping the wood?
13		can you think of any reasons why?
14	J:	yes . because the . it's . er . the November and the December
15		and so the fire is . er . in the grate

Although J is able to use verbs which describe a state (e.g. *is*), he appears to have a specific problem with expressing actions. His use of the novel form *axeing* in line 5 derives from the nominal concept of *axe*. He is only able to access the correct verb in line 11 following visual and auditory self-cueing.

6.4.2   Semantic impairment and its pragmatic consequences

Semantic impairment impacts on the communicative interaction of people with a wide range of impairments including Alzheimer's disease (Guendouzi and Müller, 2002), aphasia (Oelschlaeger and Damico, 2003), autism (Menyuk and Quill, 1985), multiple sclerosis (Laakso *et al.*, 2000), RHD (Joanette and Goulet, 1993), schizophrenia (Meilijson *et al.*, 2004), SLI (Perkins, 2001) and TBI (Chobor and Schweiger, 1998).

Impairments may result in both restriction or deviance in lexical access and use. Transcript 6.7 provides an example of word-finding problems in W, a 74-year-old man with expressive and receptive aphasia.

Transcript 6.7

```
 1  T:  so what did you make? what did the factory make?
 2  W:  what did we make was not a lot because we only made things for the
 3      thing that were [ded] so we all made things that were out our . out of our
 4      um things
 5  T:  what was it . kind of selling then rather than making things?
 6  W:  no . we're selling . taking out taking out the taking out of the [dʒɒŋɒn] . no
 7      can't do that . taking out of the selling
 8  T:  taking out the
 9  W:  taking out of the [dʒɒŋɒn] but couldn't take the [dʒɒŋɒn] out of it cos
10      there was no [dʒɒŋɒn] in it – cos he said we're taking a bit of [dʒɒŋɒn]
11      out of it and putting a lot of interesting things in it
```

W's word-finding problems are manifested in two different ways. In lines 2–3, the semantically vague *things* is used instead of a more specific noun. In lines 6 and 9–11, he uses the jargon word [dʒɒŋɒn] in the same way. In both cases the semantic underspecification is evidence of a severe limitation in lexical choice, with concomitant interpretation problems for the conversational partner. A contrasting, but similarly disruptive, semantic problem is illustrated in Transcript 6.8, where K, a 39-year-old man with chronic paranoid schizophrenia, is talking about a friend's tendency to give bizarre and aggravating replies.

Transcript 6.8

```
K:  he'd come up with something offensive or sort of make it wet and sour and
    bland and dumb and stupid
```

Such cumulative use of words with loose semantic associations – sometimes referred to as 'clanging' or 'glossomania' (Covington *et al.*, 2005) – is also linked to frequent topic changes and can make K very hard to follow.[9] Another kind of lexical 'excess' has been noted in Williams syndrome, where lexical ability has often been seen as exceptionally good when compared with cognitive ability. Temple *et al.* (2002: 489) found that, although lexical retrieval in Williams syndrome is fast, it is also 'sloppy' in that it is far more easily derailed by semantically related distracters than in healthy individuals.

6.4.3   Semantics: interactions in the intrapersonal domain

Semantic processing involves interaction between multiple elements within the intrapersonal domain, as noted above. One of the most pervasive interactions is between lexis and grammar. Indeed, based on a wide range of evidence from language development and language impairment which shows close correlations between vocabulary size and grammatical performance, it has been argued that grammar is essentially a by-product of the lexicon (Bates and Goodman, 1997; van Lancker, 2001). Such a view is also reflected in syntactic theories such as head-driven phrase structure grammar (Pollard and Sag, 1994) and construction grammar (Kay and Fillmore, 1999). As Bates (2001: 394) puts it, '[t]he grammar still exists, but it exists as part of a complex and heterogeneous lexical machinery'.

Interactions between semantics and grammar are perhaps most clearly evident in verb argument structure. It has often been reported that children with SLI and adults with aphasia are more restricted in their use of verbs than nouns (as shown in Transcript 6.6 above), and this is largely attributed to the fact that verbs are involved in more complex co-occurrence patterns than nouns.[10] Thompson (2003), for example, found that verbs with more complex argument structure were avoided by agrammatic aphasics in a story retelling task. Argument structure, however, is only one of several factors involved. Black and Chiat (2003) point out that, in addition, verbs are both semantically/conceptually distinct from nouns – i.e. they tend to have less concrete and bounded meanings (cf. *button* vs *accept*), and phonologically distinct – i.e. they tend to have less typical stress patterns, are of shorter duration and have fewer syllables.

---

[9] In some ways this is not unlike poetic language, as has been pointed out by Hens (2000) in a study of the Austrian poet Ernst Herbeck, who also happened to be schizophrenic.

[10] For example, the verb *give* requires the specification of a giver, a recipient and a thing given, at least implicitly, whereas a noun such as *cup* can stand alone.

A range of cognitive factors are also implicated in semantic processing impairments. Problems with both memory and executive function were found to underlie poor performance in word recall by people with mild Alzheimer's disease (Hashimoto *et al.*, 2004), and Buckingham (1993: 195) observes that '[a]bnormalities in short-term verbal memory, in disinhibition, and in self-monitoring will all play one role or another in disorders of word form processing in aphasia'. Locke (1993) has argued that a specialization in social cognition is a prerequisite for lexical acquisition generally, and Bloom (2000) that the meaning of artefact terms cannot be fully appreciated without a theory of mind (see Chapter 5, footnote 8). Problems in both of these cognitive areas have been implicated in lexical anomalies found in autism (Locke, 1997; Perkins *et al.*, 2006). Processing speed and overall cognitive capacity are also important factors. For children with SLI, Montgomery (2005) showed that word recognition in sentences was more successful if the stimulus sentence was spoken more slowly, and Weismer (1996) found that rate of presentation was also important in learning novel words.

Finally, sensorimotor elements are also involved in interactions jointly with cognitive and lexical processing. Franklin *et al.* (1996) describe the case of 'word meaning deafness' in an aphasic patient with intact written comprehension of words and good auditory lexical access (e.g. he could accurately repeat a word he had just heard) but impaired auditory comprehension (e.g. he was unable to understand the word he had just heard, despite being able to repeat it accurately).

6.4.4   Semantics: interactions in the interpersonal domain

Several examples have been given above of the impact of semantic impairment on interpersonal interaction. However, the direction of causation is not only one-way. Social interaction is itself a prerequisite for semantic development in the first place. Tomasello (2000: 401) argues that '[l]anguage acquisition in general, and word learning in particular, is best seen as a special case of cultural learning in which children attempt to discern adults' intentions toward their intentions toward things in the world' – i.e. lexical acquisition is an interpersonal achievement. Furthermore, when viewed in the interpersonal domain, semantic impairments such as word-finding difficulties may not be such a problem as it might at first appear. In aphasia, for example, word searches are typically a joint activity drawing on the collaborative efforts of both (or all) conversational partners, and they are frequently successful. Transcript 6.9 is from Oelschlaeger and Damico (2000: 213) and shows Ed, MG and M talking about what happened when Ed had his stroke.

Transcript 6.9

MG: Then they realized, then they put you in the hospital.
M: Uh huh
Ed: Yeah but then they did uh (1.2) the uh (1.9) uh what do you call it (2.1) the uh-
M: MRI?
Ed: No
M: Angioplasty?
Ed: No
MG: EEG?
Ed: No (1.5) The irr, no (tsk, tsk) srays, what do you call it? (1.0)
M: An x-ray?
Ed: X-ray.

The word search is initiated by Ed, but the retrieval of the word and agreement that it is the correct one is the product of an alternative guessing strategy carried out jointly by all three participants.

Individuals experiencing problems with lexical retrieval – whether or not they are language impaired – commonly indicate whether they require interlocutor assistance through use of eye contact (Goodwin, 1981, 1995). Withdrawal of gaze typically signals a desire to retain the conversational floor, and return of gaze signals turn completion and return of the floor. Other devices which may also coincide with turn ending are the use of falling intonation and pausing. However, sometimes this may go awry. In Transcript 6.10, C, a 55-year-old woman with RHD, is discussing decorating the house for Christmas with L, a student.

Transcript 6.10

1 L: and what 'else?
2 C: er (.) put Father Christmas on er on er on (.) on er (1.0) *(withdraws eye*
3   *contact)* me er (4.0) like 'videos (2.0)
4 L: what on the (1.0) so you've got a video (1.0) [cabinet?
5 C: [no on the (.) on your er (10) like
6   a (.) a chest (.) 'there *(returns eye contact)* (1.0) [what we keep 'videos in
7 L: [oh O'K

C withdraws her gaze in lines 2–3 and L, despite a subsequent four-second pause, does not take a turn until after C says 'videos' with a falling tone followed by a two-second pause. The overlap between lines 4 and 5 is reasonable, since 'video' carries no falling tone and is followed by a pause. However, the overlap between lines 6 and 7 is less expected. A likely interpretation is that L perceives the re-establishment of eye contact by C, in conjunction with a falling tone and a pause, as a clear signal that C is yielding the floor.

Apparently accurate and proficient lexical use may mask anomalies which may only come to light as a result of interpersonal interaction.

Perkins *et al.* (2006) report instances of adults with autism using a word appropriately, then later asking what it means. Tests of semantic ability are typically based on responding to or producing single lexical items in laboratory conditions where the response is scored either right or wrong. However, when one observes carefully the interactional context in which the test takes place, things can be far more complex. Beeke (2005) describes the administration of a picture-naming test in which the testee, a man with aphasia, manages to indirectly solicit information from the tester across several turn exchanges which helps to guide him towards the right answer. Both the tester and testee appear unaware that there is any manipulation involved.

Semantic ability has been shown to have more wide-ranging interpersonal consequences extending beyond single conversational encounters. Bosacki (2003) examined the links between receptive vocabulary and self-understanding and social competence in pre-adolescents and found a significant relation between vocabulary ability and popularity for boys, though not for girls. Armstrong (2005) reports that people with aphasia can have difficulty with mental state verbs expressing opinions, feelings and attitudes. This results in a limited ability to express their identity in social encounters, with negative consequences for their psychosocial competence and wellbeing.

6.5   Discourse

6.5.1   Introduction

As we saw in Chapter 2, aspects of communication impairment that may be subjected to discourse analysis are very similar – if not identical – to those which are amenable to pragmatic analysis. The use of one term or the other can sometimes appear arbitrary. For example, in the following definition from a study of discourse in RBD, one could easily substitute 'pragmatics' for 'discourse': '[d]iscourse includes the production and comprehension of language in contexts that extend beyond the literal meaning of individual words or sentences' (Brownell and Martino, 1998: 309). A key factor in determining which term is used in clinical studies is the type of test material used. Discourse studies typically elicit production of some kind of narrative (e.g. story retelling, picture description) or test comprehension of a 'text' (e.g. a spoken or written account of some kind). The difference therefore is essentially one of scope, in that 'discourse' tends to be used when an extended sequence of utterances or sentences is examined, while 'pragmatics' is more likely to involve examination of a single utterance. However, both are equally subserved by linguistic, cognitive, sensory and motor processes. So-called 'discourse' disability is reported in a wide range of communication impairments – e.g. Alzheimer's disease (Ripich *et al.*, 2000), aphasia (Ulatowska, Allard, and Chapman, 1990), autism (Losh and Capps, 2003), hydrocephalus (Barnes and Dennis, 1998), multiple sclerosis (Arnott *et al.*, 1997), schizophrenia (Caplan, 1996), RHD (Stemmer and Joanette, 1998), SLI (Bishop, 1997), TBI (Coelho, 1999) and Williams syndrome (Stojanovik, Perkins and Howard, 2001)[11] – though, as pointed out in Perkins (1985), discourse disability is almost invariably a secondary consequence of an underlying deficit elsewhere.

In this section I will focus on the specifically linguistic features of discourse – i.e. 'cohesive' devices which contribute to a string of utterances or sentences being regarded as a 'coherent' piece of discourse (Halliday and Hasan, 1976). These include anaphora, ellipsis, lexical chaining and other co-referential devices, information structure and discourse markers (Brown and Yule, 1983). Cohesion may be considered part of the language system, since it is realized through the use of explicit linguistic devices, whereas coherence relies in addition on cognitive systems such as memory and executive functions such as planning, sequencing and self-monitoring in conjunction with linguistic and sensorimotor systems.

Problems with cohesion are probably the most commonly identified manifestation of discourse impairment, and may be seen either as a gobal phenomenon (as measured, for example, by Armstrong's (1987) 'cohesive harmony index', which provides a single numerical score representing the amount of cohesion in a piece of discourse) or broken down into separate categories which may be differentially impaired. De Santi *et al.* (1994), for example, analysed different types of cohesion in patients with Alzheimer's disease, including reference, lexical cohesion, substitution, ellipsis and conjunction. They found that one particular type of cohesion (lexical) was actually more frequent than in normal controls, though this was accounted for by the fact that the Alzheimer's patients tended to repeat the same words, thus reflecting an apparent limitation of lexical choice.

Insofar as cohesive devices are part of the linguistic system, albeit with suprasentential scope, it follows that individuals with linguistic deficits – and therefore a diminished range of expressive and/or receptive options – are also likely to have concomitant discourse problems, and this is generally borne out by the research evidence. For example, in a typical study of discourse ability in impaired populations, Chapman *et al.* (1998) compared groups of people with aphasia and Alzheimer's disease on

---

[11] For a more extensive list of communication impairments, see Table 2.2.

various discourse production tasks, and found that, whereas the aphasic group (i.e. linguistically impaired) were poor on discourse formulation, the Alzheimer's group (i.e. primarily cognitively impaired) were worse on inference. Hudson and Murdoch (1992) similarly attribute the paucity, and erroneous use, of cohesive ties by children with posterior fossa tumour to underlying poor syntactic and semantic abilities. In a longitudinal study of patients with early to midstage Alzheimer's disease, Ripich et al. (2000) found that over a period of eighteen months the use of all cohesive devices (e.g. ellipsis, coordinating and subordinating conjunctions, anaphora) declined, but that this correlated closely with a concomitant reduction in linguistic complexity of utterances produced. A major feature of the discourse output of the linguistically impaired is its underspecification, and the consequent inferential load placed on the hearer. In a study of spoken narrative in the language of children with SLI, Miranda et al. (1998) noted a higher frequency of 'implicit propositions' compared with normal controls, which 'place a considerable burden on their listeners, a burden so great that it is sometimes not possible to identify the missing or misrepresented parts during an oral exchange of ideas' (1998: 659). Links between linguistic and discourse performance are evident in comprehension as well as expression. Story-recall performance was correlated with syntactic comprehension ability in both typically developing children and children with Down's syndrome in a study by Seung and Chapman (2003).

Although discourse structure is heavily dependent on linguistic ability, there may also be additional levels of organization required depending on the discourse genre. A story, for example, typically requires a setting, theme, plot, complication and resolution in a particular sequence – i.e. it conforms to a 'story grammar' (Mandler and Johnson, 1977). Hayward and Schneider (2000) were able to improve the story-telling ability of a group of language impaired school children by teaching them story grammar explicitly. They used cue cards to identify story grammar components, for example, and provided practice in putting scrambled story card sequences into their proper order. Another discourse genre commonly elicited in clinical contexts is 'procedural' discourse – a description of some procedure or process. Transcript 6.11 provides an account of how to make a sandwich, spoken by a man with moderate aphasia:

Transcript 6.11

two slices of bread – open the peanut butter jar – and get the knife – and dip the spread it on the slices – and fold it – and sandwiches   (from Ulatowska et al., 1990: 196)

Despite a limited use of cohesive devices (e.g. some lexical chaining (bread – slices – sandwiches) and overuse of 'and') and a degree of syntactic and semantic underspecification, the discourse is still reasonably coherent thanks to there being sufficient information conveyed and appropriate event sequencing. However, the more reduced one's linguistic competence becomes, the harder it is to produce adequately coherent discourse unaided.[12] Transcript 6.12 shows a retelling of the story represented in the *Cat Story* picture sequence by a man with severe posterior aphasia.[13]

Transcript 6.12

Little girl – she is a hurting. She's holler – hoow-haa-haa. So maybe somebody'd hear. So he look each other. So he turn away. She look at. So he gonna turn around. He started working it. So he gonna turn around. Work inside each other. He kinda got a little bit back there. He's gonna watch out. But he could see it. Really didn't do anything. But it jumped off right quick. Ahh – beautiful. Ahh – I love it. Oh – fellow right there trying to tell the police "Throw that back there". (From Ulatowska *et al.*, 1990: 196)

Unless one is already familiar with the story, it is impossible to reconstruct it from the transcript alone, largely because of overuse of referentially vague pronouns and omission of essential lexical content.

6.5.2   *Discourse: interactions in the intrapersonal domain*

A key interaction between discourse and grammar in both intrapersonal and interpersonal domains is evident in information structure – i.e. the way in which the relative salience of different items of meaning is signalled. 'Given' information tends to be presented before 'new' information (Clark and Haviland, 1977) and 'light' (i.e. short and grammatically simple) phrases tend to occur before 'heavy' (i.e. long and grammatically complex) phrases within clauses.[14] Arnold *et al.* (2000) attribute this to two complementary factors: (1) lighter material is easier to produce (i.e. intrapersonal constraint), and (2) hearing given/light material first also makes it easier for interlocutors to process and comprehend (interpersonal constraint).

In addition, cognitive factors play an important role. Discourse production problems are common in adults with RBD despite relatively intact

---

[12] We shall see below that even story telling is typically a joint activity, and that inadequate linguistic resources can trigger compensation within the interpersonal domain.

[13] The content of the *Cat Story* picture sequence is represented by Ulatowska *et al.* (1990: 194) as follows: 'The little girl is crying because her cat is in the tree. She tells her father, who decides to help. The father climbs the tree, but as he approaches the cat it begins hissing at him. When the father reaches for the cat, it jumps down. The little girl holds out her arms to catch the cat. Then the father slips and gets hung up on the tree. The little girl begins crying. The fire department has to come and rescue the father, while the cat sits on the ground licking itself.'

[14] This tendency is particularly evident in languages with canonical VO (Verb–Object) order, but can be partly offset in OV languages (Hawkins, 1994).

grammar. Brownell and Martino (1998) attribute this to an inferential deficit which affects the comprehension of gist and the processing of affective information, knowledge states and causal attribution, though Dressler *et al.* (2004) propose that a more specific deficit in distinguishing between 'figure and ground' is responsible for problems in expressing the given–new relationship in RBD. Memory is also a key contributory factor in discourse production, as is evident in a case study of an individual with global amnesia by Caspari and Parkinson (2000) in which poor episodic memory particularly affected the ability to sustain conversational discourse.

Paucity of content in discourse production may be a function of reduced linguistic capacity in some communication impairments, as noted above, but it is also a feature of conditions such as RBD (Joanette and Goulet, 1990), TBI (Body and Perkins, 2004), hydrocephalus (Barnes and Dennis, 1998) and PLI (Botting, 2002), where it has been attributed to problems with nonlinguistic elements such as inference, social cognition and memory. Transcript 6.13 shows a conversation between Edith, an 89-year-old woman with Alzheimer's disease, and T, a care assistant.

Transcript 6.13

```
 1   T:      I'm going to go next door
 2   Edith:  next door? what are you doing there?
 3   T:      sleeping
 4   Edith:  oh . so you'll be alright . as long as you're comfortable that's the main
 5           er . thing because things can get upset and disturbed quite easy er .
 6           at times if something goes wrong and there's a lot of things seem
 7           to go wrong occasionally these days . it's surprising how . er . they
 8           do go than what you think they would . but of course . it's n .
 9           when you study it and think about it . it's like nature isn't it .
10           it is nature when all's said and done . but when you're in somebody
11           else's place . you seem to think now then . oh I wonder if they're
12           wanting any more doing . if they didn't mind us being here . cos
13           they said we could come when we wanted and I said . you
14           were madly wanted I suppose . on the other hand we tried it . but
15           when we did er . call and . er . we called and we . er . asked them
16           and everything were OK . well it just suited me down to the ground
```

The impression of a relative lack of substance in what Edith says comes from an excess of pronouns with unclear reference, which in turn affects cohesion (which pronouns are co-referential?) and gives an appearance of 'topic drift'; a relatively high proportion of high frequency/low content to low frequency/high content words; and overuse of formulaic sequences (e.g. 'when all's said and done', 'it just suited me down to the ground'). Although it could be the case that Edith's vocabulary is limited, the meandering nature of her discourse is more indicative of cognitive than linguistic impairment.

Finally, there is also evidence of interactions between discourse output and sensorimotor factors. Kretschmer and Kretschmer (1994) cite a study by Klecan-Aker and Blondeau (1990), who reported a 'conspicuous absence' of subordinate conjunction use in the written narratives of hearing impaired students.

6.5.3   *Discourse: interactions in the interpersonal domain*

We have seen above that interpersonal, as well as intrapersonal, factors can influence discourse production in that speakers seem to be implicitly aware that 'light-before-heavy' structures are easier for their interlocutors to process. Ethnographic studies have revealed that interlocutor involvement, in fact, goes far beyond this. Clinical research on discourse has tended to focus on genres like narrative and picture description primarily because they *exclude* interlocutors and therefore supposedly provide a clearer account of individual ability. However, research which has compared formal test scores with performance in mundane conversation has tended to show that the former is a very poor predictor of the latter (e.g. Beeke *et al.*, 2003b; Schegloff, 2003; Wilkinson, 1995), and also that interlocutor involvement in narrative discourse production even under formal testing conditions is far greater than is generally assumed (Beeke, 2005). Transcript 6.14 shows the retelling of the *Bus Story* (Renfrew, 1997) by Lucy, a girl aged 4;10 who has SLI and whose case was discussed in Chapter 4, and by Amy, a typically developing child of the same age. They are 'facilitated' by Sara, an adult.

Transcript 6.14

	LUCY			AMY	
1	Lucy:	bus	1	Amy:	once upon a time when the driver
2	Sara:	yeah	2		was mending the bus . it ran off
3	Lucy:	been naughty	3		and it and the driver said "Stop!
4	Sara:	the bus was naughty	4		Stop!" and then . the bus ran on
5		what did he do?	5		and it met . a train and they pulled
6	Lucy:	bus want run away	6		faces at each other
7	Sara:	aah yeah . he did	7	Sara:	they did
8		where did he go?	8	Amy:	and then . it . they went . it soon
9	Lucy:	train (1 syllable)	9		had to go on the road again
10	Sara:	mhm	10		because the train was going into a
11	Lucy:	and then bus went	11		tunnel and then . he went . and a
12		[sticks tongue out]	12		policeman whistled his whistle
13	Sara:	[laughs] he did	13		and . he said "Stop! Stop, bus!"

#	Speaker	Utterance	#	Speaker	Utterance
14		he made a face	14		and then . but the bus took no
15		then what happened?	15		notice and just ran on and then he
16	Lucy:	police blowing whistle	16		said he got tired of goneing on the
17		[gestures blowing whistle]	17		road so he went onto the gr . over
18		stop stop bus [shouting]	18		a fence and he met a cow and the
19		[shakes fists in time with her	19		cow said 'Moo' *and then
20		speech]	20	Sara:	*he did
21	Sara:	yeah	21	Amy:	em . he was going down a hill
22		stop bus	22	Sara:	yep
23	Lucy:	bus went up – street	23	Amy:	and [1 syllable] there was a big
24		and the bus on the grass	24		some water and he didn't know
25	Sara:	and who's there? [whispered]	25		how to put his brakes on so he fell
26	Lucy:	cow	26		in the water and then when the
27	Sara:	yeah	27		driver saw what happened he
28	Lucy:	. bus fall in the . mud	28		called for help and the bus was a
29		fire pull it out the mud	29		good bus
30	Sara:	they pulled him out of the mud			
31		didn't they?			
32	Lucy:	. went on road			
33	Sara:	well done			

Leaving aside the differences in syntactic and morphological competence, the fact that Amy's story is approximately four times longer than Lucy's (170 and 43 words respectively), and the extensive use Amy makes of anaphora to marshall her utterances into a coherent story, a key difference in the two narratives is the role played by Sara. Amy is able to tell her story unaided and Sara's role is minimal, consisting simply of three 'backchannel' utterances of encouragement (lines 7, 20 and 22). In Lucy's narrative, on the other hand, Sara's role is extensive and crucial. Lucy is unable to produce a narrative unaided, and relies heavily on Sara's prompts and questions in the right sequence. Sara's contributions include:

- providing backchannel feedback and encouragement (e.g. lines 2, 10, 21)
- asking questions to help Lucy focus on the next part of the story (e.g. lines 5 and 15)
- reformulating some of Lucy's utterances to provide model sentences (e.g. lines 4 and 30–31)
- providing a linguistic formulation when Lucy is only able to produce a gesture (e.g. line 14)

Sara thus effectively provides the scaffolding which, in conjunction with Amy's contributions, results in a coherent narrative. The story is a joint achievement.

6.6   Conclusion

In this chapter we have seen that co-dependency between different areas of language is extensive. What we perceive and categorize as – say – a grammatical impairment may be a means, or the effect, of producing a lexically and phonologically complex set of utterances whose discourse and prosodic features need to be carefully adapted to the communicative needs of a specific interlocutor. Every moment requires the resolution of a vast number of potential decisions which in addition involve attention, inference, memory and other cognitive functions. Although a particular aspect of such a complex communicative event may be singled out for comment and analysis, it can only be fully understood in its embedded context. Thus language plays no less an important role in pragmatics than cognition. And indeed, there is even more to pragmatics than contextually embedded language and cognition. In Chapter 7 we consider the contribution of sensory and motor systems.

7 Sensorimotor systems and pragmatics

7.1 Introduction

Apart from obvious examples such as the use of gesture to compensate for linguistic output problems and the use of facial expression and tone of voice to interpret the attitudinal or emotional state of a speaker during comprehension, sensory input and motor output systems are rarely included in discussions of pragmatic ability and disability. However, once pragmatic functioning is seen as an emergent phenomenon it is clear that sensorimotor systems provide a range of communicative choices in the same way that cognitive and linguistic systems do; that restriction in choice as a result of impairment is pragmatically constraining and can have a knock-on effect both within the sensorimotor domain and in cognitive and linguistic domains; and that sensorimotor systems are as vulnerable as language and cognition to the effects of compensatory adaptation during interpersonal communication. The role of this chapter is therefore to round out and complete the emergentist model of pragmatics. However, because this is a relatively unexplored area, the chapter is of necessity considerably shorter than the preceding ones on cognition and language and aims to do no more than provide a programmatic outline with pointers for future research.

As outlined in Chapter 4, motor output systems govern the movements of the vocal tract, hands, arms, face, eyes and body, and sensory input includes auditory and visual perception. These are the key sensorimotor systems involved in communication and the ones that will be considered here. A fully comprehensive account would also need to include the sensory systems of touch, taste and smell and the range of body movements employed by users of augmentative and alternative communication (AAC) devices. Numerous examples of interactions involving sensorimotor systems have already been mentioned in preceding chapters, which attests to their integral role in pragmatics. To reiterate just a few examples:

- Visual and auditory perception play a key role in inferential processing – for example, misreading of facial expression or voice quality could result in failure to detect irony (Chapter 5).
- The expression of emotion and attitude is particularly multimodal, with meaning being conveyed via articulation, voice quality, prosody, facial expression, gesture, posture and gaze (Chapter 5).
- Lexical retrieval can be enhanced through the use of visual and/or auditory cueing (Chapter 6).
- Both visual and auditory impairment may affect theory of mind ability (Chapter 5) and the acquisition and production of grammar (Chapter 6), and cognitive and linguistic problems may in turn result in more extensive use being made of alternative motor output systems such as gesture to convey meaning (Chapters 4 and 6).

This chapter will focus briefly on the separate contributions of hearing, vision and motor systems to pragmatic processing.

7.2   Hearing

The influence of auditory perception on language and cognition is considerable, as can be seen in the range of concomitant impairments frequently experienced by those with deficient hearing. Poor auditory discrimination is widely seen as a key contributory factor in SLI (Bishop and McArthur, 2005) with consequences for the development of phonology (Dollaghan, 1998), grammar (Mogford-Bevan, 1993), semantics (Chiat, 2001) and discourse (Klecan-Aker and Blondeau, 1990). The effect of auditory impairment on subsequent language development is not always easy to foresee, and may involve a chain reaction of compensatory adaptations. Ebbels (2000), for example, reports a case study of a severely hearing impaired child with language difficulties over and above what was predictable on the basis of her hearing impairment alone. Wilbur (1977) describes how hearing impaired children's problems with definite and indefinite articles – which are not very acoustically salient and are sometimes omitted in hearing impaired children's writing (see Transcript 6.4 in Chapter 6) – meant that they also had difficulties in indicating cohesive relationships across sentences in narratives.

An inability to hear speech in particular can have indirect negative consequences for early language development. Feagans, Kipp and Blood (1994) found that young children with chronic otitis media had a limited attention span for joint activities such as book reading which are conducive to language development. It has also been found that 12-month-old infants with chronic otitis media use fewer nonverbal gestures to communicate than their healthy peers (Yont, Snow and Vernon-Feagans, 2001).

Since pre-linguistic gestures are a predictor of later language acquisition, this may well be developmentally significant.

A number of studies have also now established that deaf children are delayed in acquiring theory of mind and perform no better than autistic children matched for mental age, which suggests that auditory access to the use of language in conversational settings may play a role in theory of mind development (Peterson and Siegal, 2000; Russell *et al.*, 1998). It also appears to be the case that impaired auditory perception is implicated in autism (Siegal and Blades, 2003), though it plays a rather different role from that reported for SLI above. Čeponiene *et al.* (2003) found that children with high-functioning autism were unable to discriminate between speech sounds and non-speech sounds, though this is unlikely to be a purely sensory problem but linked to an inability to identify the social significance of specific sounds. Similarly, Kuhl *et al.* (2005) found that children with ASD had problems distinguishing motherese from non-motherese speech. A not dissimilar problem occurs in adults with acquired right hemisphere damage who sometimes have problems identifying familiar voices (phonagnosia) (van Lancker and Canter, 1982) and can find it difficult to detect whether an utterance is ironic from tone of voice alone (Tompkins and Mateer, 1985).

The interpersonal consequences of hearing impairment are also significant. Yont *et al.* (2003) found that parents of infants with chronic otitis media engaged with them less in joint activity and tended to direct their attention elsewhere. Mogford-Bevan (1993) also describes how difficulties in hearing others and being heard themselves affect the conversational performance of hearing-impaired children – e.g. providing fewer initiations and taking shorter conversational turns, as well as that of their interlocutors – e.g. being more directive and imposing a higher degree of control.

7.3   Vision

Although most research on language processing has focused on the vocal-auditory channel, vision also plays a key role in communication, either as an adjunct to another modality – for example, in interpreting gestural meaning that co-occurs with verbal meaning – or as the sole input modality, as in the case of reading. In the latter case, the limitations of verbal auditory memory can be avoided, since in the written modality words just read are not evanescent but remain permanently accessible as an externalized memory resource.

The complex interactions between vision, language and cognition and also other sensorimotor capacities can be seen in a wide range of constraints on communicative choice triggered by visual impairment. For example, very young blind children make more errors than sighted children when producing speech sounds whose articulation is highly visible (e.g. bilabials and labiodentals) and also produce fewer words containing labial consonants (Mills, 1983). Poor visuo-spatial ability can also impact on semantic development, as in the case of children with Williams syndrome (reported in Chapter 6) who have problems interpreting spatial prepositions (Phillips *et al.*, 2004). Visual processing deficits which affect communication in adults are often found following right hemisphere damage. 'Hemispatial neglect' – i.e. failure to detect visual signals in the spatial area opposite the site of the lesion (typically the right hemisphere) (Robertson and Rafal, 2000) – reduces the scope for eye contact and other visual input in multi-party conversations. People with RHD can also have problems reading emotion in facial expressions (Borod *et al.*, 1998), and in identifying familiar faces (prosopagnosia) (van Lancker and Canter, 1982).

Visual impairment can have particularly far-reaching effects within the interpersonal domain. It has been noted that young blind children are often more imitative – and even echolalic – than sighted children and use more formulaic language (Perez-Pereira, 1994). Such symptoms are also typical of autism, and Hobson and Bishop (2003) have reported a number of striking parallels in the communicative behaviour of some congenitally blind children and children with autism, such as the rarity of comments on things and events, and a lack of 'reciprocal engagement with others'.

The effect of blindness on conversational partners is also striking. As was reported for deaf children above, parents of blind children appear to exercise more control over their communicative interaction than parents of sighted children. In one study it was found that adults introduced more topics than their visually impaired children, and that a significant proportion of the topics related to visible situations and events that the children were unable to perceive (Kekelis and Andersen, 1984). Such modified parental input can in turn affect language development, as in the case reported in Chapter 6 where the tendency of parents of blind children to produce more imperatives and ask fewer questions had the indirect consequence of reducing the number of auxiliary verbs heard by the children and thereby delaying their acquisition (Landau and Gleitman, 1985).

Intact visual processing can be an important compensatory resource in the face of cognitive, linguistic or other sensorimotor deficits. In Transcript 7.1 (from Perkins, 1998a) a child with a diagnosis of semantic-pragmatic disorder is unable to carry out a particularly obvious inference until relevant information is presented visually.

Transcript 7.1

T (therapist) and P (child) are playing a picture guessing game
T: this one is an animal
P: oh
T: and it barks – it goes woof woof
P: oh dear
T: what kind of animal is that?
P: it's gonna run and run
T: it's an animal – and it can run
P: yes
T: and it goes woof woof woof woof woof
P: yes
T: what kind of animal is it?
P: a lion?
T: a lion? it might be or it might be . . .
P: the lion – the lion
T: *(shows picture)*
P: a dog

Further examples of the compensatory use of vision will be discussed in Chapter 8.

7.4 Motor ability

In discussing motor processing in the context of communication, it is important to distinguish between specific symbolic systems such as phonology, grammar, semantics, gesture, posture and facial expression, and the physical means of expressing them. Motor ability refers only to the latter. This is not an unproblematic distinction, since in some cases at least anatomy and physiology may partially determine the properties of the associated symbolic system, as has been argued, for example, for the relationship between articulation and phonology (e.g. Scobbie, 2005). For present purposes, though, it should suffice. In the emergentist account of pragmatics, communication is achieved via multiple yet simultaneous and integrated motor systems – for example, the use of articulation to express linguistic meaning, the use of hand and arm movement to express gestural meaning and the use of face and eye movement to express emotional and attitudinal meaning. We have seen various examples in previous chapters of impaired linguistic ability resulting in an increase and qualitative change in the use of gesture, though this is for linguistic/cognitive reasons rather than motoric ones. However, the way in which meaning is distributed across these different symbolic systems *may* be at least partly determined by the availability, capacity and proficiency of their related motor systems. For example, individuals with congenital and profound hearing loss may of necessity be forced to opt for sign language as their primary means of communication rather than spoken language, because lack of auditory feedback has prevented them from acquiring the level of control over their articulatory movements necessary for normal speech. Impairment of specific motor systems for anatomical reasons, such as glossectomy or cleft palate, or for neurological reasons as in the case of selective paralysis of vocal tract or limbs, will also directly affect the allocation of meaning to different symbolic systems. More pervasive conditions such as cerebral palsy and Parkinson's disease may affect all motoric systems equally with simultaneous diminution of function in vocal tract, face, limbs and body generally with concomitant reduction in compensatory capacity, at least in the intrapersonal domain. Kegl and Poizner (1998), in a study of deaf signers of American Sign Language who also had Parkinson's disease (PD) (also mentioned in Chapter 5), describe how their signing partners would assume responsibility for clarifying and expanding the minimally signed utterances of the individuals with PD.

We saw in the case of Len in Chapter 4 the pragmatic consequences – both in terms of intrapersonal and interpersonal interactions – of impaired articulation resulting from glossectomy. Another common cause of pragmatic problems following speech impairment is dysarthria, which simultaneously disrupts the motor functions of respiration, phonation, resonance, articulation and prosody (Murdoch, 1990). In a study of conversational interaction involving J, a man with severe dysarthria resulting from motor neurone disease, Bloch (2005) shows how J and his conversational partner deal with his reduced intelligibility by jointly breaking down sentence production into incremental stages to ensure understanding of each part before continuing. In Transcript 7.2 (from Bloch, 2005: 41–2), J waits after saying 'in a' in line 3 until receiving confirmation from S in line 5 that she has understood and that he can continue. The same process begins again with the addition of 'few days' in line 7, after which S recapitulates in line 9 by producing the phrase 'in a few days' in its entirety.[1] The final product is a joint achievement.

Transcript 7.2

```
1   S:   so when (0.5) do you know when you're going to be moving?
2        (0.6)
3   J:   ((1 syllable)) (in a)
4        (0.3)
5   S:   in a,
6        (0.4)
```

---

[1] This rather simplistic summary does not do full justice to the complexity of the data. Readers are referred to Bloch (2005) for a more comprehensive account.

7   J: (few days.)
8   (0.5)
9   S: in a few days.

The relationship between symbolic expression using the vocal tract and other motor output modalities is complex, and research increasingly suggests that speech and gesture, for example, constitute an integrated system (see Chapter 4) in which each may constrain the other and jointly co-determine meaning. Kelly *et al.* (1999) found that information conveyed through speech was better remembered when accompanied by gesture. Furthermore, participants in their experiment were unable to recall what information had been conveyed via speech and what information via gesture, suggesting that memory stores a derivative of both in a format that does not distinguish between the different output modalities. A link between memory and motor output has also been established in SLI. Following an extensive literature review, Hill (2001: 149) concluded that 'substantial co-morbidity exists between SLI and poor motor skill', and Ullman and Pierpont (2005) also found a strong link in SLI between motor impairment, procedural memory and auditory processing.

7.5   Conclusion

Multimodal approaches to the nature of communication such as those of McNeill (2000a), Clark (1996) and Goodwin (2000a) have begun to erode the still entrenched language-centric view that linguistically encoded meaning conveyed via the vocal-auditory channel is in some sense more privileged and central than meaning conveyed visually via gesture, gaze, facial expression, posture and body orientation.[2] It is this latter type of nonlinguistic meaning that has come to be seen as the domain of pragmatics and regarded as more implicit than linguistically encoded meaning. However, all of these semiotic systems encode meaning explicitly, and it is because of the flexibility of the overall communicative system including its range of sensorimotor output and input modalities that they are able to work in concert to enable the expression and reception of composite multimodal meanings. Motor output and auditory and visual input systems are no different from semiotic systems in terms of being providers of pragmatic choices as part of the process of communicative interaction.

---

[2] Prosodically encoded meaning is also commonly grouped with these nonlinguistic systems (cf. its common alternative label 'paralinguistic') despite its vocal-auditory instantiation.

8 Compensatory adaptation

8.1   Introduction

The focus in Chapters 5 to 7 has been on the elements whose interactions contribute to pragmatic behaviour. Here, we shift attention from the elements themselves to the nature and motivation of the interactions between them. These were introduced and discussed in Chapter 4 in terms of the notions of equilibrium and compensation. Let us briefly summarize the position presented there. An individual may be seen as an intrapersonal domain – i.e. the sum total of all his or her interacting cognitive, semiotic and sensorimotor capacities. A group of two or more communicating individuals comprises an interpersonal domain in which the individuals' capacities interact with those of the other individual(s). Any interaction which is interpersonally motivated – whether it is seen at the intrapersonal or interpersonal level – is pragmatic in nature. All domains are inherently equilibrium-oriented. In pragmatic terms, equilibrium may be seen as the state most conducive to maximally effective and efficient interpersonal communication. Disequilibrium results when one or more elements in either domain malfunctions or otherwise fails to achieve optimal performance. The natural response to this is compensation, whereby there is a reconfiguration and/or redistribution of resources across the domain as a whole. Compensation may be more or less successful depending on the nature of the deficit and the capacity of the domain to reorganize.

Compensation, therefore, is – or should be – key to any discussion of pragmatic disability, and also, by implication, of pragmatic ability. However, this tends not to be the case. Compensatory behaviour is certainly widely acknowledged as an important factor in recovery from communication impairments – in fact, a great deal of remedial activity is predicated upon it (e.g. Davis and Wilcox, 1985; Penn, 1999) – but its role in the development and aetiology of specific impairments, while often alluded to, is not typically seen as a core factor. For example, in a review of Ullman and Pierpont's (2005) procedural deficit hypothesis of SLI,

Thomas (2005a) singles out for particular comment the fact that 'compensation is placed centre stage in explaining observed behavioural impairments in a developmental disorder' (p. 435) since 'other explanations of developmental deficits frequently omit the possibility of compensation for simplicity's sake' (p. 436). The tendency to ignore compensation is also reflected in the fact that there is inconsistency in how 'compensation' and cognate terms are used and understood. There are several reasons for this. Firstly, most models of impairment assume there to be a fairly direct link between an underlying deficit and a consequent behaviour. For example, the PALPA assessment tool (Kay *et al.*, 1992), used for identifying underlying deficits in aphasia, maps performance on a range of tests on to a set of very specific underlying modular capacities such as the 'semantic buffer' and 'phonological output lexicon'. The possibility that test performance could be an indirect consequence of overall capacity limitations or a secondary effect of disruption elsewhere in the system is not explicitly recognized. Secondly, few theories of communication impairment see compensation as integral, two notable exceptions being connectionist accounts of developmental disorders (e.g. Elman *et al.*, 1996; Thomas and Karmiloff-Smith, 2002) and Kolk's adaptation theory of agrammatism in aphasia (Kolk, 1995). Modular theories in particular take little account of compensation. Thirdly, compensation tends to be difficult to characterize, and it is often hard to identify underlying compensatory processes purely on the basis of observed behaviour. Indeed, the nature of such processes may actually be quite counter-intuitive (Thomas, 2005a). Connectionist modelling of communication impairments, one of the few serious contenders available for testing hypotheses about compensatory processing at the intrapersonal level and for providing detailed characterization of the processes themselves (Thomas and Karmiloff-Smith, 2003), is still viewed with suspicion by many, particularly in the modularist camp.

In this chapter, I will first of all address various inconsistencies in the way terms such as compensation are used and suggest some terminological clarification. I will then consider the neurological basis of compensation, and why it appears to be successful in some cases but not others. Thirdly, I will argue that both intrapersonal and interpersonal accounts of compensation should be integrated, and finally I will provide a detailed case study of compensatory adaptation to illustrate these points.

8.2   Definition of terms

The general notion of compensation in communication disorder is not very precise. For example, it may be seen as a conscious or unconscious strategy; a process that occurs within the individual or in interaction with others; an autonomic adaptation within an organism in response to internal or external influences; or as a successful or unsuccessful outcome. A number of partially overlapping terms have been used by language pathologists and others to refer to the process of readjustment within an organism in response to dysfunction. *'Compensation'*, *'compensatory strategy'* and *'compensatory behaviour'* are often used interchangeably, though while *'compensation'* is fairly general in meaning, the latter two terms have quite specific connotations. *'Compensatory strategy'* suggests an intentional plan of action, but is also commonly used to include the resulting behaviour – i.e. the execution of the strategy (cf. Simmons-Mackie and Damico's (1997: 770; my italics) definition of compensatory strategy as 'a new or expanded communicative *behaviour*, often spontaneously acquired and systematically employed, to overcome a communicative barrier in an effort to meet both transactional and interactional communicative goals').[1] In addition, it is sometimes used figuratively to refer to plans or behaviours which may not be conscious. Some prefer *'adaptation'* or *'adaptive behaviour'* (e.g. Penn, 1999), which imply an unconscious and involuntary process. *'Forced adaptation'* is used by Simmons-Mackie and Damico (1995) to refer to adjustments which are typically unconscious and ineffective, and also has connotations of involuntariness. The main parameters of compensation to take into account, therefore, and which are often conflated, appear to be as follows:

- behaviour or state
- conscious or unconscious
- voluntary or involuntary
- intention or execution
- intrapersonal or interpersonal
- effective or ineffective
- learnable/teachable or unlearnable/unteachable.

The term I prefer is *'compensatory adaptation'* – or, more simply and shorthandedly, *'compensation'* – which I will define as 'adjustment to new conditions resulting in a counterbalancing of opposing forces within an organism as a whole'. The term is deliberately neutral with regard to issues such as whether or not the adjustment is effective, whether it is under conscious control and/or voluntary, how it is brought about and whether it may be learned or taught. To avoid connotations of consciousness, volition, intentionality, effectiveness, achievability and mode of realization is not to deny the importance of such parameters, but simply for the purpose

---

[1] *'Transactional'* refers to 'message transmission' (Simmons-Mackie and Damico, 1997: 770), while *'interactional'* refers to behaviours which 'promote social interaction and contribute to the flow or organization of discourse' (Simmons-Mackie and Damico, 1997: 771).

of clear exposition without becoming needlessly embroiled in these contentious issues.

8.3   Brain plasticity: the neurology of intrapersonal compensation

The account of compensatory adaptation in Chapter 4 and above – at least for the intrapersonal domain – is reasonably compatible with current neurological accounts of brain plasticity. This is defined by Thomas (2003: 96) (after Huttenlocher (2002)) as 'the adjustment of the nervous system to changes in the external milieu (through sensory inputs) or internal milieu (through the effects of damage to the system)' and is regarded as 'mainly a property of the cerebral cortex rather than subcortical structures' (2003: 96). Despite the overwhelming evidence that infants and young children manifest a much greater degree of neural plasticity than older children and adults, there appear to be definite constraints on compensation in certain communication disorders in children, which suggests that plasticity is not limitless. While some impairments appear to be easily compensatable, others do not. Elman *et al.* (1996) cite studies (Reilly, Bates and Marchman, 1998; Thal, Wulfeck and Reilly, 1993) in which children with early focal injury to the classical language areas of the brain, children with SLI and normal controls between the ages of 4 and 9 were tested on a range of measures including lexical diversity, morphological productivity, syntactic complexity and discourse coherence. On most of these measures, although the children with early focal lesions lagged behind the normal controls to some extent, they were still far ahead of SLI children in the same age range. In other words, early focal brain injury is easier to compensate for than SLI. Elman *et al.* (1996) speculate that this may be because SLI results from diffuse rather than focal cortical abnormalities such that 'healthy cortical tissue cannot take over the functions normally subserved by impaired regions because there simply isn't enough healthy cortical tissue to go around' (p. 313) – i.e. the neurological version of the cognitive overload hypothesis. Another possibility (they suggest) is that congenital deficits such as SLI may be a result of abnormalities outside the cortex, in the cerebellum and/or various subcortical structures, such that 'healthy cortex cannot play its usual role in language and cognitive development because of blockage or improper gating of the inputs that are crucial for normal learning to take place' (pp. 313–14). Locke (1997) suggests a somewhat different explanation in terms of maturational asynchrony; namely, that in order to activate a 'grammatical analysis mechanism' infants need to have acquired and stored a sufficiently large number of simple utterances. Children in whom this process is delayed for whatever reason 'have too little stored utterance material to activate their analytic mechanism at the optimum biological moment, and when sufficient words have been learned, this modular capability has already begun to decline' (p. 266). Each of these hypotheses has somewhat different compensatory implications, though all would account for why compensation in SLI is not particularly successful.

The various interactions observed in developmental disorders which were reviewed in Chapters 5 to 7 and elsewhere provide a very preliminary sketch of what may be able to compensate for what, but to extrapolate from correlations apparent in test results to the assumption that a specific element is in some sense capable of making up for a deficit in another element is in many cases oversimplistic. For example, if a statistically significant correlation is found between – say – performance on a specific test of productive syntax and a test of false belief in a group of children with ASD, this does not necessarily mean that syntax and ToM exist as discrete mental entities (i.e. performance mirrors competence in a Chomskyan sense), that one is a prerequisite for the other, that a correlation will also be evident outside the strict test conditions, or that the same individual will perform similarly in all circumstances and on all occasions. Furthermore, the neuroconstructivist account (see Chapter 3) argues that any imbalance within a system will have repercussions for the organism as a whole and will also affect the entire developmental trajectory. In other words, to talk of an intact element compensating for a malfunctioning element (whether or not we assume an element to be modular) is not quite accurate in that the integrity of the compensating element may be altered by the very process of compensation. As Thomas (2003: 117) puts it, '[w]ith respect to developmental disorders, it is important to realize that compensatory changes may lead to atypical cognitive processes, rather than normalization, because the limits on plasticity may have been changed during early brain development.'

Autism is another developmental disorder where the possibility of compensatory adaptation is limited. One attempt to account for this in neurological terms is the 'temporal binding hypothesis' (Brock *et al.*, 2002), according to which local neural networks fail to integrate and thus develop in relative isolation from one another, resulting in a state of neural 'hypocoupling' (Nunez, 2000), which has been described in cognitive terms as 'weak central coherence' (see Chapter 5). Such an account does not sit easily with attempts to explain autism as resulting from a specific deficit in a theory of mind module. However, if poor performance on ToM tasks is construed as a partial consequence of more basic problems with disengaging and switching attention, as predicted by the temporal binding hypothesis – i.e. as a set of complex interactions rather than a single deficit – we may be closer to the truth.

The relative lack of brain plasticity in adults compared to that found in young children clearly constitutes a barrier to intrapersonal compensation in cases of communication disorders acquired in adulthood as a result of brain damage. Karbe *et al.* (1998) compared the effectiveness of two distinct neurological compensatory adaptations[2] in adults with aphasia resulting from stroke, which they monitored using PET (positron emission tomography) brain scans. Spontaneous structural regeneration of the damaged left hemisphere regions, where this proved possible, turned out to be far more effective than recruitment of right hemisphere regions in cases where the left hemisphere regions were permanently damaged and beyond repair. However, in adult acquired disorders, despite the lack of neural plasticity and consequent unavailability of intrapersonal compensation, considerable scope for compensation exists in the interpersonal domain, to which we now turn.

8.4   Intrapersonal and interpersonal compensation

Accounts of compensation tend to focus exclusively on either the intrapersonal domain, as in the neurocognitive studies discussed above, or the interpersonal domain, as is found, for example, in the research paradigm of Conversation Analysis (see Chapter 2). Even the groundbreaking attempt by Lesser and Milroy (1993) to examine aphasia from the joint perspectives of the intrapersonal (psycholinguistics) and the interpersonal (pragmatics) treats them as distinct, parallel domains, more marked by their differences than similarities. (The latter are allocated no more than a short section of less than three pages in the concluding remarks of a 400-page book.) In the emergentist model of pragmatics proposed here, the two domains are seen as working in synergy and in fact as being identical in terms of the dynamic processes by which they are governed. Although pragmatics is driven by interpersonal considerations, its constituency extends throughout the intrapersonal and interpersonal domains. To limit one's focus to either domain in isolation can lead to an incomplete and distorted view of compensation and its scope. This becomes evident when we consider judgements of compensatory failure and success. What may be seen as failed compensation if viewed only at the intrapersonal level may in fact appear quite the opposite when viewed from an interpersonal perspective. Let us consider some examples.

Boscolo, Ratner and Rescorla (2002), in a study of 9-year-old children with a history of expressive SLI, found that they were significantly more

---

[2] Karbe *et al.* actually refer to these as 'strategies' used by the brain, which seems an odd way of putting it.

dysfluent during a story retelling task than their normally developing peers. This is explained in terms of an overload model according to which children who are pushed to the limits of their expressive linguistic ability will reduce resources in other areas, with a consequent degradation in performance – a kind of negative or subtractive compensation, as it were. If we see this within an interpersonal context, however, there may be another interpretation. Clark (2002) has argued that most speech dysfluencies, far from being evidence of communicative deficiency on the part of speakers, actually constitute a systematic means of synchronizing their actions with those of their interlocutors, and are precisely designed to help others analyse and understand what the speaker is saying. For example, in producing the following utterance, 'it would be a good thing if u:h . if Oscar went', Clark points out that, although the speaker 'could have suspended speaking after *thing* and resumed when he was ready again, he did not. Instead, he did four things: (1) before suspending his speech, he produced *if* to commit himself to producing a conditional clause; (2) he produced *uh* to signal that he was delaying the resumption of his speech; (3) he prolonged *uh* to signal that he was continuing an ongoing delay; and (4) on resuming speech, he repeated *if* to restore continuity to the conditional clause' (Clark, 2002: 6). In other words, dysfluencies such as these are not in themselves speech problems – they are *solutions* to problems that arise as a result of planning what we want to say within a limited time frame, and are specially tailored to accommodate the needs of our hearers. It might well be, therefore, that the more difficulty one has with the planning and execution of speech – as is the case for children with SLI – the more one needs to signal this (for example, via so-called dysfluencies) to help interlocutors work out what one is trying to say. Thus an apparent intrapersonal compensatory failure may in fact be recast as an interpersonal compensatory success story.

Lesser and Milroy (1993) report several instances of what they regard as failed attempts at compensation in people with aphasia which they interpret as being counter-productive to communicative success. One man would talk excessively until interrupted as a way of dealing with lexical retrieval problems (Edwards and Garman, 1989). Another patient managed to decrease his production of neologisms over a period of three years by increasing his use of stereotyped phrases, but only at the expense of reducing the variety of his vocabulary (Panzeri, Semenza and Butterworth, 1987). Yet another aphasic patient would use an introductory filler ('this is') when she was unable to access a following verb (e.g. 'This is Eddie the telephone' for 'Eddie worked for the telephone company') and also substituted the same form for prepositions (e.g. 'I was born this is Charlton Avenue' for 'I was born on Charlton Avenue') (Hand, Tonkvich and Aitchison, 1979).[3] However, we should be very cautious about dismissing these as instances of compensatory failure without detailed analysis of the interactions in which they occurred. Simmons-Mackie and Damico (1996) describe the atypical use by two aphasic speakers of neologisms, stereotyped phrases, repetition, gesture, posture and other devices to signal discourse functions such as turn initiation and termination, participant role and propositional attitude. Although such behaviours are not normally thought of as discourse markers, they were clearly used as such by the aphasic speakers, and also treated as such by their conversational partners. Interestingly, when the partners' attention was drawn to the devices, they proved either to have been completely unaware of them or else to have regarded them simply as aphasic symptoms, a direct reflection of the underlying intrapersonal deficit. A further example of an apparently aberrant intrapersonal behaviour which on closer examination turns out to be communicatively facilitative is the use of echolalia by people with autism. A number of studies have now shown that, despite the perceived oddness and even disruptiveness of echolalia, its deployment is almost invariably systematic, functionally motivated and oriented to by interlocutors, whether they are consciously aware of it or not (Dobbinson, Perkins and Boucher, 1997; 2003; Local and Wootton, 1995; Schuler and Prizant, 1985; Violette and Swisher, 1992).

The tenor of this discussion should not be taken to imply that any apparent intrapersonal compensatory failure can necessarily be transmuted to compensatory success once the interpersonal context is taken into account – merely that failure should not be assumed until the interpersonal context has been analysed in detail. It has long been an article of faith in clinical linguistics that 'a disordered language system is still a rule-governed one' (Perkins and Howard, 1995: 23) and there is no reason to assume that this does not equally apply in a broader pragmatic context. Consider the following extract in Transcript 8.1, from the same conversation as the one between Peter and Sara discussed in Chapter 4. Peter, it may be recalled, is aged 9½ and has word-finding problems.

Transcript 8.1

1 Peter: *but there was like . you know . like a hedgehog . but it were*[4] *really big*
2   *and that . it . and me mum were like eeeeee* [mimics fear and horror]
3 Sara: (laughs) and where was this hedgehog?

---

[3] Hand *et al.* (1979) suggest that this strategy may have been inadvertently carried over from therapy where picture naming using the frame: 'This is … [picture name]' had been frequently used.

[4] '*Were*' is an acceptable third person singular past tense form of '*be*' in Peter's dialect. However, he does also occasionally use '*was*', as in line 7.

4   Peter: *it was at the top . you know where the toilet is? i . it was at the top there .*
5   *and me mum were really frightened*
6   Sara: was that in the hotel?
7   Peter: *and . and then the next day I were m I was feeling . I felt sick*
8   Sara: oh dear

In Chapter 4, we saw that successful lexical retrieval can result from the conjoint actions of Peter and Sara. Transcript 8.1, in contrast, could be interpreted as a case of conversational breakdown, and therefore of compensatory failure. The story might go something like this: Peter's first turn comes in the middle of a conversation about the relative merits of English and Bulgarian food, and the apparent sudden topic change to his mother being frightened by a hedgehog is unexpected. In line 3, Sara responds empathetically with laughter to Peter's humorously dramatic portrayal of fear and horror, but also seeks to contextualize the new topic. Peter's response in lines 4–5 is treated as inadequate by Sara, as in line 6 she reformulates her wh-question from line 3 as a yes–no question (and therefore easier to answer), querying whether the location is the same as that of the previous topic – i.e. a hotel in Bulgaria. In line 7, Peter appears to ignore Sara's question completely, and to introduce yet another topic. In line 8, Sara does not challenge this, and the topic of 'feeling sick' continues for the next few turns. In other words, she makes no attempt to explore the potential topic links between restaurant food, hedgehogs and feeling sick. (Could it be that feeling sick was a result of eating hedgehog? Surely they don't eat hedgehogs in Bulgaria?) As it turned out, a subsequent conversation with Peter's mother revealed that the incident described involved a spider, not a hedgehog. Peter had retrieved the wrong word, but failed to monitor this, even when it was repeated back to him by Sara in line 3. In other words, Peter's lexical retrieval error contributed to a conversational breakdown which Sara failed to compensate for, as she had earlier (in Transcript 4.5).

But is there another way of looking at this? Let us provide a little more context. Part of Sara's motivation for carrying out this video-recorded conversation with Peter was to collect data which could be later used as a teaching aid and for research. Although this is an 'authentic' conversation in which Sara is interested in what Peter has to say, she is also interested in just getting him to talk. Compensating directly for Peter's word retrieval error is not even on the agenda, as she is not aware of the substitution of 'hedgehog' for 'spider', though it clearly has conversational consequences. However, despite Sara's clarification requests in lines 3 and 5 and Peter's topic shifts, there is nothing really 'wrong' with this conversation. Although Sara could have directly queried or challenged Peter's topic maintenance, she didn't. For whatever reason (maybe she just wants him to go on talking – it doesn't really matter), she implicitly accepts, by her response in line 8, Peter's new topic in line 7. The conversation continues in an orderly manner. If we avoid comparisons with subjective norms and focus purely on the turn construction and turn transition of both participants, there is nothing untoward here. Despite Peter's putative intrapersonal difficulties, there is no interpersonal breakdown if we take as our evidence the conversational behaviour of the participants.

There is an increasing number of published accounts of perceived intrapersonal communication problems being compensated for interpersonally, as evident in article titles such as 'Aphasic agrammatism as interactional artifact and achievement' (Heeschen and Schegloff, 2003) and 'Conversational success in Williams syndrome: communication in the face of cognitive and linguistic limitations' (Tarling *et al.*, 2006). Sometimes success is achieved after an interim period of mutual adaptation – or 'tuning in'– by both interlocutors, as described in the case of Len (Chapter 4), who, following his glossectomy, was able to remap his phonological system on to a novel set of phonetic realizations in such a way that he was once again intelligible to hearers after a short period of familiarization. If the damaged intrapersonal system is sufficently rich and flexible, interpersonal equilibrium may be restored following compensation. A similar case is reported in Howard (1993), where a 6-year-old girl with a repaired cleft palate initially appeared unintelligible. This impression gradually disappeared, however, once the interlocutor adapted to the highly systematic, yet very unusual, articulatory realization of her phonological system.

Judgements of what counts as abnormal or atypical – and therefore potentially compensatable – always require a precise frame of reference, and can vary as the frame shifts. We have focused here on the effect of shifting from the individual to the dyad, but the interpersonal resolution of an intrapersonal problem via compensation is not the end of the line. The paradigmatic scale of intrapersonal and interpersonal interactions may be extended further into the macrosocial domain, as is evident in differing societal and cultural attitudes towards disability, and in which intervention may be effected via social policy decisions through the medium of legal and political action. In addition to the 'interactions all the way down' referred to by Elman *et al.* (1996: 319), there are also interactions all the way up.

8.5   Case study

One of the best ways to see compensatory adaptation at work is through a holistic single case study. Experimental group studies are good at spotting trends, but, because of their tendency to see cognitive and linguistic capacities solely as reflections of test results, are incapable of homing in on what makes each individual case unique and can miss the crucial dimension of real-time, moment-by-moment activity. The following case study is data-driven – i.e. it emerged from the scrutiny of data of different kinds collected in different ways in different contexts with the sole purpose of trying to characterize, explicate and explain what was happening. It began with a puzzle: here was a child who was not coping well at school, possibly as a result of communication difficulties. However, the nature of his communication difficulties and their putative link to his academic performance were not at all clear. It started with no clear hypothesis, other than that something was not quite right. Various hypotheses did emerge during the course of the study and were subsequently revised as further data were brought to bear on them. A central hypothesis which received increasing support as the case study progressed was that intrapersonal and interpersonal compensatory adaptation between cognitive, semiotic and sensorimotor elements was pervasive, and this turned out to be the key to understanding and treating his problems.

8.5.1   Background

The subject of this case study is Peter,[5] the same child we have already encountered in Transcripts 8.1 and 4.5. By the age of 2;4 he was still only using one word – 'mummy'. He was referred for speech and language therapy, diagnosed as having developmental language difficulties/SLI and received treatment intermittently over the next two years. At 3;4 he was reported as being able to understand strings of three content words and was beginning to produce SV and SVO structures such as *pussycat sleeping* and *I like that*. Six months later he was using four- or five-word sentences together with negative and interrogative constructions. By 4;1 his phonology was reported as being near normal for his age apart from a few residual immaturities such as [gɒg] for 'dog'. At 4;7 Peter had occasional problems making himself understood with unfamiliar interlocutors and still produced a few grammatical errors, but his overall level of communication was felt to be adequate for him to attend mainstream school. Here, despite being a willing and well-behaved pupil, there was concern over his academic progress, particularly in reading, and at 6;5 he was once again referred for speech and language therapy. When assessed on a story retelling task (BS)[6] he performed at the level of a child two years

---

[5] A brief sketch of Peter's case was published as Perkins (2001).

[6] Initials in parentheses in this chapter denote formal tests and assessments. See the Appendix for the full list.

younger. A year later, his teachers expressed concern over his poor comprehension, and at 8;8 a vocabulary assessment (BPVS) showed him once again to be lagging approximately two years behind his peers. Eventually, it was felt that other factors might be contributing to his poor communication over and above his specific linguistic problems, and at the age of 9 ½ Peter underwent extensive investigation by an educational psychologist, a speech and language therapist and a clinical linguist. As a result, at the age of 10;6 he was finally provided with a 'statement of special educational needs'.[7]

Peter's case is interesting for a number of reasons, but in particular because (a) although his problems are not particularly severe, they are extensive and complex with no obvious single underlying cause, (b) his communicative performance is inconsistent and can vary considerably from one occasion to another, and (c) immediate impressions of his ability do not square with what the formal test results appear to tell us. The educational psychologist reports that 'on first meeting Peter, his language difficulties are not so apparent', and that, despite his poor performance on a range of individual tests, when viewed in the round 'Peter does not seem unusual'. The story is clearly not a straightforward one.

The case study is based on a range of assessments carried out during the second half of Peter's ninth year. The formal test results, however, were only the starting point of the analysis, which also takes into account Peter's performance during the administration of the tests and in more informal conversational settings. First we will review his linguistic, then cognitive, abilities, and subsequently consider the interactions between them.

8.5.2   Language

Notwithstanding the 'veneer of normality' (as the educational psychologist put it) that Peter can sometimes convey, a detailed scrutiny of his communicative behaviour soon reveals ample evidence of linguistic anomalies at all levels.

8.5.2.1 Syntax Peter's syntactic errors include wrong word order:

Transcript 8.2

a new brand window (for 'a brand-new window')

lack of subject–verb agreement:

---

[7] This means that a child is entitled to receive additional learning support specially tailored to his/her needs as laid out in the report.

Table 8.1 *Sample performance on a comprehension test of reversible passives*

Test stimulus	Peter's response
Jim was taught by Mary. Bill was taught by Ellen. Who was taught?	*Mary. Ellen.*

Table 8.2 *Sample performance on a test of sentence formulation*

Test stimulus	Peter's response
but	*but I've got a CD*
before	*before I went to bed*
although	*although you haven't got any shopping*
either	*either have I got anything for you*

Transcript 8.3

there's two <u>men</u> who'<u>s</u> got yellow hair and two <u>men</u> who'<u>s</u> got red hair

double marking of the comparative:

Transcript 8.4

it helps me <u>more better</u>

and use of a reflexive object pronoun with a non-reflexive verb:

Transcript 8.5

she'll be tired and she'll <u>bump into herself</u>

On a test of comprehension of reversible passives (CELF-R), Peter scored only 3 out of 8. An example is shown in Table 8.1. When asked to make up sentences using coordinating or subordinating conjunctions (CELF-R), in nearly every case he provided only a single dependent clause. An example is given in Table 8.2.

8.5.2.2 *Morphology* Peter sometimes regularizes irregular nouns and verbs, both in response to specifically targeted test stimuli (CELF-R), as in Table 8.3, and also spontaneously in discursive picture descriptions:

Transcript 8.6

there's two yellow-haired <u>mans</u> and two other red <u>mans</u> who's got red hair

and in conversation:

Transcript 8.7

I think they got a stone and lit it really quick and <u>throwed</u> it

Table 8.3 *Sample performance on a test of word structure production*

Test stimulus	Peter's response
Here is a tooth. Here are some ...	*toothes*
Here is a foot. Here are two ...	*foots*
Here is Butch making an airplane. This is the airplane Butch ...	*builted*

8.5.2.3 Vocabulary As already seen in Chapter 4 and earlier in the current chapter, one of Peter's most noticeable problems is word finding. Sometimes, he fails to retrieve a word altogether, but on other occasions he may use the right words but in the wrong order, as in Transcript 8.8,

Transcript 8.8

I had peas on my sugar (for 'I had sugar on my peas')

or else he may simply select the wrong word, as shown in Transcript 8.9.

Transcript 8.9

if you break through a shop (for 'break into')

and then . the tram and the bus are . pulling faces at each other (referring to a train)

he doesn't know how to s . stop the brakes (for 'put the brakes on')

if there was a City playing in m . in me bag or something (for 'player')

Context: Sara and Peter are looking at a picture of a man holding a fish
Sara: what will he have to do to them to make them nice to eat?
Peter: *he'll have to take all the skin off and all the. hairs off* (for 'scales'?)
Sara: and then what's on the end of the line to help catch the fish? (points to the hook)
Peter: *erm the . erm rope?*

Sara: what room do you keep food in at home?
Peter: *might be . in the fridge*
Sara: you're right . you keep yoghurts in the fridge
Peter: *you k you keep cheese*
Sara: you do keep . why do you keep those kind of things in the fridge?
Peter: *they might melt*

About half an hour after the previous example, Peter used '*melt*' wrongly again but in a different sense, as shown in Transcript 8.10.

Transcript 8.10

they're making a . sandcastle . then they've made it then erm they might be making another one . then it melts . and then it's gone

8.5.2.4 Discourse Peter also has problems with discourse and, according to some assessment profiles, pragmatic problems. Peter would perform poorly, for example, on Penn's (1985) 'Profile of communicative appropriateness', which includes the categories 'Cohesion', 'Response to interlocutor', 'Control of semantic content' and 'Fluency'. The lack of semantic coherence in Peter's narratives is illustrated in Transcript 8.11, which is Peter's attempt to describe the route he takes when he walks to school.

Transcript 8.11

right . there's . it's called Cedar Close . so i it's like a path . you go . down this like road . you turn . right . keep going . then there's Grange Road . and . you k you keep . o you keep going . don't go up Grange Road don't . you keep going that way . and then . there's like . there's shops . erm . hairdresser's . so you . but you keep going . that way . you nee . so you keep going that way . and there's all flats here . you can . keep going that way . and then . there's Mark Law's here . and there's sh . all shops and and ma like Mark Law's and . like a pub . and . so you keep . you keep going that way . up . there's like . erm . ramp . and . you go . right . keep going up . that road . keep going still . then you turn left . and then . it's like . a road called Laburnum Road . so you go a bit . to the right . you go up . and then there's school . and then erm . you k . you keep going that way and then . you go into school and then you're there

Despite accompanying gestures (not shown in the transcript), the excessive use of anaphoric and exophoric pro-forms (e.g. *there, it, that*) makes his description very difficult to follow. It would certainly be impossible to identify or follow the route based solely on the information conveyed.

Peter's responses to questions are sometimes inappropriate either in terms of their topical relevance, as in Transcript 8.12,

Transcript 8.12

Sara: so how did you get into the football ground?
Peter: *and me grandad came with me too*
Sara: right
Peter: *it was me dad . me and me grandad*

or in terms of their form. In Transcript 8.13, for example, Peter's answer seems to presuppose a question with similar meaning but differently formulated, such as 'What is the function of an iron?'

Transcript 8.13

Sara: he . what does an iron do?
Peter: *to make it flat . not creasy*

In narrative expositions of more than a sentence or two, Peter often loses his thread and wanders off topic as illustrated in Table 8.4 (BAS).

Table 8.4 *Sample performance on a test of social reasoning*

Stimulus	Peter's response
Colin and Dave like reading a lot and Colin goes to the library every Friday. One week, Dave went with him and saw a lot of books he wanted to read. Colin showed him where to go to get tickets for the library, but Dave said 'not likely' and took the books he wanted out under his coat. What do you think?	*You shouldn't steal and it's the wrong thing to do but if you . it's . it's I . you have to pay for the book because they're very interesting books and . erm it will be very good and if I . if . you paid for you can read it in bed or something . something like that . or if it was just a pound for about Saturday . and he brought it back in it . it would be quite good because some people can read fast . some people can't . and . but . it's best if you read . and then you can write that down . that's what I usually do . if I rea . if I want that book I draw a picture . and I write all the words neat . then I can read it all the time instead of the book.*

Table 8.5 *Sample performance on a test of reading accuracy*

Written target	Peter's read version
convenient	*convented*
cellars	*clennars*
important	*impossilant*
reduce	*red course*
heat	*het*
raise	*rise*
cover	*covern*

8.5.2.5 Phonology and reading Although Peter rarely makes phonological errors, when formally assessed (PAB) he showed some problems with onset and rime, i.e. in correctly identifying initial sounds and phonologically similar word endings. This may be linked to errors he makes when he reads aloud, as in Table 8.5 (BAS) where he achieved a score equivalent to two years below his chronological age.

8.5.2.6 Fluency Peter is often dysfluent with frequent pauses, hesitations, false starts and repetitions. In the following brief conversational extract, there is even an intra-word pause of about a second between 'Bulgaria' and 'n', as shown in Transcript 8.14.

Transcript 8.14

sh she wasn't p . f . sh . I don't think . she was Bulgaria . n

8.5.2.7 Comprehension In addition to his problems with expressive communication, Peter frequently finds comprehension hard, too. For example, at the age of 9;10 he achieved the score of a child aged 8;2 on a test of reading comprehension (BAS). On a formal comprehension test (CELF-R) in which he was required to answer questions about a short paragraph which was read out to him, he only managed one accurate response out of eight – well below the norm for his age group. His teachers reported that he found it difficult to follow instructions, which was confirmed by a test (CELF-R) in which he was able to respond correctly, for example, to 'Point to a blue line before you point to a yellow line' but not to 'After I point to a red line, you point to a blue line after you point to a yellow line'.

8.5.3   Cognition

Some of Peter's linguistic problems start to fall into place once we examine his cognitive strengths and weaknesses, though a full account of interactions will be left until the next section.

On the *British Ability Scales* (BAS), which assess the processing of information visually and verbally, Peter's overall performance put him at the 9th centile – in other words, on these measures he would be outperformed by 91 per cent of his peer group. Of particular significance, though, are his extremes of performance on specific subsections. Peter's highest BAS score was on the 'Visualization of cubes' subtest, where he scored at the 84th centile. This required him to use visual information to match three-dimensional objects (cubes with pictures on) with a number of two-dimensional pictures. His visuo-spatial abilities, therefore, proved to be exceptionally good. His lowest score, on the other hand, was on the 'Immediate visual recall' subtest, where he was shown a card containing pictures for a set time before it was taken away and he was asked to recall as many items as he could. Here his performance was only at the 3rd centile. Short-term memory therefore clearly appears to be a problem for Peter, even when deployed in the visual domain, where he has obvious strengths. Long-term memory seems to be less of an issue. Although he could only remember six items once the card had been taken away, when asked twenty minutes later what he could remember ('Delayed visual recall' subtest) he was able to recall accurately five of those six, and scored a little higher, at the 11th centile.

Difficulty retaining more than a few items in short-term memory may also help to explain lapses in attention and failure to focus on more than one or two features at a time in either a visual ensemble or a sequence of events. On the 'Block design' subtest, Peter was required to look at a two-dimensional design, and use cubes to create a matching three-dimensional version. He seemed to pick up on the key visual information needed to

Table 8.6 *Performance on a test of auditory selective attention aged 13;9*

Type of background noise	Number of words identified	Percentile rank	Age equivalent in years
None	11/11	100	
Fan-like	27/33	1	
Cafeteria-like	27/33	1	
Voice	30/33	7	
		Total	6;7

Two-dimensional design   Peters versions

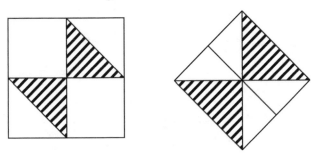

Fig. 8.1 Replication of a block design

reproduce the patterns appropriately. However, rather than completing the task with the cubes placed in the correct orientation – an important requirement – he appeared to forget this and focused only on the central section of the design, replicating it in isolation as shown in Figure 8.1.

Not being able to take full account of context is also evident when Peter loses track of what he's been told to do, misses the point of explanations or loses the thread of what he is saying.

A further weakness in Peter's cognitive profile lies in his ability to process auditory information. This was not assessed at the same time as the other measures reported here, but at the later age of 13;9. Although the results discussed below are not, therefore, a direct reflection of Peter's abilities four years earlier, they are unlikely to under-represent them. Peter was still performing below his mental age level at 13;9 and, given that his communication had improved considerably during the intervening period, if anything his auditory processing abilities at the age of 9½ are likely to have been at a lower level than those described here.

Tables 8.6 and 8.7 give Peter's scores on two subtests from the *Goldman-Fristoe-Woodcock Auditory Skills Test Battery* (GFW) (Goldman, Fristoe

Table 8.7 *Performance on a test of auditory memory aged 13;9*

	Number of words remembered	Percentile rank	Age equivalent in years
Recognition memory	98/110	3	
Memory for content	21/32	10	
Memory for sequence	49/84	11	
		Total	9;1

Table 8.8 *Performance on a test of auditory and visual sequential memory aged 13;9*

	Span	Age equivalent in years
Visual sequential memory	8	> 10;6
Auditory sequential memory	4	4;8

Table 8.9 *Sample performance on tests of syntactic processing*

Stimulus	Peter's response
The pencil on the shoe is blue. (TROG) (Subject is required to point to the correct matching picture)	Chose the picture with the blue shoe.
After you point to a yellow line, point to a red line. (CELF-R)	Only pointed to the red line.

and Woodcock, 1974). The 'Selective attention' subtest assesses the ability to listen to, and understand, a message against a noisy background, whereas the 'Auditory memory' subtest assesses auditory word recognition, recall of word content and position of words in a sequence.

The results in Table 8.6 show that Peter had no difficulty identifying words without background noise, but had tremendous problems when the noise of a fan or cafeteria was present in the background, and only slightly less difficulty with a background voice. Table 8.7 shows that Peter also performed poorly on some aspects of auditory recall. His slightly better performance on 'Memory for content' and 'Memory for sequence' may be explained by the presence of picture aids (there are none in the 'Recognition memory' subsection) which could have played to his visual strengths.

Peter's auditory and visual memory were also explicitly compared at 13;9 using the *Illinois Test of Psycholinguistic Abilities* (ITPA) (Kirk, McArthur and Kirk, 1968), as shown in Table 8.8.

Although short-term memory is impaired in both modalities, Peter's auditory short-term memory is particularly severely affected. This can be clearly seen in Table 8.9, where Peter shows a recency effect in processing complex and/or long syntactic structures – i.e. he appears to remember the last part and ignores the first part.

8.5.4   Intrapersonal interactions and compensatory adaptations

Now that we have a clearer picture of Peter's cognitive and linguistic abilities in isolation, we can start to explore why his performance is often inconsistent and how he is able on occasion to mask some of the problems revealed by his poor test results.

With regard to the latter point, one difficulty with formal tests is that they can only show part of the picture, and strict scoring methods can mean that important relevant information has to be ignored or discarded. For example, Peter only scored at the 4th centile on the BAS 'Word definition' subtest, but some of his 'wrong' responses show that this score may not reflect his true ability. When asked to define *massive*, he said: 'when somebody small then er . when you look up and they're giant . they're like a giant and they look really really big'. He clearly knew what the word meant, but was not able to express it succinctly. His definition of *error*: 'I'm frightened . there's like when someone comes up to you and they like . they'd kill you' was wrong for a different reason – he had clearly misheard it as *terror*, possibly as a result of background noise. It is perhaps for such reasons that a number of researchers have found that formal language scores do not always correlate well with clinicians' assessment of SLI (Gray *et al.*, 1999) and that analysis of spontaneous speech samples provide better material for diagnosis (Dunn *et al.*, 1996). And yet, even during spontaneous speech Peter's performance can vary considerably. We have noted above how dysfluent and grammatically illformed his language can be, but there are also frequent instances of grammatically flawless sentences delivered both rapidly and fluently, as shown in Transcript 8.15.

Transcript 8.15

his dad might have bought something for him to give to his mother (spoken rapidly)

then . this boy or a girl or the mum or the dad (spoken rapidly). *picks a flower off*

this boy at Norton did that and he had to pay for it but he didn't have any money (spoken rapidly)

Why such variability? There are already clues in the cognitive test results above. Recall that Peter has poor short-term memory, particularly in the auditory modality, but is good at visual processing and is also able to recall things reasonably well once he has stored them in long-term memory. The following extracts from the educational psychologist's report are instructive here:

Peter finds it easier to make up stories if he is given physical things, for instance toys or cars or other objects, to focus upon.

Peter himself has told me that, at times, he knows what he wants to say, but he can't always say it. Sometimes his thoughts get distracted by others chatting, for instance, and his thoughts go out of his head.

Peter also seems to become overloaded when increasing demands are made on his attention. For instance, his parents report that Peter finds it difficult to watch and listen to television at the same time.

Information gathered from the classroom and teacher reports indicates that Peter finds it hard to group things if others speak quickly to him. He can follow three-part instructions if these are presented to him slowly, and this also perhaps gives him more time to rehearse them before carrying them out.

Peter seemed to make more errors as the passage got harder – which is obvious – but he also made errors on the types of words which he had read very easily in earlier passages.

These observations confirm what is already implicit in the account of Peter's communicative abilities provided above. They depict a child whose language processing is constrained by limited working memory and whose auditory processing is distracted by background noise, whose attention is easily diverted and whose overall processing capacity is overloaded by multiple demands. At the same time, he is helped when there is visual support and ample time to plan and rehearse what he says and to process what he hears. There is clearly some capacity for compensation here. What we are at last in a position to do is map out the various ways in which Peter is able to achieve no little degree of communicative success through a complex counterbalancing of his inherent strengths and weaknesses, both intrapersonally and in conjunction with others.

There is an interesting trade-off between syntactic complexity and lexical content in much of what Peter says. These in turn interact with other factors, such as fluency and speed of delivery. For example, although, as we have seen, Peter's word retrieval is often unsuccessful, sometimes after a long drawn-out struggle there are also occasions when he produces a whole string of content words with apparent ease, as in Transcript 8.16.

Transcript 8.16

Sara: why d'you think that man's doing some shopping?
Peter: *to get some fe . some . cos he might . he might have drunk all . coke or anything or shandy or beer* (last two items spoken quickly)
Sara: right
Peter: *or lager*

Peter: *cos me dad goes football training*
Sara: oh does he? right
Peter: *not like <u>Aston Villa or Arsenal or United</u>*

Peter: *then . <u>this boy or a girl or the mum or the dad</u>* (spoken quickly) . *picks a flower off*

There are two rather telling points to be made about these examples. Firstly, the syntax of the underlined sections is very basic, coordination being the simplest form of syntactic adjunction. Secondly, the words used are all co-hyponyms – i.e. they belong to the same superordinate semantic category. This makes good processing sense: Peter only has to access a single semantic field and doesn't have to worry about inserting each word into a precise position in a complex syntactic structure. It is hardly surprising that such strings are often delivered rapidly and fluently. However, such a compensatory adaptation can also have negative consequences. In the following lexical tour de force, shown in Transcript 8.17, Peter appears to get so caught up in listing items of clothing that he loses track of what the question was and thus ends up in a topical cul-de-sac of his own making.

Transcript 8.17

M: what are you good at when you write stories?
Peter: *I get me names in . country . ages . where they live . are they married . is hot or snow . nice house very nice clothes . brother or sister . any shoes or any hair . any coats socks trousers jumpers T-shirts shorts . . .*

In addition to offsetting syntactic simplicity against lexical density, the opposite effect can also be found as shown in Transcript 8.18.

Transcript 8.18

the man who's got yellow hair wants to go out with the yellow-haired lady and the boy who's got yellow hair wants to go out with the red-haired lady . and the man with red hair wants to go out with the lady who's got yellow hair

The syntax here is quite complex, with both relative clauses and nominal postmodification in evidence. On the face of it, some of the lexis appears fairly advanced too. However, what we see here is the same few words being repeated again and again in similar syntactic frames. In addition, this extract is taken from the ninth item of a test of formal operational thinking (BAS) in which all preceding items have also made use of similar pictures, and Peter has had ample opportunity to rehearse these words and structures (compare, for example, the adequacy of his response to the first item: 'the boys is red hair and the girls is yellow hair . . .'). Furthermore, there are pictures of the people referred to which reduces pressure on short-term memory – temporary storage can be outsourced, as it were, to the visual modality where Peter is more adept. In fact, Peter often uses visual props and cues to facilitate his lexical retrieval, though not always to good effect. For example, when asked what he found difficult about school, he looked around the room, noticed some musical instruments and then said he found music difficult. In the same sentence completion task mentioned earlier (CELF-R), when he was asked, 'give me a sentence beginning with *neither*', he looked around, saw some books and said, 'neither some books'.

A further way of reducing pressure on lexical selection is to use more high-frequency words such as pro-forms. A good example of this is Peter's narrative account of how to get to school, shown above in Transcript 8.11. If we further discount frequent repetition of '(you) keep going (that way)' (discussed further below) and a few instances of proper names for roads and shops, there is hardly any lexical content left in his description. There is also precious little syntax remaining either, but here we also need to factor in the added processing burden that comes from constructing a lengthy but orderly narrative with each item in its appropriate place in the sequence – quite a tall order for an already challenged working memory.

Further evidence of repetition abounds. Peter frequently uses stereotypes or 'formulaic sequences' (Wray and Perkins, 2000) such as '(you) keep going (that way)',[8] which are a well-attested means of reducing linguistic processing demands (Perkins, 1999; Wray, 2002). One common example is '(you) know (when)', as in Transcript 8.19.

Transcript 8.19

Peter: *yeah . you know the tickets?*
Sara: yeah
Peter: *they tell you where to go*

     you know when it's no school?

     I have . erm . d'you know a boiled egg?

     you know when . it's a servant?

     mm no . well do you know the sausages?

     know when it was a wa °hh we went on erm . (tuts) . a ship

Another, 'one('s) (called)', is shown in Transcript 8.20.

Transcript 8.20

Peter: *erm it . he just plays like . erm . well look . I'll . one who's joined is Simon . one called Tim*
Sara: mhm

---

[8] This formulaic phrase is used by Peter on other occasions, too – e.g. in his retelling of the Bus Story: '*the . the . bus is not very pleased so he keeps going that way*'.

Peter: *one called Banner . one called John*
Sara: right
Peter: *one called . I think there's five a side . and there's me dad as the goalkeeper*

Sara: have you ever had a dog?
Peter: *. well . one's called . Cindy and one's called Bonny . er . and they're me grandma and me grandad's*
Sara: oh that's nice . what colour are they
Peter: *er . one's black and . another one's black . then the . they're big and they're fluffy*

Sara: so you'd like to be an actor? what's your favourite programme that you'd like to be an actor in?
Peter: *. one's called the Mask . cos I like that . it's funny*

Peter: *but .hh we . e we did like the dinner and that . but erm . there were . a . there was one called Mike . one called . oh erm . erm . I don't know his name now*
Sara: right
Peter: *other one*
Sara: right
Peter: *but there was . ff oh and one was called John . I don't know the other one*
Sara: and who were they?

This formula is idiosyncratic, nearly always semantically underspecified and enables Peter to avoid using a superordinate category term – namely, '(football) player', 'dog', 'programme/film' and 'waiter' respectively in the examples shown in Transcript 8.20. The interlocutor is charged with inferring the missing category.

Peter makes use of various other devices which appear to facilitate his language production and/or comprehension. Many of us may talk to ourselves occasionally, but Peter does this frequently, and during face-to-face interaction, which is less usual. One possible reason for this is that it is a type of rehearsal, and also an alternative to short-term memory as a form of temporary storage – effectively a way of 'thinking aloud', in true Vygotskyan fashion (Clark, 1998). The educational psychologist made the following observation:

On some tasks, I have noticed that Peter talks to himself as the demands increase. I have suggested to him that he should do this more. One reason for this is that it could be a way of him capturing his thoughts, instead of having them go out of his head. Perhaps if he hears what he has said, he stands a better chance of processing it. When I followed up the suggestion with Peter, he told me 'it helps me more better'. He also added that 'it helps me more better if you don't think'.

Four years later, at the age of 13;9, Peter showed evidence of a more refined version of this technique. When asked a question, he would often repeat part of it before responding, as in Transcript 8.21.

Transcript 8.21

Tanya: what was your room like? what did it look like?
Peter: er . *the room* . *what it looked like* . *it was . er . i . it were a bit like this actually .*
         er . just a bit bigger

Tanya: can you tell me about the last holiday you went on? did you go on one over
         the summer?
Peter: *the last holiday I went on* . *what do you mean with the school or do you mean*
         with
Tanya: with your family
Peter: *er* . *with me family* . *I . I . er I went to Spain . I think it was*

Thinking aloud is not uncommon in ordinary conversation as a means of
creating 'thinking time', but is marked in Peter's discourse by its frequency.
Another device found in typical interaction as a complement or alternative
to language, but which Peter uses with atypical frequency, is gesture. This
can be as a straightforward lexical replacement, as in Transcript 8.22.

Transcript 8.22

Context: Describing a picture in which a man is using a kettle instead of an iron to
iron clothes
he's not ironing he's like . putting . he's doi . he's got like a kettle and doing that
(mimes ironing)

and erm there was erm – the boat was going like that (rocking gesture) *and wa . and*
we all felt sick

Getsure can also be used to be more semantically precise about what is
being said, as in Transcript 8.23.

Transcript 8.23

Sara: wh what shape's a fishing hook?
Peter: (gestures the shape of a hook) *it's . down and it's . like a hook*

Sara: °hh oh dear – so where was the boat? o- on the sea or . .
Peter: *it was on the sea* (gestures wave motion with left hand)

So far we have considered interactions and compensatory adaptations
only within the intrapersonal domain. While this is convenient for expository purposes, it is only part of the story. For example, Peter's account of
how to get to school was actually a dialogue (albeit with minimal 'backchannel' contributions from his interlocutor) and all the test results were
collected in an interactive setting. The *raison d'être*, after all, of all the
processes described above is optimal communication with others – i.e. they
are pragmatically motivated. To complete Peter's profile, we now turn
to the interpersonal domain, where he is no more – nor less – than a
co-dependent participant.

8.5.5   Interpersonal interactions and compensatory adaptations

Peter is a slow processor. His dysfluencies and frequent pausing mean that his spoken language is long-drawn-out by normal standards. For example, his 177-word account of how to get to school, shown in Transcript 8.11, took 4 minutes and 56 seconds – a rate of only 38.2 words per minute.[9] Likewise, his comprehension improves when interlocutors speak slowly. We have already seen that there are good intrapersonal reasons for this, but there are also interpersonal consequences. In communication, time is not an individual preserve but a shared commodity. A speaker can't just take extra time unilaterally, but must ensure the hearer's compliance too. How does this happen in Peter's case? In Transcript 8.24, repeated from Transcript 8.1, further crucial information has been added – namely, the pattern of Peter's eye contact. One or more dashes (– – –) above the line indicates that Peter's gaze is averted from Sara, while one or more crosses (+ + +) shows that he is making eye-contact with her.

Transcript 8.24

```
          ---- +------------------+----------------
1   Peter:  cos I felt sick . know when it was a wa °hh we went on erm (0.1)
          --------+++
2          (tuts) (1.0) a ship
          ----
3   Sara:   mhm
```

Towards the end of line 1 and continuing into line 2, Peter is clearly searching for the word 'ship'. The gap between 'on' and 'a ship' lasts two seconds and contains a filled pause ('erm'), a short silence, a 'tutting' noise (more specifically, a voiceless alveolar click) and a longer one-second silence. Although we have seen in Chapter 4 that Sara sometimes assists Peter in his word searches, she doesn't take the opportunity to help him out here. There are several likely reasons. Firstly, filled pauses have been identified as signals to one's interlocutor that a delay in speaking is anticipated (Clark and Fox Tree, 2002). Although such signals are often interpreted as 'transition relevance places' (Hutchby and Wooffitt, 1998) where the interlocutor may intervene and take a turn, Sara fails to do so here. The most obvious explanation for this is Peter's averted gaze. In fact, not only does he fail to make eye contact during this two-second period, but during the longer pause he even closes his eyes and covers them with his hands as if to emphasize gaze withdrawal. Averted gaze by a speaker has been shown

---

[9] Speech rate can obviously vary enormously, but for spoken English the average is often quoted as being somewhere around 150 words per minute (Miller, 1981).

to be a concomitant of word searching, and the re-establishment of eye contact a signal that the interlocutor may take the floor (Goodwin, 1981).[10] As soon as Peter looks at Sara at the end of line 2, this is exactly what she does. The two instances of eye contact shown in line 1 are very brief, fleeting glances, possibly to monitor Sara's continued attention and reactions. The same pattern is repeated again and again throughout an hour's worth of transcribed dialogue between Peter and Sara. Transcript 8.25, which repeats Transcript 4.5 already shown in Chapter 4, but with Peter's gaze pattern added, provides a more extended illustration.

Transcript 8.25

```
                                 -----------------------------+++++++-------
1   Peter:  but (0.8) .hh [wɪʔ] (.) [ægˑ] we did like the dinner and (.) that (0.6) but erm
            ------------------------------------------------------------
2           (1.6) there were (.) [ʔæ] (.) there was (.) one called Mike (1.5) one called
            ---------------+----+++++++++++++++
3           (2.1) oh (.) erm (3.4) erm (2.5) I don't know his name now
            +++
4   Sara:   right
            +++++
5   Peter:  other one
            ---
6   Sara:   right
            -----------+----------------------+++++++
7   Peter:  but there was (2.0) ff oh (.) and one was called John (1.6) I don't know the
            +++ +----
8           (0.5) other one
            +++++++++
9   Sara:   and who were they?
            --- ++++----------------+--------------------
10  Peter:  (1.4) they was do you know (.) erm (.) when you (.) do you know when
11          +--+++++++++++
            (1.6) it's a servant (0.5) [and]
12                              ++++---
13  Sara:                         [right] (0.8) yeah
14          ----------++++++++++++++++
15  Peter:  and (.) and they bring the dinner in for you
16          ++++
17  Sara:   a waiter?
18          ------+++
19  Peter:  waiter (.) yeah
```

Here Peter is unable to retrieve the word 'servant' but he is eventually able to provide Sara with enough information for her to guess, and finally

---

[10] See Chapter 6 for further examples and discussion of the role of gaze in conversation.

produce, the word herself. Apart from line 8, Sara only takes a turn when Peter is making eye contact. In this isolated instance, Sara's response is qualitatively different from her previous 'backchannel' contributions. The impression one gets is that Peter is admitting defeat in his word search, only to be rallied by Sara to try again.

Thinking aloud – another device referred to earlier as an instance of intrapersonal compensation for inadequate working memory – may play a similar interpersonal role of signalling to the interlocutor that Peter is not yet ready for her to intervene. Sometimes such implicit signals are made explicit by Peter in the form of metalinguistic statements. The educational psychologist reports that 'on one occasion, when asking Peter for an explanation, . . . he prefaced his statement with "I think it's gonna be a long one", indicating to me that he was aware that he was going to have to give me quite a lengthy explanation'.

Peter's formulaic sequence '(you) know (when)', which incidentally appears in both the above examples, is another intrapersonal compensatory device which plays an interpersonal role. Firstly, once the interlocutor becomes familiar with it, it provides evidence that Peter may be having word-finding problems. In addition, though, it is often used to elicit a reaction from the interlocutor before continuing, as in Transcript 8.26.

Transcript 8.26

Peter: yeah . you know the tickets?
Sara: yeah
Peter: they tell you where to go
Sara: right
Peter: do you know when . it's a servant . [and]
Sara: [right] . yeah
Peter: and (.) and they bring the dinner in for you?

'You know' immediately precedes and flags up a noun phrase which can later be referred to anaphorically using a pronoun. Since use of pro-forms reduces lexical density (see earlier discussion), this means that the subsequent sentence is easier to produce. Rather than a single speaker presenting information in a single sentence, speaker and hearer cooperate to distribute the load incrementally across conversational turns in simpler structures.[11] Further evidence of cross-turn sentence formulation can be seen in Transcript 8.27.

---

[11] A similar phenomenon was reported in Chapter 7 in Bloch's (2005) account of a conversation involving a man with motor neurone disease, and has also been noted in the emergence of syntax in early language development, where it has been referred to using terms such as 'propositions across utterances' (Ochs, Schieffelin and Platt, 1979) and 'vertical constructions' (Scollon, 1979).

Transcript 8.27

1 Sara: and was that different?
2 Peter: . mm no . well do you know the sausages?
3 Sara: mm
4 Peter: they wasn't
5 Sara: they were the same?
6 Peter: yeah [(unintelligible)]

Sara's clarification request in line 5 suggests that she assumes Peter's prior utterance is an (overly) elliptical version of 'they wasn't different' – which is subsequently confirmed by Peter in line 6. Here, the elided 'different' is picked up from Sara's earlier utterance in line 1, rather than being provided by Peter himself. Line 4 is effectively a composite, incorporating elliptical and anaphoric reference to elements from lines 1 and 2. The continuation of this example in Transcript 8.28 reveals a further instance of the same type of process.

Transcript 8.28

6   Peter: yeah [(unintelligible)]
7   Sara: [as English] right was there anything different?
8   was it [quite]
9   Peter: [hm] – it was quite the same
10 Sara: right

In line 9 Peter copies 'quite' from Sara's prior turn to produce a rather odd-sounding sentence, presumably meaning something like 'they were not really different at all'. Here the composite has not worked so well, with the immediate availability of relevant lexical material apparently overriding its formal shortcomings. However, it has clearly worked well enough for Sara, who accepts it in line 10.

Because we are aware that Peter has communication difficulties, it is easy to fall into the trap of seeing the various compensatory adaptations described above as examples of Peter – as the source of the 'deficit' – simply using his interlocutor as an external resource (as is often presumed in the use of terms like 'compensatory strategy'), just as he uses thinking aloud and repetition as external resources for temporary storage and visual displays as reminders. However, this is a one-sided and incomplete view. It is unlikely that Peter – or Sara, for that matter – is consciously aware that any overt direction or manipulation on his part is taking place, at least while the activity is occurring. As Clark (1996) points out (see Chapter 3 for discussion), when one person signals to another and the other recognizes the meaning of the signal, these are not two autonomous actions but are inextricably bound together. In order for communication to work, it is not enough for a signal to be sent: it must also be received, be shown and seen to have been received, and if necessary be acted upon, be shown and seen to have been acted upon, and so on.

8.6   Conclusion

It is not possible – or even necessary, for present purposes – to apply a straightforward diagnostic label to Peter's communication impairment. He certainly has problems with language, but 'SLI' will not do, since he also has cognitive difficulties, and in any case, as Leonard (1998: 23) points out: 'the category of SLI is little more than a terminological way station for groups of children until such time as finer diagnostic categories can be identified'. Furthermore, if we use descriptive categories from pragmatic theories and commonly used clinical pragmatic assessments, he would appear to have pretty extensive pragmatic difficulties, too. For example, his lengthy and meandering descriptions could be seen as breaking Grice's Maxim of Quantity in that he says more than is strictly necessary, and yet he sometimes also says too little as, for example, in his overly elliptical 'they wasn't' in Transcript 8.27. He also breaks the Maxim of Manner by being unclear. In terms of Speech Act Theory, the illocutionary point of what he says is not always clear – for example, when confronted with his long list of 'one (was) called . . .' expressions in Transcript 8.20, an initial reaction might well be, 'Why is he telling me this now?' From a Relevance Theory perspective, he could certainly be seen as causing his interlocutors considerable processing effort for a comparatively small return. He also performs badly in terms of the following items selected from various profiles of pragmatic impairment: referential inadequacy, lack of coherence, topic introduction and maintenance problems, dysfluency, incomplete phrases, word-finding difficulties and use of repetitions, stereotypes and long pauses. And yet, at the same time, Peter has clear pragmatic strengths: in particular, his turn-taking proficiency and use of repair, gaze, prosody and gesture to manage turn taking; and the skilful way he coordinates his own behaviour with that of interlocutors during conversation. When seen in the light of the detailed analysis provided above in terms of specific but interlinked cognitive and semiotic strengths and weaknesses, which are both the source and the outcome of a complex of compensatory adaptations, all of these labels and categories prove to be overly superficial, often contradictory and of limited practical use for clinical intervention.

9   Conclusions

The main thesis of this book is that pragmatics is emergent. That is to say, it is not a discrete entity but the product of many interacting variables. When we communicate with others, we draw on a range of capacities including (a) signalling systems such as language, gesture and facial expression, (b) cognitive systems such as theory of mind, inference and memory, (c) motor output systems such as the vocal tract and hand movement, and (d) sensory input systems such as hearing and vision. All of these 'elements' exist within the individual – i.e. they constitute an intrapersonal domain, but during communication they combine with those of other individuals to form an interpersonal domain. Interpersonal communication involves many choices – for example, which meanings are explicitly encoded, and which left implicit; which signalling system(s) are used; which meanings are most salient and relevant. The exercise of such choices requires multiple interactions between the various underlying semiotic, cognitive and sensorimotor capacities both within and between individuals. Intrapersonal and interpersonal domains are dynamic systems whose integrity and equilibrium are maintained via a continuous process of compensatory adaptation. The effect of this is most plainly seen when one or more individual elements malfunction and create an imbalance within the system as a whole.

In the preceding chapters I have attempted to map out in detail this emergentist model of pragmatic ability and disability, to compare it with other approaches and to provide extensive evidence for why it is useful to account for pragmatics in this way. In this concluding chapter, I will briefly highlight some of the key ways in which emergentist pragmatics (EP) differs from other accounts of pragmatics, and also comment on its potential relevance for researchers and professionals involved with communication impairment.

9.1   Issues for pragmatics and pragmatic theory

9.1.1   Scope

By using pragmatic impairment as the starting point of this enquiry, rather than the more usual focus on the concerns and practices of mainstream pragmatics, we have ended up with a view of the scope and constituency of pragmatics which differs in a number of ways from that found in pragmatics textbooks and most theories of pragmatics. It is a perspective that will perhaps feel more familiar to psychologists, cognitive neuroscientists and speech and language pathologists than to linguists and philosophers, but it may also encourage theorists and practitioners of non-clinical pragmatics to take account of aspects and areas of their discipline that they might not otherwise have considered. One consequence of its basis in pathology is that the EP model is broader in scope than many other approaches to pragmatics, and indeed has the potential to be even broader. Although the version presented here has been restricted to the intrapersonal and interpersonal domains, it could be extended both 'downwards' into a neurological domain and 'upwards' into a sociocultural domain, following the emergentist principle outlined in Chapter 4 that an element within a domain may itself constitute a domain to the extent that it is also a by-product of interactions at a lower level. By following this approach through to its logical conclusion, pragmatics turns out to be largely equivalent to 'usage' (in the sense of Newmeyer (2003)) and all that entails. In fact, it is even broader, since Newmeyer focuses only on *language* usage.

Despite its breadth, however, EP is not broad in the sense used by Sperber and Wilson when they refer to pragmatics as 'a range of loosely related research programmes' (Sperber and Wilson, 2005: 468). Instead, it aims to be coherent by specifying principled ways in which its various components and subcomponents are interrelated.

EP is not necessarily incompatible with other narrower approaches to pragmatics. In theory, one could create a typology of pragmatics based on specific underlying cognitive, semiotic or sensorimotor capacities such as theory of mind pragmatics, linguistic pragmatics and gestural pragmatics – similar to that proposed in Perkins (2000) – but as was pointed out there, and in Chapter 5 above, these would be somewhat idealized accounts, omitting central features such as interactions and compensations between the various elements.

9.1.2   Multimodality

The tendency of most work in pragmatics to focus exclusively on language – and in particular on linguistically encoded propositions – has provided a particular view of the distinction between implicit and explicit meaning. In addition to inferred meaning, pragmatics has sometimes been associated with meaning conveyed by gesture, gaze, facial expression and prosody, which is seen as complementing a more primary or central linguistically encoded meaning conveyed through speech and writing.

In contrast, EP takes the view, following Clark (1996), McNeill (1992), Goodwin (2000a) and others, that meaning may be made explicit not only through language but also through other semiotic systems, using a range of output modalities, and in fact that all of these together comprise a composite, flexible signalling system. The simple boundary between what is explicit and implicit is thus shifted, with greater emphasis placed on the nature of, and links between, the various different types of explicit meaning.

9.1.3   Causation as explanation

Most theories of pragmatics are couched in terms of the behaviour of speakers and hearers. The emergentist account, on the other hand, attempts to explain such behaviours by identifying the cognitive, semiotic and sensorimotor systems and processes which subserve them. Identification of underlying causes affords a strong sense of explanation. Relevance Theory similarly explains pragmatic processing by reference to underlying cognitive principles – i.e. the first and second principles of relevance together with theory of mind. EP extends the range of cognitive processes seen as playing a central role in pragmatics, and also views semiotic and sensorimotor processes as integral. Furthermore, rather than focusing on a multiple set of separate underlying determinants, EP sees pragmatics crucially as the product of the interactions between them.

9.1.4   Intrapersonal and interpersonal synergy

Pragmatic theories have tended to treat the intention-driven agenda of speakers and the inference-driven agenda of hearers as central yet separate components of communicative interaction. Ethnographic approaches such as Conversation Analysis, on the other hand, have focused more exclusively on the interaction itself, giving short shrift to the mental states of participants except in so far as they are reflected in empirically observable behaviours. EP combines both perspectives and sees pragmatics as the integrated product of both the intrapersonal and interpersonal, taking equal account of communicative behaviour as a joint activity and the underlying cognitive, semiotic and sensorimotor processes from which it derives. We saw in Chapter 8, for example, that compensatory adaptation in communication disorder can only be fully accounted for by seeing the intrapersonal and interpersonal domains as acting in synergy.

9.1.5   Pragmatic ability and disability

So far, no theories of pragmatics have been explicitly designed to account
for pragmatic impairment.[1] Instead, language pathologists have had to
make do with theories of normal pragmatic functioning which, as shown in
Chapter 2, at best provide only a partial fit. By focusing on impairment
from the outset, EP encompasses not only the pragmatically atypical, but
also, by default, the pragmatically typical. This is partly because the study
of pragmatic impairment throws up a wider range of phenomena to be
accounted for than is normally addressed in theories of non-impaired
pragmatic behaviour. As a by-product, EP thus adds to the agenda of
mainstream pragmatics a number of issues which any comprehensive
theory should aim to incorporate.

9.2   Issues for clinical practice

9.2.1   Terminology

In Chapter 2 we saw that terms such as 'pragmatic impairment' and their
cognates are too vague, and used too inconsistently, to be effective diagnostic labels. Although individual groups of clinicians or researchers may
adopt a particular definition and apply it rigorously, their use of the term
'pragmatic' will still lead many to assume that they are referring to the
same specific behaviours as other groups who may, in fact, be working
with only a partly overlapping – or even entirely different – definition. In
studies of communicative impairment, pragmatics will often be represented by a single phenomenon such as turntaking, inference or the use
of clarification requests, and yet conclusions drawn are often discussed as
though they applied to pragmatic impairment as a generic phenomenon. It
is perfectly acceptable for a particular type or instance of communicative
behaviour to be reported as an illustration of pragmatics, but not for it to
be thereby implied that pragmatics is all and only what this one type or
instance represents. Another approach is to define pragmatics implicitly by
providing an illustrative list of instances. For example, in a study of
communicative behaviour in aphasia, Menn et al. (2005: 488) refer to
narrative structure, new/old referents, recognition of humour and sarcasm, emotional expression and empathy as 'basic aspects of pragmatics'.

---

[1] Cf. Bara et al. (1999: 522), who observe that 'no single theory covers systematically the
emergence of pragmatic capacity' and note the absence of 'a systematic account of the
deficits of communicative performance in children with traumatic brain injury, hydrocephalus, focal brain damage, [and] autism'.

The assumption is that pragmatics is 'to do with' phenomena such as these, but there is no clear sense of what pragmatics actually *is* beyond this particular set of manifestations. To adopt as a diagnostic category the broad emergentist definition of pragmatics used in this book would not help matters, since it views pragmatic impairment as a concomitant of *all* communication disorders. One potential solution would be to avoid terms such as 'pragmatic impairment' altogether – though this would be unlikely to succeed, given their widespread currency. An alternative would be to take on board the broad scope of pragmatics within the emergentist account, and to establish a typology of pragmatic impairment based on the contributions of (a) its underlying cognitive, semiotic and sensorimotor elements, and (b) interactions and compensatory adaptations among these elements in both the intrapersonal and interpersonal domains. The model presented in Chapters 4 to 7 and illustrated in Chapter 8 might then be used as a heuristic for approaching the assessment, diagnosis and treatment of pragmatic impairment.

9.2.2   The multiple causes of pragmatic impairment

The development of such a typology will not be easy, particularly given the complex – and sometimes obscure – role of compensatory adaptation. However, it is unavoidable if we wish to go beyond a superficial labelling procedure based on behaviour alone. The emergentist model is at least indirectly supported by an ever-increasing number of research studies, particularly of developmental disorders, which suggest that divisions between diagnostic categories once seen as completely distinct are becoming increasingly blurred, and that symptoms at one time taken to be a direct reflection of a specific underlying cause may in fact be the tip of a multi-factorial iceberg. For example, in a study involving a large group of children with a range of communication disorders, Norbury *et al.* (2004: 361) found that '60% of children with PLI [pragmatic language impairment] (with or without autistic features) had significant structural impairments. This is in line with mounting evidence that clear boundaries between SLI, PLI and indeed autistic disorder simply do not exist.' Overlap has also been reported between SLI and Williams syndrome (WS) (Stojanovik *et al.*, 2004) and between SLI, WS and Down's syndrome (Laws and Bishop, 2004). A similar conclusion is reached by Reuterskiöld-Wagner and Nettelbladt (2005) in a case study of a boy diagnosed as language impaired at the age of 3, then as autistic at the age of 6, and eventually seen at the age of 8 as displaying a range of subtle symptoms, both linguistic and cognitive in nature, which varied according to interactional context. In other words there is a growing trend away from seeing communication disorders as a set of discrete, mutually exclusive syndromes, each with its own distinct aetiology. Instead, there is a need for models which accept, and can account for, the fact that for any single manifestation of communication impairment: (a) multiple underlying factors are frequently implicated; (b) even a single underlying cause will have widespread ramifications, particularly given the inevitability of compensatory adaptation; and (c) pragmatic impairment of one kind or another is an inescapable consequence. The emergentist model of pragmatics is ideally suited to mapping out this complex terrain.

9.2.3   Intrapersonal and interpersonal perspectives

In common with most theories of normal pragmatic functioning, clinical approaches to pragmatic impairment tend to focus either on the cognitive and linguistic capacities of the individual with minimal reference to interlocutor contributions, or else on the properties of the interaction in which the individual is involved without taking account of his or her underlying cognitive or linguistic problems. Despite their obvious clinical potential (as pointed out in Perkins (1998b)), approaches such as Clark's Joint Action Theory (Clark, 1996), which unites both perspectives, so far appear not to have attracted the interest of language pathologists. There are a few exceptions, such as the CAPPA (Whitworth et al., 1997) and CAPPCI (Perkins et al., 1997) profiles for analysing the communicative behaviour of individuals with aphasia and cognitive impairments respectively, which specifically target the interactional consequences of linguistic and cognitive disorders, but these are rare. By focusing on the synergy between the intrapersonal and the interpersonal, the EP model provides a starting point for developing clinical assessment and intervention protocols that take equal account not just of linguistic and cognitive processing within the communicative dyad seen as a whole, but also the contribution of non-linguistic signalling systems together with their associated motor output and sensory input modalities. Such a comprehensive approach means taking on board extremely challenging levels of complexity. However, the alternative, as we saw in Chapter 2, is to focus on individual systems, processes and perspectives in isolation, which results in only a partial and fragmentary picture.

9.2.4   The centrality of compensatory adaptation

One of the most complex aspects of pragmatic impairment is compensatory adaptation. One practical reason why it is important to know how well compensation works both intrapersonally and interpersonally is that it is an essential prerequisite for designing intervention strategies. Indeed, the rationale for therapeutic intervention and facilitation derives from the view that successful compensation can be induced. The potential value of incorporating compensation as a central aspect of any analysis or assessment of pragmatic impairment has hopefully been demonstrated in the case study in Chapter 8, where we saw that to address potential contributory causes independently of how they trade off across modalities, within the individual, between the individual and his or her interlocutor and in real time, is to miss the most crucial feature of all. The view that compensatory adaptation plays a central role in determining the symptoms of communication impairment is not yet widely shared, though there are some influential recent converts to the idea (e.g. Ullman and Pierpont, 2005). One problem lies in the fact that compensatory adaptation is hard to characterize and pin down, though connectionist modelling appears to have considerable potential (e.g. Thomas and Karmiloff-Smith, 2003). From a clinical perspective, it is important to note that the full extent of compensation only becomes apparent through the study of individuals interacting with others on specific occasions. In other words, establishing how closely a person's symptoms match the shared characteristics of a particular diagnostic group is only a starting point. In addition, we also need to focus on what makes that individual unique.

Although this book provides no easy answers, what it does hopefully provide is a broad yet comprehensive framework within which it is possible to pose new and worthwhile questions about pragmatics in a coherent and realistic manner. It does so by linking pragmatic behaviour with underlying causes, and acknowledging that the causal link is rarely straightforward but instead involves complex interactions between cognitive, semiotic and sensorimotor processes. Furthermore, these interactions draw on the cognitive, semiotic and sensorimotor resources of pairs and groups of individuals as well as those of each individual separately. Finally, by treating pragmatic ability and disability as two sides of the same coin, it marks out common ground between the study of communication and communication disorder in a way that may benefit linguists and clinicians alike.

Appendix

Key to abbreviations for tests and assessments referred to in Chapter 8

BAS   *British Ability Scales* (Elliott, Murray and Pearson, 1977)

BPVS   *The British Picture Vocabulary Scale* (BPVS) (Dunn *et al.*, 1982)

BS   *The Bus Story* (Renfrew, 1997)

CELF-R   *Clinical Evaluation of Language Fundamentals – Revised* (Semel *et al.*, 1987)

GFW   *Goldman-Fristoe-Woodcock Auditory Skills Test Battery* (Goldman *et al.*, 1974)

ITPA   *Illinois Test of Psycholinguistic Abilities* (Kirk *et al.*, 1968)

PAB   *Phonological Assessment Battery* (Frederickson, Frith and Reason, 1997)

References

Adams, A.-M. and Gathercole, S. E. (2000). Limitations in working memory: implications for language development. *International Journal of Language and Communication Disorders*, 35(1), 95–116.

Adams, M. R. (1990). The demands-capacities model I: theoretical elaborations. *Journal of Fluency Disorders*, 15, 135–44.

Adams, C. and Bishop, D. V. M. (1989). Conversational characteristics of children with semantic-pragmatic disorder. I: Exchange structure, turntaking, repairs and cohesion. *British Journal of Disorders of Communication*, 24, 211–39.

Adams, C., Green, J., Gilchrist, A. and Cox, A. (2002). Conversational behaviour of children with Asperger syndrome and conduct disorders. *Journal of Child Psychology and Psychiatry*, 43(5), 679–90.

Ahlsén, E. (1991). Body communication as compensation for speech in a Wernicke's aphasic – a longitudinal study. *Journal of Communication Disorders*, 24, 1–12.

(1993). Conversational principles and aphasic communication. *Journal of Pragmatics*, 19, 57–70.

(2005). Argumentation with restricted linguistic ability: performing a role play with aphasia or in a second language. *Clinical Linguistics and Phonetics*, 19(5), 433–51.

Alderman, N. and Ward, A. (1991). Behavioural treatment of the dysexecutive syndrome: reduction of repetitive speech using response cost and cognitive overlearning. *Neuropsychological Rehabilitation*, 1(1), 65–80.

Alexopoulos, G. S., Kiosses, D. N., Klimstra, S., Kalayam, B. and Bruce, M. L. (2002). Clinical presentation of the 'depression-executive dysfunction syndrome' of late life. *American Journal of Geriatric Psychiatry*, 10, 98–106.

Allan, K. (1998). Speech Act Theory: an overview. In J. L. Mey (ed.), *Concise Encyclopedia of Pragmatics* (pp. 927–39). Amsterdam: Elsevier.

Allen, H. A. (1983). Do positive and negative symptom subtypes of schizophrenia show qualitative differences in language production? *Psychological Medicine*, 13, 787–97.

Allen, J. and Seidenberg, M. S. (1999). The emergence of grammaticality in connectionist networks. In B. MacWhinney (ed.), *The Emergence of Language* (pp. 115–51). Mahwah, NJ: Lawrence Erlbaum.

Almor, A., Kempler, D., MacDonald, M. C., Andersen, E. S. and Tyler, L. K. (1999). Why do Alzheimer patients have difficulty with pronouns? Working memory, semantics, and reference in comprehension and production in Alzheimer's disease. *Brain and Language*, 67, 202–27.

Armstrong, E. (1987). Cohesive harmony in aphasic discourse and its significance to listener perception of coherence. In R. H. Brookshire (ed.), *Clinical Aphasiology* (pp. 210–15). Minneapolis: BRK Publishers.

(2005). Expressing opinions and feelings in aphasia: linguistic options. *Aphasiology*, 19, 285–95.

Armstrong, E. M. (1991). The potential of cohesion analysis in the analysis and treatment of aphasic discourse. *Clinical Linguistics and Phonetics*, 5(1), 39–51.

Arnold, J. E., Wasow, T., Losongco, A. and Ginstrom, R. (2000). Heaviness vs newness: the effects of structural complexity and discourse status on constituent ordering. *Language*, 76, 28–55.

Arnott, W. L., Jordan, F. M., Murdoch, B. E. and Lethlean, J. B. (1997). Narrative discourse in multiple sclerosis: an investigation of conceptual structure. *Aphasiology*, 11, 969–91.

Atkinson, M. and Heritage, H. (eds.) (1984). *Structure of Social Action: Studies in Conversation Analysis*. Cambridge: Cambridge University Press.

Audet, L. R. and Ripich, D. N. (1994). Psychiatric disorders and discourse problems. In D. N. Ripich and N. A. Creaghead (eds), *School Discourse Problems*, 2nd Edition (pp. 191–227). San Diego, CA: Singular.

Austin, J. L. (1962). *How to Do Things with Words*. Oxford: Clarendon Press.

Baddeley, A. (1986). *Working Memory*. Oxford: Oxford University Press.

(2003). Working memory and language: an overview. *Journal of Communication Disorders*, 36, 189–208.

Baddeley, A., Harris, J., Sunderland, A., Watts, K. P. and Wilson, B. (1987). Closed head injury and memory. In H. S. Levin, J. Grafman and H. M. Eisenberg (eds), *Neurobehavioral Recovery from Head Injury* (pp. 295–317). Oxford: Oxford University Press.

Baddeley, A. D. (2000). The episodic buffer: a new component of working memory? *Trends in Cognitive Sciences*, 4, 417–23.

Baddeley, A. D. and Hitch, G. J. (1974). Working memory. In G. H. Bower (ed.), *The Psychology of Learning and Motivation* (vol. VIII, pp. 47–90). London: Academic Press.

Baddeley, A. D. and Wilson, B. (1988). Frontal amnesia and the dysexecutive syndrome. *Brain and Cognition*, 7, 212–30.

Baltaxe, C. A. M. and Simmons, J. Q. (1985). Prosodic development in normal and autistic children. In E. Schopler and G. Mesibov (eds), *Issues of Autism*, vol. III, *Communication Problems in Autism* (pp. 95–125). New York: Plenum.

Bar-On, R., Tranel, D., Denburg, N. L. and Bechara, A. (2003). Exploring the neurological substrate of emotional and social intelligence. *Brain*, 126(8), 1790–1800.

Bara, B. G. (2000). Neuropragmatics: brain and communication. *Brain and Language*, 71, 10–14.

Bara, B. G., Bosco, F. M. and Bucciarelli, M. (1999). Developmental pragmatics in normal and abnormal children. *Brain and Language*, 68, 507–28.

Bara, B. G., Tirassa, M. and Zettin, M. (1997). Neuropragmatics: neuropsychological constraints on formal theories of dialogue. *Brain and Language*, 59, 7–49.

Barkley, R. A. (1997). Behavioral inhibition, sustained attention, and executive functions: constructing a unifying theory of ADHD. *Psychological Bulletin*, 121(1), 65–94.

Barnes, M. A. and Dennis, M. (1998). Discourse after early-onset hydrocephalus: core deficits in children of average intelligence. *Brain and Language*, 61, 309–34.

Baron-Cohen, S. (1989). Do autistic children have obsessions and compulsions? *British Journal of Clinical Psychology*, 28, 193–200.

  (1991). Do people with autism understand what causes emotion? *Child development*, 62, 385–95.

  (1995). *Mindblindness: An Essay on Autism and Theory of Mind*. Cambridge, MA: MIT Press.

Bates, E. (2001). Tailoring the emperor's new clothes. *Aphasiology*, 15(4), 391–5.

  (2003). Natura e cultura nel linguaggio [On the nature and nurture of language]. In E. Bizzi, P. Calissano and V. Volterra (eds), *Frontiere della Biologia: Il Cervello di Homo Sapiens [Frontiers of Biology: The Brain of Homo Sapiens]* (pp. 241–65). Rome: Istituto della Enciclopedia Italiana fondata da Giovanni Trecanni S. p. A.

Bates, E., Dick, F. and Wulfeck, B. (1999). Not so fast: domain-general factors can account for domain-specific deficits in grammatical processing. *Behavioral and Brain Sciences*, 22(1), 96–7.

Bates, E. and Goodman, J. C. (1997). On the inseparability of grammar and the lexicon: evidence from acquisition, aphasia and real-time processing. *Language and Cognitive Processes*, 12(5/6), 507–84.

Bates, E. and MacWhinney, B. (1987). Competition, variation, and language learning. In B. MacWhinney (ed.), *Mechanisms of Language Acquisition*. Hillsdale, NJ: Lawrence Erlbaum.

  (1989). Functionalism and the competition model. In B. MacWhinney and E. Bates (eds), *The Cross-Linguistic Study of Sentence Processing* (pp. 3–73). Cambridge: Cambridge University Press.

Bates, E., Wulfeck, B., Hernandez, A. and Andanova, E. (1996). The Competition Model: implications for language processing, language development and language breakdown. In B. Kokinov (ed.), *Perspectives on Cognitive Science* (vol. II, pp. 7–72). Sofia: New Bulgarian University.

Bayles, K. A., Tomoeda, C. K., Kaszniak, A. W., Stern, L. Z. and Eagans, K. K. (1985). Verbal perseveration of dementia patients. *Brain and Language*, 25, 102–16.

Bechara, A., Dolan, S., Denburg, N., Hindes, A., Anderson, S. W. and Nathan, P. E. (2001). Decision-making deficits, linked to a dysfunctional ventromedial prefrontal cortex, revealed in alcohol and stimulant abusers. *Neuropsychologia*, 39, 376–89.

Beeke, S. (2005). Rethinking Agrammatism: Using Conversation Analysis to Investigate the Talk of Individuals with Aphasia. Unpublished Ph.D. dissertation, Department of Human Communication Science, University College London.

Beeke, S., Wilkinson, R. and Maxim, J. (2003a). Exploring aphasic grammar 1: a single case analysis of conversation. *Clinical Linguistics and Phonetics*, 17(2), 81–107.

(2003b). Exploring aphasic grammar 2: do language testing and conversation tell a similar story? *Clinical Linguistics and Phonetics*, 17(2), 109–34.

Beeman, M. (1998). Coarse semantic coding and discourse comprehension. In M. Beeman and C. Chiarello (eds), *Right Hemisphere Language Comprehension: Perspectives from Cognitive Neuroscience* (pp. 255–84). Mahwah, NJ: Erlbaum.

Beeson, P. M., Bayles, K. A., Rubens, A. B. and Kazniak, A. W. (1993). Memory impairment and executive control in individuals with stroke-induced aphasia. *Brain and Language*, 45, 253–75.

Bellugi, U., Marks, S., Bihrle, A. and Sabo, H. (1988). Dissociation between language and cognitive functions in Williams syndrome. In D. V. M. Bishop and K. Mogford (eds), *Language Development in Exceptional Circumstances* (pp. 177–89). London: Churchill Livingstone.

Ben Shalom, D. (2003). Memory in autism: review and synthesis. *Cortex*, 39, 1129–38.

Benjamin, L., Debinski, A., Fletcher, D., Hedger, C., Mealings, M. and Stewart-Scott, A. (1989). The use of the Bethesda Conversational Skills Profile in closed head injury. In V. Anderson and M. Bailey (eds), *Theory and Function: Bridging the Gap. Proceedings of the Fourteenth Annual Brain Impairment Conference* (pp. 57–65). Melbourne: Australian Society for the Study of Brain Impairment.

Berko Gleason, J., Goodglass, H., Obler, L., Green, E., Hyde, M. R. and Weintraub, S. (1980). Narrative strategies of aphasic and normal speaking subjects. *Aphasiology*, 23, 370–82.

Bibby, H. and McDonald, S. (2005). Theory of mind after traumatic brain injury. *Neuropsychologia*, 43, 99–114.

Biddle, K. R., McCabe, A. and Bliss, L. S. (1996). Narrative skills following traumatic brain injury in children and adults. *Journal of Communication Disorders*, 29(6), 447–69.

Bird, H., Howard, D. and Franklin, S. (2000). Why is a verb like an inanimate object? Grammatical category and semantic category deficits. *Brain and Language*, 72, 246–09.

(2003). Verbs and nouns: the importance of being imageable. *Journal of Neurolinguistics*, 16(2–3), 113–49.

Bishop, D. V. M. (1987). Childhood language disorders: classification and overview. In W. Yule and M. Rutter (eds), *Language Development and Disorders*. Oxford: MacKeith Press.

(1997). *Uncommon Understanding: Development and Disorders of Language Comprehension in Children*. Hove: Psychology Press.

(1998). Development of the Children's Communication Checklist (CCC): a method for assessing qualitative aspects of communicative impairment in children. *Journal of Child Psychology and Psychiatry*, 39(6), 879–91.

(2000). Pragmatic language impairment: a correlate of SLI, a distinct subgroup, or part of the autistic continuum? In D. V. M. Bishop and L. B. Leonard (eds), *Speech and Language Impairments in Children: Causes, Characteristics, Intervention and Outcome* (pp. 99–113). Hove: Psychology Press.

Bishop, D. V. M. and Adams, C. (1989). Conversational characteristics of children with semantic-pragmatic disorder, II: What features lead to a judgement of inappropriacy? *British Journal of Disorders of Communication*, 24, 241–63.

(1992). Comprehension problems in children with specific language impairment – literal and inferential meaning. *Journal of Speech and Hearing Research*, 35, 119–29.

Bishop, D. V. M., Bishop, S. J., Bright, P., James, C., Delaney, T. and Tallal, P. (1999). Different origin of auditory and phonological processing problems in children with language impairment: evidence from a twin study. *Journal of Speech, Language, and Hearing Research*, 42, 155–68.

Bishop, D. V. M., Carlyon, R. P., Deeks, J. M. and Bishop, S. J. (1999). Auditory temporal processing impairment: neither necessary nor sufficient for causing language impairment in children. *Journal of Speech, Language and Hearing Research*, 42, 1295–310.

Bishop, D. V. M., Chan, J., Adams, C., Hartley, J. and Weir, F. (2000). Conversational responsiveness in specific language impairment: evidence of disproportionate pragmatic difficulties in a subset of children. *Development and Psychopathology*, 12, 177–99.

Bishop, D. V. M. and Edmundson, A. (1987). Language-impaired 4-year-olds: distinguishing transient from persistent impairment. *Journal of Speech and Hearing Disorders*, 52, 156–73.

Bishop, D. V. M. and McArthur, G. M. (2005). Individual differences in auditory processing in specific language impairment: a follow-up study using event-related potentials and behavioural thresholds. *Cortex*, 41(3), 327–41.

Bishop, D. V. M. and Norbury, C. F. (2005a). Executive functions in children with communication impairments, in relation to autistic symptomatology 1: Generativity. *Autism*, 9(1), 7–27.

(2005b). Executive functions in children with communication impairments, in relation to autistic symptomatology 2: Response inhibition. *Autism*, 9(1), 29–43.

Bissett, J. D. and Novak, A. M. (1995). Drawing inferences from emotional situations: Left versus right hemisphere deficit. *Clinical Aphasiology*, 23, 217–25.

Black, M. and Chiat, S. (2003). Noun-verb dissociations: a multi-faceted phenomenon. *Journal of Neurolinguistics*, 16(2–3), 231–50.

Blackwell, A. and Bates, E. (1995). Inducing agrammatic profiles in normals: evidence for the selective vulnerability of morphology under cognitive resource limitation. *Journal of Cognitive Neuroscience*, 7(2), 228–57.

Blank, M., Gessner, M. and Esposito, A. (1979). Language without communication: a case study. *Journal of Child Language*, 6, 329–52.

Bloch, S. (2005). Co-constructing meaning in acquired speech disorders: word and letter repetition in the construction of turns. In K. Richards and P. Seedhouse (eds), *Applying Conversation Analysis* (pp. 38–55). Basingstoke: Palgrave Macmillan.

Bloom, P. (1996). Intention, history, and artifact concepts. *Cognition*, 60, 1–29.

(2000). *How Children Learn the Meanings of Words*. Cambridge, MA: MIT Press.

Bloom, R. L., Obler, L. K., De Santi, S. and Ehrlich, J. S. (eds). (1994). *Discourse Analysis and Applications: Studies in Adult Clinical Populations*. Hillsdale, NJ: Erlbaum.

Bloom, R. L., Pick, L. H., Borod, J. C., Rorie, K. D., Andelman, F., Obler, L. K., Sliwinski, M., Campbell, A. L., Tweedy, J. R. and Welkowitz, J. (1999). Psychometric aspects of verbal pragmatic ratings. *Brain and Language*, 68, 553–65.

Bock, J. K. (1982). Toward a cognitive psychology of syntax: information processing contributions to sentence formulation. *Psychological Review*, 89, 1–47.

Body, R. and Parker, M. (2005). Topic repetitiveness after traumatic brain injury: an emergent, jointly managed behaviour. *Clinical Linguistics and Phonetics*, 19(5), 379–92.

Body, R. and Perkins, M. R. (1998). Ecological validity in assessment of discourse in traumatic brain injury: ratings by clinicians and non-clinicians. *Brain Injury*, 12(11), 963–76.

    (2004). Validation of linguistic analyses in narrative discourse after traumatic brain injury. *Brain Injury*, 18(7), 707–24.

Body, R., Perkins, M. R. and McDonald, S. (1999). Pragmatics, cognition and communication in traumatic brain injury. In S. McDonald, L. Togher and C. Code (eds), *Communication Disorders Following Traumatic Brain Injury* (pp. 81–112). Hove: Psychology Press.

Borod, J. C., Bloom, R. L. and Haywood, C. S. (1998). Verbal aspects of emotional communication. In M. Beeman and C. Chiarello (eds), *Right Hemisphere Language Comprehension: Perspectives from Cognitive Neuroscience* (pp. 285–307). Mahwah, NJ: Lawrence Erlbaum.

Bosacki, S. L. (2003). Psychological pragmatics in preadolescents: sociomoral understanding, self-worth, and school behavior. *Journal of Youth and Adolescence*, 32(2), 141–55.

Boscolo, B., Ratner, N. B. and Rescorla, L. (2002). Fluency of school-aged children with a history of expressive language impairment: an exploratory study. *American Journal of Speech-Language Pathology*, 11, 41–9.

Botting, N. (2002). Narrative as a tool for the assessment of linguistic and pragmatic impairments. *Child Language Teaching and Therapy*, 18(1), 1–21.

Boucher, J. (1989). The theory of mind hypothesis of autism: explanation, evidence and assessment. *British Journal of Disorders of Communication*, 24, 181–98.

Boucher, J., Cowell, P., Howard, M., Broks, P., Farrant, A., Roberts, N. and Mayes, A. (2005). A combined clinical, neuropsychological, and neuroanatomical study of adults with high functioning autism. *Cognitive Neuropsychiatry*, 10(3), 165–213.

Brady, M., Armstrong, L. and Mackenzie, C. (2005). Further evidence on topic use following right hemisphere brain damage: procedural and descriptive discourse. *Aphasiology*, 19(8), 731–47.

Brady, M., Mackenzie, C. and Armstrong, L. (2003). Topic use following right hemisphere brain damage during three semi-structured conversational discourse samples. *Aphasiology*, 17(9), 881–904.

Brewster, K. R. (1989). Assessment of Prosody. In K. Grundy (ed.), *Linguistics in Clinical Practice*. London: Taylor and Francis.

Brinton, B. and Fujiki, M. (1994). Ability of institutionalized and community-based adults with retardation to respond to questions in an interview context. *Journal of Speech and Hearing Research*, 37(2), 369–77.

Brock, J., Brown, C. C., Boucher, J. and Rippon, G. (2002). The temporal binding deficit hypothesis of autism. *Development and Psychopathology*, 14, 209–24.

Brook, S. L. and Bowler, D. M. (1992). Autism by another name: semantic and pragmatic impairments in children. *Journal of Autism and Developmental Disorders*, 22, 61–81.

Browman, C. P. and Goldstein, L. (1992). Articulatory phonology: an overview. *Phonetica*, 49, 155–80.

Brown, G. and Yule, G. (1983). *Discourse Analysis*. Cambridge: Cambridge University Press.

Brownell, H. and Martino, G. (1998). Deficits in inference and social cognition: the effects of right hemisphere brain damage on discourse. In M. Beeman and C. Chiarello (eds), *Right Hemisphere Language Comprehension: Perspectives from Cognitive Neuroscience* (pp. 309–28). Mahwah, NJ: Erlbaum.

Brownell, H. and Stringfellow, A. (1999). Making requests: illustrations of how right-hemisphere brain damage can affect discourse production. *Brain and Language*, 68, 442–65.

Bryan, K. L. (1989). *The Right Hemisphere Language Battery*. Kibworth: Far Communications.

Buckingham, H. W. (1993). Disorders of word-form processing in aphasia. In G. Blanken, J. Dittmann, H. Grimm, J. C. Marshall and C.-W. Wallesch (eds), *Linguistic Disorders and Pathologies: An International Handbook* (pp. 187–97). Berlin: Walter de Gruyter.

Bunton, K., Kent, R. D. and Kent, J. F. (2000). Perceptuo-acoustic assessment of prosodic impairment in dysarthria. *Clinical Linguistics and Phonetics*, 14(1), 13–24.

Butterworth, B. and Howard, D. (1987). Paragrammatisms. *Cognition*, 26, 1–37.

Campbell, T. F. and Shriberg, L. D. (1982). Associations among pragmatic functions, linguistic stress and natural phonological processes in speech-delayed children. *Journal of Speech and Hearing Research*, 25, 547–53.

Caplan, D. (1987). *Neurolinguistics and Linguistic Aphasiology: An Introduction*. Cambridge: Cambridge University Press.

(1995). Issues arising in contemporary studies of disorders of syntactic processing in sentence comprehension in agrammatic patients. *Brain and Language*, 50, 325–38.

Caplan, D. and Hildebrandt, N. (1988). *Disorders of Syntactic Comprehension*. Cambridge, MA: MIT Press.

Caplan, R. (1996). Discourse deficits in childhood schizophrenia. In J. Beitchman, N. Cohen, M. Konstantareas and R. Tannock (eds), *Language, Learning and Behavior Disorders: Developmental, Biological and Clinical Perspectives* (pp. 156–77). Cambridge: Cambridge University Press.

Capps, L., Kehres, J. and Sigman, M. (1998). Conversational abilities among children with autism and children with developmental delays. *Autism*, 2(4), 325–44.

Caramazza, A. (2000). The organization of conceptual knowledge in the brain. In M. S. Gazzaniga (ed.), *The New Cognitive Neurosciences*, 2nd edition (pp. 1037–46). Cambridge, MA: MIT Press.

Carlomagno, S. (1994). *Pragmatic Approaches to Aphasia Therapy*. London: Whurr.

Carroll, J. B. (1993). *Human Cognitive Abilities: A Survey of Factor-Analytic Studies*. Cambridge: Cambridge University Press.

Carruthers, P. and Smith, P. K. (eds). (1996a). *Theories of Theories of Mind*. Cambridge: Cambridge University Press.

(1996b). Introduction. In P. Carruthers and P. K. Smith (eds), *Theories of Theories of Mind* (pp. 1–8). Cambridge: Cambridge University Press.

Carston, R. (1997). Relevance-theoretic pragmatics and modularity. *UCL Working Papers in Linguistics*, 9, 1–27.

Carston, R., Guttenplan, S. and Wilson, D. (2002). Introduction: special issue on pragmatics and cognitive science. *Mind and Language*, 17, 1–2.

Caspari, I. and Parkinson, S. R. (2000). Effects of memory impairment on discourse. *Journal of Neurolinguistics*, 13(1), 15–36.

Caspari, I., Parkinson, S. R., LaPointe, L. L. and Katz, R. C. (1998). Working memory and aphasia. *Brain and Cognition*, 37, 205–23.

Čeponiene, R., Lepistö, T., Shestakova, A., Vanhala, R., Alku, P., Näätänen, R. and Yaguchi, K. (2003). Speech-sound-selective auditory impairment in children with autism: they can perceive but do not attend. *Proceedings of the national Academy of Sciences*, 100(9), 5567–72.

Champagne, M., Desautels, M.-C. and Joanette, Y. (2003). Accounting for the pragmatic deficit in RHD individuals: a multiple case study. *Brain and Language*, 87(1), 210–11.

Channon, S., Pellijeff, A. and Rule, A. (2005). Social cognition after head injury: Sarcasm and theory of mind. *Brain and Language*, 93(2), 123–34.

Chapman, S. B., Culhane, K. A., Levin, H. S., Harward, H., Mendelsohn, D., Ewing-Cobbs, L., Fletcher, J. M. and Bruce, D. (1992). Narrative discourse after closed head injury in children and adolescents. *Brain and Language*, 43, 42–65.

Chapman, S. B., Highley, A. P. and Thompson, J. L. (1998). Discourse in fluent aphasia and Alzheimer's disease: linguistic and pragmatic considerations. *Journal of Neurolinguistics*, 11, 55–78.

Chenery, H. J. and Murdoch, B. E. (1994). The production of narrative discourse in response to animations in persons with dementia of the Alzheimer's type: preliminary findings. *Aphasiology*, 8(2), 159–71.

Cherney, L. R. and Canter, G. J. (1990). *Informational Content and Cohesion in the Discourse of Alzheimer's Disease*. Paper presented at the 1990 ASHA Convention, Seattle.

Chiat, S. (1983). Why *Mikey*'s right and *my key*'s wrong: the significance of stress and word boundaries in a child's output system. *Cognition*, 14, 275–300.

(2001). Mapping theories of developmental language impairment: premises, predictions and evidence. *Language and Cognitive Processes*, 16(2/3), 113–42.

Chobor, K. L. and Schweiger, A. (1998). Processing of lexical ambiguity in patients with traumatic brain injury. *Journal of Neurolinguistics*, 11, 119–36.

Chomsky, N. (1995a). Bare phrase structure. In G. Webelhuth (ed.), *Government and Binding Theory and the Minimalist Program* (pp. 383–439). Oxford: Blackwell.

(1995b). Language and nature. *Mind*, 104, 1–61.

(2002). *On Nature and Language*. Cambridge: Cambridge University Press.

Christiansen, J. A. (1995). Coherence violations and propositional usage in the narratives of fluent aphasics. *Brain and Language*, 51, 291–317.

Christman, S. S. (2002). Dynamic systems theory: application to language development and acquired aphasia. In R. G. Daniloff (ed.), *Connectionist Approaches to Clinical Problems in Speech and Language: Therapeutic and Scientific Applications* (pp. 111–46). Mahwah, NJ: Erlbaum.

Clahsen, H. and Almazan, M. (1998). Syntax and morphology in Williams syndrome. *Cognition*, 68, 167–98.

Clark, A. (1997). *Being There: Putting Brain, Body, and World Together Again*. Cambridge, MA: MIT Press.

(1998). Magic words: how language augments computation. In P. Carruthers and J. Boucher (eds), *Language and Thought: Interdisciplinary Themes* (pp. 162–83). Cambridge: Cambridge University Press.

(1999). Where brain, body, and world collide. *Journal of Cognitive Systems Research*, 1, 5–17.

Clark, A. and Chalmers, D. J. (1995). *The Extended Mind: Philosophy-Neuroscience-Psychology Research Report*. Washington University, St Louis.

Clark, H. H. (1987). Relevance to what? *Behavioral and Brain Sciences*, 10, 714–15.

(1996). *Using Language*. Cambridge: Cambridge University Press.

(2002). Speaking in time. *Speech Communication*, 36, 5–13.

Clark, H. H. and Fox Tree, J. E. (2002). Using *uh* and *um* in spontaneous speaking. *Cognition*, 84, 73–111.

Clark, H. H. and Haviland, S. E. (1977). Comprehension and the given–new contrast. In R. O. Freedle (ed.), *Discourse Production and Comprehension* (pp. 1–40). Hillsdale, NJ: Lawrence Erlbaum.

Coelho, C. A. (1999). Discourse analysis in traumatic brain injury. In S. McDonald and L. Togher and C. Code (eds), *Communication Disorders Following Traumatic Brain Injury* (pp. 55–79). Hove: Psychology Press.

Coelho, C. A., Liles, B. Z. and Duffy, R. J. (1991a). Discourse analyses with closed head injured adults: Evidence for differing patterns of deficits. *Archives of Physical Medicine and Rehabilitation*, 72, 465–8.

(1991b). The use of discourse analyses for the evaluation of higher level traumatically brain-injured adults. *Brain Injury*, 5(1), 381–92.

Coggins, T. E., Friet, T. and Morgan, T. (1998). Analysing narrative productions in older school-age children and adolescents with fetal alcohol syndrome: an experimental tool for clinical applications. *Clinical Linguistics and Phonetics*, 12(3), 221–36.

Cohen, A. S. and Docherty, N. M. (2004). Affective reactivity of speech and emotional experience in patients with schizophrenia. *Schizophrenia Research*, 69(1), 7–14.

Cohen, N. J., Menna, R., Vallance, D. D., Barwick, M. A., Im, N. and Horodezky, N. B. (1998). Language, social cognitive processing, and behavioral characteristics of psychiatrically disturbed children with previously identified and unsuspected language impairments. *Journal of Child Psychology and Psychiatry*, 39(6), 853–64.

(2002). Phonetic representations in the mental lexicon. In J. Durand and B. Laks (eds), *Phonetics, Phonology, and Cognition* (pp. 96–130). Oxford: Oxford University Press.

(2003). Discovering the acoustic correlates of phonological contrasts. *Journal of Phonetics*, 31, 351–72.

Coltheart, M. (1999). Modularity and cognition. *Trends in Cognitive Sciences*, 3, 115–20.

Conti-Ramsden, G. and Friel-Patti, S. (1983). Mothers' discourse adjustments to language-impaired and non-language-impaired children. *Journal of Speech and Hearing Disorders*, 48, 360–7.

Conti-Ramsden, G. and McTear, M. F. (1995). Assessment of pragmatics. In K. Grundy (ed.), *Linguistics in Clinical Practice*, 2nd edition (pp. 206–33). London: Whurr.

Cornish, K. M., Turk, J., Wilding, J., Sudhalter, V., Munir, F., Kooy, F. and Hagerman, R. (2004). Annotation: deconstructing the attention deficit in fragile X syndrome: a developmental neuropsychological approach. *Journal of Child Psychology and Psychiatry*, 45(6), 1042–53.

Corrin, J., Tarplee, C. and Wells, B. (2001). Interactional linguistics and language development: a conversation-analytic perspective on emergent syntax. In M. Selting and E. Couper-Kuhlen (eds), *Studies in Interactional Linguistics* (pp. 199–225). Amsterdam: Benjamins.

Coulmas, F. (2005). *Sociolinguistics: The Study of Speakers' Choices*. Cambridge: Cambridge University Press.

Couper-Kuhlen, E. and Selting, M. (eds). (1996). *Prosody in Conversation: Interactional Studies*. Cambridge: Cambridge University Press.

Covington, M. A., He, C., Brown, C., Naçi, L., McClain, J. T., Fjordback, B. S., Semple, J. and Brown, J. (2005). Schizophrenia and the structure of language: the linguist's view. *Schizophrenia Research*, 77, 85–98.

Crick, B. (1997). Obituary of Isaiah Berlin (1909–97). *The Guardian*, 20 November.

Croker, V. and McDonald, S. (2005). Recognition of emotion from facial expression following traumatic brain injury. *Brain Injury*, 19(10), 787–99.

Crystal, D. (1979). *Working with LARSP*. London: Edward Arnold.

(1981). *Clinical Linguistics*. London: Whurr.

(1987). Towards a 'bucket' theory of language disability: taking account of interaction between linguistic levels. *Clinical Linguistics and Phonetics*, 1, 7–22.

(1992). *Profiling Linguistic Disability*, 2nd edition. London: Whurr.

(1997). *A Dictionary of Linguistics and Phonetics*, 4th edition. Oxford: Blackwell.

(2001). Clinical linguistics. In M. Aronoff and J. Rees-Miller (eds), *The Handbook of Linguistics* (pp. 673–82). Oxford: Blackwell.

Damasio, A. R. (1994). *Descartes' Error: Emotion, Reason, and the Human Brain.* New York: Quill.

Damico, J. S. (1985). Clinical discourse analysis: a functional approach to language assessment. In C. S. Simon (ed.), *Communication Skills and Classroom Success* (pp. 165–204). Basingstoke: Taylor and Francis.

Damico, J. S. and Nelson, R. L. (2005). Interpreting problematic behavior: systematic compensatory adaptations as emergent phenomena in autism. *Clinical Linguistics and Phonetics*, 19(5), 405–17.

Damico, J. S., Oelschlaeger, M. and Simmons-Mackie, N. (1999). Qualitative methods in aphasia research: conversation analysis. *Aphasiology*, 13(9–11), 667–79.

Dapretto, M., Davies, M. S., Pfeifer, J. H., Scott, A. A., Sigman, M., Brookheimer, S. Y. and Iacoboni, M. (2006). Understanding emotions in others: mirror neuron dysfunction in children with autism spectrum disorders. *Nature Neuroscience*, 9, 28–30.

Davis, G. A. and Wilcox, M. J. (1985). *Adult Aphasia Rehabilitation: Applied Pragmatics.* San Diego: College Hill Press.

de Santi, S., Koenig, L., Obler, L. K. and Goldberger, J. (1994). Cohesive devices and conversational discourse in Alzheimer's disease. In R. L. Bloom, L. K. Obler, S. De Santi and J. S. Ehrlich (eds), *Discourse Analysis and Applications: Studies in Adult Clinical Populations* (pp. 201–15). Hillsdale, NJ: Erlbaum.

Deevy, P. and Leonard, L. B. (2004). The comprehension of *Wh*-questions in children with specific language impairment. *Journal of Speech, Language and Hearing Research*, 47(4), 802–15.

Dennett, D. C. (1998). Reflections on language and mind. In P. Carruthers and J. Boucher (eds), *Language and Thought: Interdisciplinary Themes* (pp. 284–94). Cambridge: Cambridge University Press.

Dennis, M. (1998). Introduction: discourse in children with neurodevelopmental disorder, early focal brain injury, or childhood acquired brain injury. *Brain and Language*, 61, 305–7.

Dennis, M. and Barnes, M. A. (1990). Knowing the meaning, getting the point, bridging the gap and carrying the message: aspects of discourse following closed head injury in childhood and adolescence. *Brain and Language*, 39(3), 428–46.

Dennis, M., Barnes, M. A., Wilkinson, M. and Humphreys, R. P. (1998). How children with head injury represent real and deceptive emotion in short narratives. *Brain and Language*, 61, 450–83.

Dennis, M., Jacennik, B. and Barnes, M. A. (1994). The content of narrative discourse in children and adolescents after early-onset hydrocephalus and in normally developing age peers. *Brain and Language*, 46, 129–65.

Dewart, H. and Summers, S. (1988). *The Pragmatics Profile of Everyday Communication Skills.* Windsor: NFER-Nelson.

(1995). *The Pragmatics Profile of Everyday Communication Skills in Pre-school and School-aged Children.* Windsor: NFER-Nelson.

Dick, F., Bates, E., Wulfeck, B., Utman, J. A. and Dronkers, N. (2001). Language deficits, localization, and grammar: evidence for a distributive model of language breakdown in aphasics and normals. *Psychological Review*, 108(4), 759–88.

Dickerson, P., Rae, J., Stribling, P., Dautenhahn, K. and Werry, I. (2005). Autistic children's co-ordination of gaze and talk: re-examining the 'asocial' autist. In K. Richards and P. Seedhouse (eds), *Applying Conversation Analysis* (pp. 19–37). Basingstoke: Palgrave Macmillan.

Dipper, L. T., Bryan, K. L. and Tyson, J. (1997). Bridging inference and Relevance Theory: an account of right hemisphere inference. *Clinical Linguistics and Phonetics*, 11(3), 213–28.

Dobbinson, S., Perkins, M. R. and Boucher, J. (1997). A comparison of two autistic language users. *Collected Papers from the Conference on Therapeutic Intervention in Autism: Perspectives from Research and Practice, 1996*, University of Durham, 231–58.

(1998). Structural patterns in conversations with a woman who has autism. *Journal of Communication Disorders*, 31(2), 113–34.

(2003). The interactional significance of formulas in adult autistic language. *Clinical Linguistics and Phonetics*, 17, 299–307.

Dollaghan, C. (1998). Spoken word recognition in children with and without specific language impairment. *Applied Psycholinguistics*, 19, 193–207.

Donahue, M. (1986). Phonological constraints on the emergence of two-word utterances. *Journal of Child Language*, 13, 209–18.

Donahue, M. L. (1994). Differences in classroom discourse styles of students with learning disabilities. In D. N. Ripich and N. A. Creaghead (eds), *School Discourse Problems*, 2nd edition (pp. 229–61). San Diego, CA: Singular.

Donlan, C. and Masters, J. (2000). Correlates of social development in children with communicative disorders: the concurrent predictive value of verbal short-term memory span. *International Journal of Language and Communication Disorders*, 35(2), 211–26.

Dressler, W. U., Stark, H. K., Vassilakou, M., Rauchensteiner, D., Tosic, J., Weitzenauer, S. M., Wasner, P., Pons, C., Stark, J. and Brunner, G. (2004). Textpragmatic impairments of figure–ground distinction in right-brain damaged stroke patients compared with aphasics and healthy controls. *Journal of Pragmatics*, 36(2), 207.

Dronkers, N. F., Ludy, C. A. and Redfern, B. B. (1998). Pragmatics in the absence of verbal language: descriptions of a severe aphasic and a language-deprived adult. *Journal of Neurolinguistics*, 11, 179–90.

Druks, J. and Carroll, E. (2005). The crucial role of tense for verb production. *Brain and Language*, 94, 1–18.

Dujardin, K., Blairy, S., Defebvre, L., Duhem, S., Noel, Y., Hess, U. and Destee, A. (2004). Deficits in decoding emotional facial expressions in Parkinson's disease. *Neuropsychologia*, 42(2), 239–50.

Dunn, J. C. and Kirsner, K. (2003). What can we infer from double dissociations? *Cortex*, 39, 1–7.

Dunn, L. M., Dunn, L. M., Whetton, C. and Pintilie, D. (1982). *British Picture Vocabulary Scale*. Windsor: NFER-Nelson.

Dunn, M., Flax, J., Sliwinski, M. and Aram, D. (1996). The use of spontaneous language measures as criteria for identifying children with specific language impairment: an attempt to reconcile clinical and research incongruence. *Journal of Speech and Hearing Research*, 39, 643–54.

Duranti, A. (1997). *Linguistic Anthropology*. Cambridge: Cambridge University Press.

Ebbels, S. (2000). Psycholinguistic profiling of a hearing-impaired child. *Child Language Teaching and Therapy*, 16(1), 3–22.

Edwards, S. and Garman, M. (1989). Case study of a fluent aphasic: the relation between linguistic assessment and therapeutic intervention. In P. Grunwell and A. James (eds), *The Functional Evaluation of Language Disorders* (pp. 163–81). London: Croom Helm.

Ehrlic, J. S., Obler, L. K. and Clark, L. (1997). Ideational and semantic contributions to narrative production in adults with dementia of the Alzheimer's type. *Journal of Communication Disorders*, 30(2), 79–99.

Eisele, J. and Aram, D. (1993). Differential effects of early hemisphere damage on lexical comprehension and production. *Aphasiology*, 7(5), 513–523.

Elliott, C. D., Murray, D. J. and Pearson, L. S. (1977). *The British Ability Scales*. Windsor: NFER-Nelson.

Elman, J. L., Bates, E. A., Johnson, M. H., Karmiloff-Smith, A., Parisi, D. and Plunkett, K. (1996). *Rethinking Innateness: A Connectionist Perspective on Development*. Cambridge, MA: MIT Press.

Emerich, D. M., Creaghead, N. A., Grether, S. M., Murray, D. and Grasha, C. (2003). The comprehension of humorous materials by adolescents with high-functioning autism and Asperger's syndrome. *Journal of Autism and Developmental Disorders*, 33(3), 253–7.

Ewing-Cobbs, L., Brookshire, B., Scott, M. A. and Fletcher, J. M. (1998). Children's narratives following traumatic brain injury: linguistic structure, cohesion, and thematic recall. *Brain and Language*, 61, 395–419.

Farrar, M. J. and Maag, L. (2002). Early language development and the emergence of theory of mind. *First Language*, 22, 197–213.

Fay, D. (1982). Substitutions and splices: a study of sentence blends. In A. Cutler (ed.), *Slips of the Tongue and Language Production*. The Hague: Mouton.

Feagans, L. V., Kipp, E. and Blood, I. (1994). The effects of otitis media on the attention skills of day-care-attending toddlers. *Developmental Psychology*, 30, 701–8.

Ferguson, A. (1996). Describing competence in aphasic/normal conversation. *Clinical Linguistics and Phonetics*, 10(1), 55–63.

(1998). Conversational turn-taking and repair in fluent aphasia. *Clinical Linguistics and Phonetics*, 12(11), 1007–31.

Fex, B. and Månsson, A.-C. (1998). The use of gestures as a compensatory strategy in adults with acquired aphasia compared to children with specific language impairment. *Journal of Neurolinguistics*, 11, 191–206.

Fey, M. E., Cleave, P. L., Ravida, A. I., Long, S. H., Dejmal, A. E. and Easton, D. L. (1994). Effects of grammar facilitation on the phonological performance of children with speech and language impairments. *Journal of Speech and Hearing Research*, 37(3), 594–607.

Fine, C., Lumsden, J. and Blair, R. J. R. (2001). Dissociation between 'theory of mind' and executive functions in a patient with early left amygdala damage. *Brain*, 124, 287–98.

Fine, J., Bartolucci, G., Ginsberg, G. and Szatmari, P. (1991). The use of intonation to communicate in pervasive developmental disorders. *Journal of Child Psychology and Psychiatry*, 32(5), 771–82.

Fix, S., Dickey, M. W. and Thompson, C. S. (2005). Impairments of derivational word formation in agrammatic aphasia. *Brain and Language*, 95, 131–2.

Fletcher, P. C., Happé, F., Frith, U., Baker, S. C., Dolan, R. J., Frackowiak, R. S. J. and Frith, C. D. (1995). Other minds in the brain: a functional imaging study of 'theory of mind' in story comprehension. *Cognition*, 57, 109–28.

Fletcher, S. G. (1988). Speech production following partial glossectomy. *Journal of Speech and Hearing Disorders*, 53, 232–8.

Fodor, J. A. (1983). *The Modularity of Mind: An Essay on Faculty Psychology*. Cambridge, MA: MIT Press.

Foldi, N. S. (1987). Appreciation of pragmatic interpretations of indirect commands: Comparison of right and left hemisphere brain-damaged patients. *Brain and Language*, 31, 88–108.

Fox, A. V., Dodd, B. and Howard, D. (2002). Risk factors for speech disorders in children. *International Journal of Language and Communication Disorders*, 37, 117–31.

Franklin, S., Turner, J., Lambon Ralph, M. A., Morris, J. and Bailey, P. J. (1996). A distinctive case of word meaning deafness. *Cognitive Neuropsychology*, 13(8), 1139–62.

Frederickson, N., Frith, U. and Reason, R. (1997). *Phonological Assessment Battery*. Windsor: NFER-Nelson.

Friedland, D. and Miller, N. (1998). Conversation analysis of communication breakdown after closed head injury. *Brain Injury*, 12(1), 1–14.

(1999). Language mixing in bilingual speakers with Alzheimer's dementia: a conversation analysis approach. *Aphasiology*, 13, 427–44.

Frith, C. D., and Done, D. J. (1990). Stereotyped behaviour in madness and in health. In S. J. Cooper and C. T. Dourish (eds), *Neurobiology of Stereotyped Behaviour*. Oxford: Clarendon Press.

Frith, U. (1989). *Autism: Explaining the Enigma*. Oxford: Blackwell.

(2003). *Autism: Explaining the Enigma*, 2nd edition. Oxford: Blackwell.

Frith, U. and Happé, F. G. E. (1994). Autism: beyond 'theory of mind'. *Cognition*, 50, 115–32.

Gallagher, H. L., Happé, F., Brunswick, N., Fletcher, P. C., Frith, U. and Frith, C. D. (2000). Reading the mind in cartoons and stories: an fMRI study of 'theory of mind' in verbal and nonverbal tasks. *Neuropsychologia*, 38(1), 11–21.

Gallagher, T. M. (ed.). (1991). *Pragmatics of Language: Clinical Practice Issues*. London: Chapman Hall.

Gallese, V. and Goldman, A. (1998). Mirror neurons and the simulation theory of mind-reading. *Trends in Cognitive Sciences*, 2, 493–501.

Garcia, L. J., Metthé, L., Paradis, J. and Joanette, Y. (2001). Relevance is in the eye and ear of the beholder: an example from populations with a neurological impairment. *Aphasiology*, 15(1), 17–38.

Gardner, H. (1997). Are your minimal pairs too neat? The dangers of phonemicisation in phonology therapy. *European Journal of Disorders of Communication*, 32, 167–75.

Gardner, H., Froud, K., McLelland, A. and van der Lely, H. K. J. (2006). The development of the Grammar and Phonology Screening (GAPS) test to assess key markers of specific language and literacy difficulties in young children. *International Journal of Language and Communication Disorders*, 41, 513–40.

Garfinkel, H. (1967). *Studies in Ethnomethodology*. Englewood Cliffs, NJ: Prentice Hall.

Garrett, M. F. (1980). Levels of processing in language production. In B. Butterworth (ed.), *Language production*, vol. I, *Speech and talk* (pp. 177–220). London: Academic Press.

Gathercole, S. E. and Adams, A.-M. (1993). Phonological working memory in very young children. *Developmental Psychology*, 29(4), 770–8.

Gathercole, S. E. and Baddeley, A. (1993). *Working Memory and Language*. Hove: Erlbaum.

Gathercole, S. E. and Baddeley, A. D. (1990). Phonological memory deficits in language-impaired children: is there a causal connection? *Journal of Memory and Language*, 29, 336–60.

Gazzaniga, M. S. (ed.). (2000). *The New Cognitive Neurosciences*. Cambridge, MA: MIT Press.

Geis, M. L. (1995). *Speech Acts and Conversational Interaction*. Cambridge: Cambridge University Press.

Gernsbacher, M. A. (1990). *Language Comprehension as Structure Building*. Hillsdale, NJ: Lawrence Erlbaum.

Gibson, E. (1992). On the adequacy of the Competition Model. *Language*, 68(4), 812–30.

Gibson, E. J. (1969). *Principles of Perceptual Learning and Development*. East Norwal, CT: Appleton-Century-Crofts.

Gillott, A., Furniss, F. and Walter, A. (2004). Theory of mind ability in children with specific language impairment. *Child Language Teaching and Therapy*, 20(1), 1–11.

Givón, T. (1999). Generativity and variation: the notion of 'rule of grammar' revisited. In B. MacWhinney (ed.), *The Emergence of Language* (pp. 81–114). Mahwah, NJ: Lawrence Erlbaum.

Godfrey, H. P. D. and Shum, D. (2000). Executive functioning and the application of social skills following traumatic brain injury. *Aphasiology*, 14(4), 433–44.

Goldman, R., Fristoe, M. and Woodcock, R. W. (1974). *GFW Sound–Symbol Tests*. Circle Pines, MN: American Guidance Service.

Goldsmith, J. A. (1990). *Autosegmental and Metrical Phonology*. Oxford: Blackwell.

Goleman, D. (1995). *Emotional Intelligence*. New York: Bantam.

Goodwin, C. (1981). *Conversational Organisation: Interaction Between Speakers and Hearers*. New York: Academic Press.

(1995). Co-constructing meaning in conversations with an aphasic man. *Research on Language and Social Interaction*, 28(3), 233–60.

(2000a). Action and embodiment within situated human interaction. *Journal of Pragmatics*, 32, 1489–522.

(2000b). Gesture, aphasia, and interaction. In D. McNeill (ed.), *Language and Gesture* (pp. 84–98). Cambridge: Cambridge University Press.

(2003b). Conversational frameworks for the accomplishment of meaning in aphasia. In C. Goodwin (ed.), *Conversation and Brain Damage* (pp. 90–116). New York: Oxford University Press.

Goodwin, C. (ed.). (2003a). *Conversation and Brain Damage.* New York: Oxford University Press.

Goodyer, I. M. (2000). Language difficulties and psychopathology. In D. V. M. Bishop and L. B. Leonard (eds), *Speech and Language Impairments in Children: Causes, Characteristics, Intervention and Outcome* (pp. 227–44). Hove: Psychology Press.

Gopnik, M. and Crago, M. B. (1991). Familial aggregation of a developmental language disorder. *Cognition,* 39, 1–50.

Grant, J., Karmiloff-Smith, A., Gathercole, S. A., Paterson, S., Howlin, P., Davies, M. and Udwin, O. (1997). Phonological short-term memory and its relationship to language in Williams syndrome. *Cognitive Neuropsychiatry,* 2(2), 81–99.

Gray, S., Plante, E., Vance, R. and Henrichsen, M. (1999). The diagnostic accuracy of four vocabulary tests administered to preschool-age children. *Language, Speech, and Hearing Services in Schools,* 30, 196–206.

Green, G. M. (1989). *Pragmatics and Natural Language Understanding.* Hillsdale, NJ: Erlbaum.

Green, R. E. A., Turner, G. R. and Thompson, W. F. (2004). Deficits in facial emotion perception in adults with recent traumatic brain injury. *Neuropsychologia,* 42(2), 133–41.

Grice, H. P. (1975). Logic and conversation. In F. Cole and J. L. Morgan (eds), *Syntax and Semantics,* vol. III *Speech Acts* (pp. 41–58). New York: Academic Press.

Griffith, P. L., Ripich, D. N. and Dastoli, S. L. (1986). Story structure, cohesion, and propositions in story recalls by learing-disabled and nondisabled children. *Journal of Psycholinguistic Research,* 15(6), 539–55.

Grodzinsky, Y. (2000). The neurology of syntax: language use without Broca's area. *Behavioral and Brain Sciences,* 23(1), 1–71.

Grundy, P. (2000). *Doing Pragmatics,* 2nd edition. London: Edward Arnold.

Grunwell, P. (1987). *Clinical Phonology,* 2nd edition. London: Croom Helm.

Grunwell, P. (ed.). (1993). *Analysing Cleft Palate Speech.* London: Whurr.

Guendouzi, J. and Müller, N. (2001). Intelligibility and rehearsed sequences in conversations with a DAT patient. *Clinical Linguistics and Phonetics,* 15, 91–5.

(2002). Defining trouble sources in dementia: repair strategies and conversational satisfaction in interactions with an Alzheimer's patient. In F. Windsor and M. L. Kelly and N. Hewlett (eds), *Investigations in Clinical Linguistics and Phonetics* (pp. 15–30). Mahwah, NJ: Erlbaum.

Gutfreund, M., Harrison, M. and Wells, G. (1989). *Bristol Language Development Scales: Manual.* Windsor: NFER-Nelson.

Hale, M. and Reiss, C. (2000). Phonology as cognition. In N. Burton-Roberts, P. Carr and G. Docherty (eds), *Phonological Knowledge: Conceptual and Empirical Issues* (pp. 161–84). Oxford: Oxford University Press.

Halliday, M. A. K. and Hasan, R. (1976). *Cohesion in English*. London: Longman.

Hamann, S., Monarch, E. S. and Goldstein, F. C. (2002). Impaired fear conditioning in Alzheimer's disease. *Neuropsychologia*, 40(8), 1187–95.

Hancher, M. (1979). The classification of cooperative illocutionary acts. *Language in Society*, 8, 1–14.

Hand, C. R., Tonkvich, J. D. and Aitchison, J. (1979). Some idiosyncratic strategies utilized by a chronic Broca's aphasic. *Linguistics*, 17, 729–59.

Hanson, R. A. and Montgomery, J. W. (2002). Effects of general processing capacity and sustained selective attention on temporal processing performance of children with specific language impairment. *Applied Psycholinguistics*, 23, 75–93.

Happé, F. G. E. (1991). The autobiographical writings of three Asperger syndrome adults: problems of interpretation and implications for theory. In U. Frith (ed.), *Autism and Asperger Syndrome* (pp. 207–42). Cambridge: Cambridge University Press.

(1993). Communicative competence and theory of mind in autism: a test of relevance theory. *Cognition*, 48, 101–19.

(1996). Studying weak central coherence at low levels: children with autism do not succumb to visual illusions: a research note. *Journal of Child Psychology and Psychiatry*, 37, 873–7.

Happé, F., Brownell, H. and Winner, E. (1999). Acquired 'theory of mind' impairments following stroke. *Cognition*, 70(3), 211–40.

Happé, F. G. E. and Loth, E. (2002). 'Theory of mind' and tracking speakers' intentions. *Mind and Language*, 17, 24–36.

Harley, T. (2001). *The Psychology of Language: From Data to Theory*, 2nd edition. Hove: Psychology Press.

Harris, R. J. (1975). Children's comprehension of complex sentences. *Journal of Experimental Child Psychology*, 19, 420–33.

Hartley, L. L. and Jensen, P. J. (1991). Narrative and procedural discourse after closed head injury. *Brain Injury*, 5(3), 267–85.

(1992). Three discourse profiles of closed-head-injury speakers: theoretical and clinical implications. *Brain Injury*, 6(3), 271–82.

Hashimoto, R., Meguro, K., Yamaguchi, S., Ishizaki, J., Ishii, H., Meguro, M. and Sekita, Y. (2004). Executive dysfunction can explain word-list learning disability in very mild Alzheimer's disease: the Tajiri Project. *Psychiatry and Clinical Neurosciences*, 58(1), 54–60.

Hawkins, J. (1994). *A Performance Theory of Order and Constituency*. Cambridge: Cambridge University Press.

Haynes, C. and Naidoo, S. (1991). *Children with Specific Speech and Language Impairments*. Oxford: Blackwell.

Haynes, W. O., Haynes, M. D. and Jackson, J. (1982). The effects of phonetic context and linguistic complexity on /s/ misarticulation in children. *Journal of Communication Disorders*, 15, 287–97.

Hayward, D. and Schneider, P. (2000). Effectiveness of teaching story grammar knowledge to pre-school children with language impairment: an exploratory study. *Child Language Teaching and Therapy*, 16(3), 255–84.

Heeschen, C. and Schegloff, E. A. (1999). Agrammatism, adaptation theory, conversation analysis: on the role of so-called telegraphic style in talk-in-interaction. *Aphasiology*, 13, 365–405.

(2003). Aphasic agrammatism as interactional artifact and achievement. In C. Goodwin (ed.), *Conversation and Brain Damage* (pp. 231–82). New York: Oxford University Press.

Hens, G. (2000). What drives Herbeck? Schizophrenia, immediacy, and the poetic process. *Language and Literature*, 9(1), 43–59.

Heselwood, B., Bray, M. and Crookston, I. (1995). Juncture, rhythm and planning in the speech of an adult with Down's syndrome. *Clinical Linguistics and Phonetics*, 9(2), 121–38.

Hewlett, N. (1985). Phonological versus phonetic disorders: some suggested modifications to the current use of the distinction. *British Journal of Disorders of Communication*, 20, 155–64.

Hill, E. L. (2001). Non-specific nature of specific language impairment: a review of the literature with regard to concomitant motor impairments. *International Journal of Language and Communication Disorders*, 36(2), 149–71.

Hirsh-Pasek, K., Nelson, D. G. K., Jusczyk, P. W., Cassidy, K. W., Benjamin, D. and Kennedy, L. (1987). Clauses are perceptual units for young infants. *Cognition*, 26, 269–86.

Hirst, W., LeDoux, J. and Stein, S. (1984). Constraints on the processing of indirect speech acts: evidence from aphasiology. *Brain and Language*, 23, 26–33.

Hobson, R. P. (1989). Beyond cognition: a theory of autism. In G. Dawson (ed.), *Autism: Nature, Treatment and Diagnosis* (pp. 22–48). New York: Guilford Press.

(1993). *Autism and the Development of Mind*. Hove: Erlbaum.

Hobson, R. P. and Bishop, M. (2003). The pathogenesis of autism: insights from congenital blindness. *Philosophical Transactions of the Royal Society, Series B358*, 335–44.

Hobson, R. P. and Lee, A. (1989). Emotion-related and abstract concepts in autistic people: evidence from the British Picture Vocabulary Scale. *Journal of Autism and Developmental Disorders*, 4, 601–24.

Hobson, R. P., Ouston, J. and Lee, A. (1988). What's in a face? The case of autism. *British Journal of Psychology*, 79, 441–53.

Hofstede, B. T. M. and Kolk, H. H. J. (1994). The effect of task variation on the production of grammatical morphology in Broca's aphasia: a multiple case study. *Brain and Language*, 46, 278–328.

Holtgraves, T. (1999). Comprehending indirect replies: when and how are their conveyed meanings activated? *Journal of Memory and Language*, 41, 519–40.

Hopper, P. J. (1998). Emergent grammar. In M. Tomasello (ed.), *The New Psychology of Language* (pp. 155–75). Mahwah, NJ: Lawrence Erlbaum.

Horowitz, L., Jansson, L., Ljungberg, T. and Hedenbro, M. (2005). Behavioural patterns of conflict resolution strategies in preschool boys with language impairment in comparison with boys with typical language development. *International Journal of Language and Communication Disorders*, 40(4), 431–54.

Howard, S. (2004). Connected speech processes in developmental speech impairment: observations from an electropalatographic perspective. *Clinical Linguistics and Phonetics*, 18(6–8), 405–17.

Howard, S. J. (1993). Articulatory constraints on a phonological system: a case study of cleft palate speech. *Clinical Linguistics and Phonetics*, 7(4), 299–317.

Huber, W. (1990). Text comprehension and production in aphasia: analysis in terms of micro- and macro-processing. In Y. Joanette and H. H. Brownell (eds), *Discourse Ability and Brain Damage: Theoretical and Empirical Perspectives* (pp. 154–98). New York: Springer-Verlag.

Hudson, L. J. and Murdoch, B. E. (1992). Spontaneously generated narratives of children treated for posterior fossa tumour. *Aphasiology*, 6(6), 549–66.

Hughes, C., Plumet, M.-H. and Leboyer, M. (1999). Towards a cognitive phenotype for autism: increased prevalence of executive dysfunction and superior spatial span amongst siblings of children with autism. *Journal of Child Psychology and Psychiatry*, 40(5), 705–18.

Hughes, C., Russell, J. and Robbins, T. W. (1994). Evidence for executive dysfunction in autism. *Neuropsychologia*, 32(4), 477–92.

Hutchby, I. and Wooffitt, R. (1998). *Conversation Analysis: Principles, Practices and Applications*. Cambridge: Polity Press.

Hutchins, E. (1995). *Cognition in the Wild*. Cambridge, MA: MIT Press.

Huttenlocher, P. R. (2002). *Neural Plasticity: The Effects of Environment on the Development of the Cerebral Cortex*. Cambridge, MA: Harvard University Press.

Ingram, D. (1976). *Phonological Disability in Children*. London: Edward Arnold.

International Phonetic Association. (2005). *International Phonetic Alphabet*, Revised to 2005. London: International Phonetic Association.

Jackendoff, R. (2002). *Foundations of Language: Brain, Meaning, Grammar, Evolution*. Oxford: Oxford University Press.

Janssen, U. and Penke, M. (2002). Phonologically conditioned omissions of inflectional affixes in German Broca's Aphasia. *Brain and Language*, 83, 99–101.

Jay, T. (2000). *Why We Curse: A Neuro-Psycho-Social Theory of Speech*. Amsterdam: John Benjamins.

Joanette, Y. and Ansaldo, A. I. (1999). Clinical note: acquired pragmatic impairments and aphasia. *Brain and Language*, 68, 529–34.

Joanette, Y. and Goulet, P. (1990). Narrative discourse in right-brain-damaged right-handers. In Y. Joanette and H. H. Brownell (eds), *Discourse Ability and Brain Damage: Theoretical and Empirical Perspectives* (pp. 139–53). New York: Springer-Verlag.

(1993). Verbal communication deficits after right-hemisphere damage. In G. Blanken, J. Dittmann, H. Grimm, J. C. Marshall and C.-W. Wallesch (eds), *Linguistic Disorders and Pathologies: An International Handbook* (pp. 383–8). Berlin: Walter de Gruyter.

Joanette, Y., Goulet, P., Gagnon, L., Leblanc, B. and Simard, A. (1999). Single or dual semantics? Brain lateralization and the semantic processing of words. In B. Maassen and P. Groenen (eds), *Pathologies of Speech and Language: Advances in Clinical Phonetics and Linguistics* (pp. 193–207). London: Whurr.

Johnson, M. H. (1995). The development of visual attention: a cognitive neuro-science perspective. In M. S. Gazzaniga (ed.), *The Cognitive Neurosciences* (pp. 735–47). Cambridge, MA: MIT Press.

Johnson, S. (2001). *Emergence: The Connected Lives of Ants, Brains, Cities, and Software*. New York: Scribner.

Jolliffe, T. and Baron-Cohen, S. (1999). The strange stories test: a replication with high-functioning adults with autism or Asperger syndrome. *Journal of Autism and Developmental Disorders*, 29(5), 395–406.

Jordan, F. M., Murdoch, B. E. and Buttsworth, D. L. (1991). Closed-head-injured children's performance on narrative tasks. *Journal of Speech and Hearing Research*, 34, 572–82.

Karbe, H., Thiel, A., Weber-Luxenburger, G., Herholz, K., Kessler, J. and Heiss, W.-D. (1998). Brain plasticity in poststroke aphasia: what is the contribution of the right hemisphere? *Brain and Language*, 64, 215–30.

Karmiloff-Smith, A. (1992). *Beyond Modularity: A Developmental Perspective on Cognitive Science*. Cambridge, MA: MIT Press/Bradford Books.

(1998). Development itself is the key to understanding developmental disorders. *Trends in Cognitive Sciences*, 2(10), 389–98.

(1999). Modularity of mind. In R. A. Wilson and F. Keil (eds), *The MIT Encyclopedia of the Cognitive Sciences* (pp. 558–60). Cambridge, MA: MIT Press.

Karmiloff-Smith, A., Grant, J., Berthoud, I., Davies, M., Howlin, P. and Udwin, O. (1997). Language and Williams syndrome: how intact is 'intact'? *Child Development*, 68(2), 246–62.

Karmiloff-Smith, A., Scerif, G. and Ansari, D. (2003). Double dissociations in developmental disorders? Theoretically misconceived, empirically dubious. *Cortex*, 39, 161–3.

Karmiloff-Smith, A., Tyler, L. K., Voice, K., Sims, K., Udwin, O., Howlin, P. and Davies, M. (1998). Linguistic dissociations in Williams syndrome: evaluating receptive syntax in on-line and off-line tasks. *Neuropsychologia*, 36(4), 343–51.

Karniol, R. (1992). Stuttering out of bilingualism. *First Language*, 12(3), 255–83.

Kasari, C., Mundy, P., Yirmiya, N. and Sigman, M. (1990). Affect and attention in children with Down syndrome. *American Journal on Mental Retardation*, 95(1), 55–67.

Kasari, C., Sigman, M., Mundy, P. and Yirmaya, N. (1990). Affective sharing in the context of joint attention interactions of normal, autistic, and mentally retarded children. *Journal of Autism and Developmental Disorders*, 20(1), 87–100.

Kasher, A. (1991). On the pragmatic modules: a lecture. *Journal of Pragmatics*, 16, 381–97.

Kasher, A., Batori, G., Soroker, N., Graves, D. and Zaidel, E. (1999). Effects of right- and left-hemisphere damage on understanding conversational implica-tures. *Brain and Language*, 68, 566–90.

Kay, J., Lesser, R. and Coltheart, M. (1992). *PALPA: Psycholinguistic Assessments of Language Processing in Aphasia*. Hove: Lawrence Erlbaum.

Kay, P. and Fillmore, C. J. (1999). Grammatical constructions and linguistic gen-eralizations: the What's X doing Y? construction. *Language*, 75(1), 1–33.

Kean, M.-L. (1977). The linguistic interpretation of aphasic syndromes: agrammatism in Broca's aphasia, an example. *Cognition*, 5, 9–46.
  (1995). The elusive character of agrammatism. *Brain and Language*, 50,
  369–84.
Kegl, J. A. and Poizner, H. (1998). Shifting the burden to the interlocutor: compensation for pragmatic deficits in signers with Parkinson's disease. *Journal of
Neurolinguistics*, 11, 137–52.
Kekelis, L. S. and Andersen, E. (1984). Family communication styles and language
development. *Journal of Visual Impairment and Blindness*, 78, 54–64.
Kelly, S. D. (2001). Broadening the units of analysis in communication: speech and
nonverbal behaviours in pragmatic comprehension. *Journal of Child
Language*, 28, 325–49.
Kelly, S. D., Barr, D. J., Church, R. B. and Lynch, K. (1999). Offering a hand to
pragmatic understanding: the role of speech and gesture in comprehension
and memory. *Journal of Memory and Language*, 40, 577–92.
Kempler, D., Van Lancker, D. and Hadler, B. (1984). *Familiar Phrase Recognition
in Brain-Damaged and Demented Adults*. Paper presented at the the 22nd
Meeting of the Academy of Aphasia, 1984, Los Angeles, CA.
Kendon, A. (2000). Language and gesture: unity or duality? In D. McNeill
(ed.), *Language and Gesture* (pp. 47–63). Cambridge: Cambridge University
Press.
  (2004). *Gesture: Visible Action as Utterance*. Cambridge: Cambridge University
  Press.
Kent, R. D., Weismer, G., Kent, J. F., Vorperian, H. K. and Duffy, J. R. (1999).
Acoustic studies of dysarthric speech: methods, progress, and potential.
Journal of Communication Disorders, 32, 141–86.
Kilborn, K. (1991). Selective impairment of grammatical morphology due to
induced stress in normal listeners: implications for aphasia. *Brain and
Language*, 41, 275–88.
Kimelman, M. D. Z. (1999). Prosody, linguistic demands, and auditory compre-
hension in aphasia. *Brain and Language*, 69, 212–21.
Kintsch, W. (1998). *Comprehension: A Paradigm for Cognition*. Cambridge:
Cambridge University Press.
Kintsch, W. and van Dijk, T. A. (1978). Towards a model of text comprehension
and production. *Psychological Review*, 85, 363–94.
Kiparsky, P. and Kiparsky, C. (1971). Fact. In D. D. Steinberg and L. A. Jakobovits
(eds), *Semantics: An Interdisciplinary Reader in Philosophy, Linguistics and
Psychology*. Cambridge: Cambridge University Press.
Kirk, S., McArthur, J. and Kirk, W. (1968). *Illinois Test of Psycholinguistic
Abilities*. Urbana, IL: University of Illinois Press.
Klecan-Aker, J. and Blondeau, R. (1990). An examination of the written stories of
hearing-impaired school age children. *Volta Review*, 92, 275–82.
Klippi, A. (1996). *Conversation as an Achievement in Aphasics*. Helsinki:
Suomalaisen Kirjallisuuden Seura.
Knight, C., Studdert-Kennedy, M. and Hurford, J. R. (eds). (2000). *The
Evolutionary Emergence of Language: Social Functions and the Origins of
Linguistic Form*. Cambridge: Cambridge University Press.

Kohn, S. and Cragnolino, A. (1998). The role of lexical co-occurrence in aphasic sentence production. *Applied Psycholinguistics*, 19, 631–46.

Kohn, S. E., Melvold, J. and Smith, K. L. (1995). Consonant harmony as a compensatory mechanism in fluent aphasic speech. *Cortex*, 31, 747–56.

Kolk, H. (1995). A time-based approach to agrammatic production. *Brain and Language*, 50, 282–303.

Kosslyn, S. M. and Smith, E. E. (2000). Introduction to higher cognitve functions. In M. S. Gazzaniga (ed.), *The New Cognitive Neurosciences*, 2nd edition (pp. 961–3). Cambridge, MA: MIT Press.

Kretschmer, R. R. and Kretschmer, L. W. (1994). Discourse and hearing impairment. In D. N. Ripich and N. A. Creaghead (eds), *School Discourse Problems*, 2nd edition (pp. 263–96). San Diego, CA: Singular.

Kuhl, P. K., Coffey-Corina, S., Padden, D. and Dawson, G. (2005). Links between social and linguistic processing of speech in preschool children with autism: behavioral and electrophysiological measures. *Developmental Sciences*, 8(1), F9–F20.

Laakso, K., Brunnegård, K. and Hartelius, L. (2000). Assessing high-level language in individuals with multiple sclerosis. *Clinical Linguistics and Phonetics*, 14, 329–49.

Labov, W. and Fanshel, D. (1977). *Therapeutic Discourse: Psychotherapy as Conversation*. New York: Academic Press.

Lacoste, M. (1998). Doctor–patient language. In J. L. Mey (ed.), *Concise Encyclopedia of Pragmatics* (pp. 266–9). Amsterdam: Elsevier.

Laine, M., Laakso, M., Vuorinen, E. and Rinne, J. (1998). Coherence and informativeness of discourse in two dementia types. *Journal of Neurolinguistics*, 11, 79–87.

Lambon Ralph, M. A. and Howard, D. (2000). Gogi aphasia or semantic dementia? Simulating and assessing poor verbal comprehension in a case of progressive fluent aphasia. *Cognitive Neuropsychology*, 17(5), 437–65.

Landau, B. and Gleitman, L. R. (1985). *Language and Experience: Evidence from the Blind Child*. Harvard: Harvard University Press.

Langdon, R., Davies, M. and Coltheart, M. (2002). Understanding minds and understanding communicated meanings in schizophrenia. *Mind and Language*, 17(1/2), 68–104.

Lawrence, K., Campbell, R., Swettenham, J., Terstegge, J., Akers, R., Coleman, M. and Skuse, D. (2003). Interpreting gaze in Turner syndrome: impaired sensitivity to intention and emotion, but preservation of social cueing. *Neuropsychologia*, 41(8), 894–905.

Laws, G. and Bishop, D. V. M. (2004). Pragmatic language impairment and social deficits in Williams syndrome: a comparison with Down's syndrome and specific language impairment. *International Journal of Language and Communication Disorders*, 39(1), 45–64.

Leech, G. N. (1983). *Principles of Pragmatics*. London: Longman.

Lehman, M. T. and Tompkins, C. A. (2000). Inferencing in adults with right hemisphere brain damage: an analysis of conflicting results. *Aphasiology*, 14, 485–99.

Leinonen, E. and Kerbel, D. (1999). Relevance theory and pragmatic impairment. *International Journal of Language and Communication Disorders*, 34(4), 367–90.

206   References

Leinonen, E., Letts, C. and Smith, B. R. (2000). *Children's Pragmatic Communication Difficulties*. London: Whurr.

Lemme, M. L., Hedberg, N. L. and Bottenberg, D. E. (1984). Cohension in narratives of aphasic adults. In R. H. Brookshire (ed.), *Clinical Aphasiology Conference Proceedings* (pp. 215–22). Minneapolis: BRK.

Lennox, P. (2001). Hearing and ENT management. In A. C. H. Watson and D. A. Sell and P. Grunwell (eds), *Management of Cleft Lip and Palate*. London: Whurr.

Leonard, L. B. (1988). Government-binding theory and some of its applications: a tutorial. *Journal of Speech and Hearing Research*, 31, 515–524.

(1995). Phonological impairment. In P. Fletcher and B. MacWhinney (eds), *The Handbook of Child Language* (pp. 573–602). Oxford: Blackwell.

(1998). *Children with Specific Language Impairments*. Cambridge, MA: MIT Press.

(2000a). Specific language impairment across languages. In D. V. M. Bishop and L. B. Leonard (eds), *Speech and Language Impairments in Children: Causes, Characteristics, Intervention and Outcome* (pp. 115–29). Hove: Psychology Press.

(2000b). Theories of language learning and children with specific language impairment. In M. R. Perkins and S. Howard (eds), *New Directions in Language Development and Disorders* (pp. 1–5). New York: Kluwer Academic/Plenum.

Leonard, L. B. and Fey, M. E. (1991). Facilitating grammatical development: the contribution of pragmatics. In T. M. Gallagher (ed.), *Pragmatics of Language: Clinical Practice Issues*. (pp. 333–55). London: Chapman and Hall.

Lerner, G. H. (1996). On the 'semi-permeable' character of grammatical units in conversation: conditional entry into the turn space of another speaker. In E. Ochs, E. A. Schegloff and S. A. Thompson (eds), *Interaction and Grammar* (pp. 238–76). Cambridge: Cambridge University Press.

Leslie, A. M. (1988). Some implications of pretense for mechanisms underlying the child's theory of mind. In J. Astington, P. Harris and D. Olsen (eds), *Developing Theories of Mind* (pp. 19–46). Cambridge: Cambridge University Press.

Leslie, A. M. and Frith, U. (1988). Autistic children's understanding of seeing, knowing and believing. *British Journal of Developmental Psychology*, 6, 315–24.

Lesser, R. and Milroy, L. (1993). *Linguistics and Aphasia: Psycholinguistic and Pragmatic Aspects of Intervention*. London: Longman.

(1998). Pragmatics and aphasia. In A. Kasher (ed.), *Pragmatics: Critical Concepts* (pp. 217–29). London: Routledge.

Letts, C. (1985). Linguistic interaction in the clinic: how do therapists do therapy? *Child Language Teaching and Therapy*, 1, 321–31.

Letts, C. and Leinonen, E. (2001). Comprehension of inferential meaning in language-impaired and language normal children. *International Journal of Language and Communication Disorders*, 36(3), 307–28.

Levelt, W. J. M. (1989). *Speaking: From Intention to Articulation*. Cambridge, MA: MIT Press.

Levine, M. J., Van Horn, K. R. and Curtis, A. B. (1993). Developmental models of social cognition in assessing psychosocial adjustments in head injury. *Brain Injury*, 7(2), 153–67.

Levinson, S. C. (1983). *Pragmatics.* Cambridge: Cambridge University Press.

Liles, B. Z., Coelho, C. A., Duffy, R. and Zalagens, M. R. (1989). Effects of elicitation procedures on the narratives of normal and closed head-injured adults. *Journal of Speeach and Hearing Disorders,* 54, 356–66.

Lind, M. (2002). The use of prosody in interaction: observations from a case study of a Norwegian speaker with a non-fluent type of aphasia. In F. Windsor, M. L. Kelly and N. Hewlett (eds), *Investigations in Clinical Phonetics and Linguistics.* Mahwah, NJ: Lawrence Erlbaum.

Lindblom, B. (1999). Emergent phonology. Unpublished manuscript.

Lloyd, J., Lieven, E. and Arnold, P. (2001). Oral conversations between hearing-impaired children and their normally hearing peers and teachers. *First Language,* 21, 83–107.

Local, J. (2003). Variable domains and variable relevance: interpreting phonetic exponents. *Journal of Phonetics,* 31, 321–39.

Local, J. and Wootton, T. (1995). Interactional and phonetic aspects of immediate echolalia in autism: a case study. *Clinical Linguistics and Phonetics,* 9(2), 155–84.

Lock, S. and Armstrong, L. (1997). Cohesion analysis of the expository discourse of normal, fluent aphasic and demented adults: a role in differential diagnosis? *Clinical Linguistics and Phonetics,* 11(4), 299–317.

Locke, J. L. (1993). *The Child's Path to Spoken Language.* Cambridge, MA: Harvard University Press.

(1994). Gradual emergence of developmental language disorders. *Journal of Speech and Hearing Research,* 37, 608–16.

(1997). A theory of neurolinguistic development. *Brain and Language,* 58, 265–326.

Loeb, D. F. and Leonard, L. B. (1988). Specific language impairment and parameter theory. *Clinical Linguistics and Phonetics,* 2(4), 317–27.

Lorch, M. P., Borod, J. C. and Koff, E. (1998). The role of emotion in the linguistic and pragmatic aspects of aphasic performance. *Journal of Neurolinguistics,* 11, 103–18.

Losh, M. and Capps, L. (2003). Narrative ability in high-functioning children with autism or Asperger's syndrome. *Journal of Autism and Developmental Disorders,* 33(3), 239–51.

Loveland, K. A., Kehres, J. and Sigman, M. (1993). Narrative language in autism and the theory of mind hypothesis: a wider perspective. In S. Baron-Cohen, H. Tager-Flusberg and D. J. Cohen (eds), *Understanding Other Minds.* New York: Oxford University Press.

Loveland, K. A., Landry, S. H., Hughes, S. O., Hall, S. K. and McEvoy, R. (1988). Speech acts and the pragmatic deficits of autism. *Journal of Speech and Hearing Research,* 31, 593–604.

Loveland, K. A., McEvoy, R. E., Tunali, B. and Kelley, M. L. (1990). Narrative story telling in autism and Down's syndrome. *British Journal of Developmental Psychology,* 8, 9–23.

Lovett, M. W., Dennis, M. and Newman, J. E. (1986). Making reference: the cohesive use of pronouns in the narrative discourse of hemidecorticate adolescents. *Brain and Language,* 29, 224–51.

Luria, A. R. (1968). *The Mind of a Mnemonist*. New York: Basic Books.

MacLure, M. and French, P. (1981). A comparison of talk at home and at school. In G. Wells (ed.), *Learning Through Interaction: The Study of Language Development* (pp. 205–39). Cambridge: Cambridge University Press.

MacWhinney, B. (1999). Preface. In B. MacWhinney (ed.), *The Emergence of Language* (pp. ix–xvii). Mahwah, NJ: Lawrence Erlbaum.

Maher, B. A. and Spitzer, M. (1993). Thought disorders and language behavior in schizophrenia. In G. Blanken, J. Dittmann, H. Grimm, J. C. Marshall and C.-W. Wallesch (eds), *Linguistic Disorders and Pathologies: An International Handbook* (pp. 522–33). Berlin: Walter de Gruyter.

Mandler, J. M. and Johnson, N. S. (1977). Remembrance of things parsed: story structure and recall. *Cognitive Psychology*, 9, 111–51.

Martin, I. and McDonald, S. (2003). Weak coherence, no theory of mind, or executive dysfunction? Solving the puzzle of pragmatic language disorders. *Brain and Language*, 85, 451–66.

  (2005). Evaluating the causes of impaired irony comprehension following traumatic brain injury. *Aphasiology*, 19(8), 712–30.

Martin, R. C. and Feher, E. (1990). The consequences of reduced memory span for the comprehension of semantic versus syntactic information. *Brain and Language*, 3, 1–20.

Marton, K. and Schwartz, R. G. (2003). Working memory capacity and language processes in children with specific language impairment. *Journal of Speech, Language and Hearing Research*, 46(5), 1138–53.

Masterson, J. J. and Kamhi, A. G. (1992). Linguistic trade-offs in school-age children with and without language disorders. *Journal of Speech and Hearing Research*, 35, 1064–75.

McCaleb, P. and Prizant, B. M. (1985). Encoding of new versus old information by autistic children. *Journal of Speech and Hearing Disorders*, 50, 230–40.

McCann, J. and Peppé, S. (2003). Prosody in autism spectrum disorders: a critical review. *International Journal of Language and Communication Disorders*, 38(4), 325–50.

McDonald, S. (1992a). Communication disorders following closed head injury: new approaches to assessment and rehabilitation. *Brain Injury*, 6(3), 283–92.

  (1992b). Differential pragmatic language loss after closed head injury: ability to comprehend conversational implicature. *Applied Psycholinguistics*, 13, 295–312.

  (1993a). Pragmatic language loss after closed head injury: inability to meet the informational needs of the listener. *Brain and Language*, 44, 28–46.

  (1993b). Viewing the brain sideways? Frontal versus right hemisphere explanations of non-aphasic language disorders. *Aphasiology*, 7(6), 535–49.

  (1999). Exploring the process of inference generation in sarcasm: a review of normal and clinical studies. *Brain and Language*, 68, 486–506.

  (2000). Exploring the cognitive basis of right-hemisphere pragmatic language disorders. *Brain and Language*, 75(1), 82–107.

McDonald, S. and Flanagan, S. (2004). Social perception deficits after traumatic brain injury: interaction between emotion recognition, mentalizing ability, and social communication. *Neuropsychology*, 18(3), 527–79.

McDonald, S. and Pearce, S. (1996). Clinical insights into pragmatic theory: frontal lobe deficits and sarcasm. *Brain and Language*, 53, 81–104.

(1998). Requests that overcome listener reluctance: impairment associated with executive dysfunction in brain injury. *Brain and Language*, 61, 88–104.

McDonald, S., Togher, L. and Code, C. (1999). The nature of traumatic brain injury: basic features and neuropsychological consequences. In S. McDonald, L. Togher and C. Code (eds), *Communication Disorders Following Traumatic Brain Injury* (pp. 19–54). Hove: Psychology Press.

McDowell, S., Whyte, J. and D'Esposito, M. (1997). Working memory impairments in traumatic brain injury: evidence from a dual-task paradigm. *Neuropsychologia*, 35(10), 1341–53.

McKoon, G. and Ratcliff, R. (1992). Inference during reading. *Psychological Review*, 99, 440–66.

McNamara, P. and Durso, R. (2003). Pragmatic communication skills in patients with Parkinson's disease. *Brain and Language*, 84(3), 414–23.

McNeill, D. (1992). *Hand and Mind: What Gesture Reveals about Thought*. Chicago, IL: University of Chicago Press.

(2000b). Catchments and contexts: non-modular factors in speech and gesture production. In D. McNeill (ed.), *Language and Gesture* (pp. 312–18). Cambridge: Cambridge University Press.

McNeill, D. (ed.). (2000a). *Language and Gesture*. Cambridge: Cambridge University Press.

McTear, M. F. and Conti-Ramsden, G. (1992). *Pragmatic Disability in Children*. London: Whurr.

Meilijson, S. R., Kasher, A. and Elizur, A. (2004). Language performance in chronic schizophrenia: a pragmatic approach. *Journal of Speech, Language and Hearing Research*, 47(3), 695–713.

Menn, L., Gottfried, M., Holland, A. L. and Garrett, M. F. (2005). Encoding location in aphasic and normal speech: the interaction of pragmatics with language output processing limitations. *Aphasiology*, 19(6), 487–519.

Menn, L., O'Connor, M., Obler, L. K. and Holland, A. (1995). *Non-Fluent Aphasia in a Multilingual World*. Amsterdam: John Benjamins.

Mentis, M., Biggs-Whitaker, J. and Gramigna, G. D. (1995). Discourse topic management in senile dementia of the Alzheimer's type. *Journal of Speech and Hearing Research*, 38, 1054–66.

Mentis, M. and Prutting, C. A. (1987). Cohesion in the discourse of normal and head-injured adults. *Journal of Speech and Hearing Research*, 30, 88–98.

Menyuk, P. and Looney, P. L. (1972). Relationships among components of the grammar in language disorder. *Journal of Speech and Hearing Research*, 15, 395–406.

Menyuk, P. and Quill, K. (1985). Semantic problems in autistic children. In E. Schopler and G. Mesibov (eds), *Communication Problems in Autism* (pp. 127–45). New York: Plenum.

Merrison, S. and Merrison, A. J. (2005). Repair in speech and language therapy interaction: investigating pragmatic language impairment of children. *Child Language Teaching and Therapy*, 21(2), 191–211.

Mey, J. L. (2001). *Pragmatics: An Introduction*, 2nd edition. Oxford: Blackwell.

Milford, S. A. (1989). Children's acquisition of the presuppositional status of factive and non-factive verbs. Unpublished MSc, Ulster, Jordanstown.

Miller, C. A. (2004). False belief and sentence complement performance in children with specific language impairment. *International Journal of Language and Communication Disorders*, 39(2), 191–213.

Miller, G. A. (1981). *Language and Speech*. San Francisco: W. H. Freeman.

Miller, N. and Docherty, G. (1995). Acquired neurogenic speech disorders. In K. Grundy (ed.), *Linguistics in Clinical Practice*. London: Whurr.

Mills, A. E. (1983). Acquisition of speech sounds in the visually-handicapped child. In A. E. Mills (ed.), *Language Acquisition in the Blind Child: Normal and Deficient*. London: Croom Helm.

Minshew, N. J., Goldstein, G. and Siegel, D. J. (1995). Speech and language in high-functioning autistic individuals. *Neuropsychology*, 9, 255–61.

Miranda, A. E., McCabe, A. and Bliss, L. S. (1998). Jumping around and leaving things out: a profile of the narrative abilities of children with specific language impairment. *Applied Psycholinguistics*, 19, 647–67.

Mitchley, N. J., Barber, J., Gray, J. M., Brooks, D. N. and Livingston, M. G. (1998). Comprehension of irony in schizophrenia. *Cognitive Neuropsychiatry*, 3(2), 127–38.

Miyake, A., Carpenter, P. A. and Just, M. A. (1994). A capacity approach to syntactic comprehension disorders: making normal adults perform like aphasic patients. *Cognitive Neuropsychology*, 11, 671–717.

   (1995). Reduced resources and specific impairments in normal and aphasic sentence comprehension. *Cognitive Neuropsychology*, 12(6), 651–79.

Moen, I. (1990). A case of 'foreign-accent syndrome'. *Clinical Linguistics and Phonetics*, 4, 295–302.

Mogford-Bevan, K. (1993). Language acquisition and development with sensory impairment: hearing-impaired children. In G. Blanken, J. Dittmann, H. Grimm, J. C. Marshall and C.-W. Wallesch (eds), *Linguistic Disorders and Pathologies: An International Handbook* (pp. 660–79). Berlin: Walter de Gruyter.

Molloy, R., Brownell, H. H. and Gardner, H. (1990). Discourse comprehension by right-hemisphere stroke patients: deficits of prediction and revision. In Y. Joanette and H. H. Brownell (eds), *Discourse Ability and Brain Damage: Theoretical and Empirical Perspectives* (pp. 113–30). New York: Springer-Verlag.

Montgomery, J. W. (2002). Examining the nature of lexical processing in children with specific language impairment: temporal processing or processing capacity deficit? *Applied Psycholinguistics*, 22, 447–70.

   (2005). Effects of input rate and age on real-time language processing of children with specific language impairment. *International Journal of Language and Communication Disorders*, 40(2), 171–88.

Morgan, J. L. (1986). *From Simple Input to Complex Grammar*. Cambridge, MA: MIT Press.

Morris, C. W. (1938). *Foundations of the Theory of Signs*. Chicago: University of Chicago Press.

Morrison-Stewart, S. L., Williamson, P. C., Corning, W. C., Kutcher, S. P., Snow, W. G. and Merskey, H. (1992). Frontal and non-frontal lobe neuropsychological test performance and clinical symptomatology in schizophrenia. *Psychological Medicine*, 22, 353–9.

Müller, N. (ed.) (2000). *Pragmatics in Speech and Language Pathology*. Amsterdam: Benjamins.

Murdoch, B. E. (1990). *Acquired Speech and Language Disorders: A Neuroanatomical and Functional Neurological Approach*. London: Chapman and Hall.

Murphy, F. C., Sahakian, B. J., Rubinsztein, J. S., Michale, A., Rogers, R. D., Robbins, T. W. and Paykel, E. S. (1999). Emotional bias and inhibitory control processes in mania and depression. *Psychological Medicine*, 29, 1307–21.

Nation, K., Marshall, C. M. and Snowling, M. J. (2001). Phonological and semantic contributions to children's picture naming skill: evidence from children with developmental reading disorders. *Language and Cognitive Processes*, 16(2/3), 241–59.

Nespoulous, J.-L., Code, C., Virbel, J. and Lecours, A. R. (1998). Hypotheses on the dissociation between 'referential' and 'modalizing' verbal behavior in aphasia. *Applied Psycholinguistics*, 19, 311–31.

Newmeyer, F. J. (2003). Grammar is grammar and usage is usage. *Language*, 79(4), 682–707.

Nicholas, M., Obler, L. K., Albert, M. L. and Helm-Estabrooks, N. (1985). Empty speech in Alzheimer's disease and fluent aphasia. *Journal of Speech and Hearing Research*, 28, 405–10.

Niemi, J. and Hägg, M. (1999). Syntax at late stages of acquisition: experiments with normal and SLI children. In B. Maassen and P. Groenen (eds), *Pathologies of Speech and Language: Advances in Clinical Phonetics and Linguistics* (pp. 76–81). London: Whurr.

Ninio, A., Wheeler, P., Snow, C. E., Pan, B. A. and Rollins, P. R. (1991). *INCA-A: Inventory of Communicative Acts – Abridged*. Cambridge, MA: Harvard Graduate School of Education.

Norbury, C. F. and Bishop, D. V. M. (2002a). Does impaired grammatical comprehension provide evidence for an innate grammar module? *Applied Psycholinguistics*, 23, 247–68.

(2002b). Inferential processing and story recall in children with communication problems: a comparison of specific language impairment, pragmatic language impairment and high-functioning autism. *International Journal of Language and Communication Disorders*, 37(3), 227–51.

Norbury, C. F., Nash, M., Baird, G. and Bishop, D. V. M. (2004). Using a parental checklist to identify diagnostic groups in children with communication impairment: a validation of the Children's Communication Checklist-2. *International Journal of Language and Communication Disorders*, 39(3), 345–64.

Nunez, P. L. (2000). Toward a quantitative description of large-scale neocortical dynamic function and EEG. *Behavioral and Brain Sciences*, 23, 371–437.

Nuyts, J. and Roeck, A. D. (1997). Autism and meta-representation: the case of epistemic modality. *European Journal of Disorders of Communication*, 32, 113–17.

O'Grady, W. (2005). *Syntactic Carpentry: An Emergentist Approach to Syntax.* Mahwah, NJ: Lawrence Erlbaum.

Ochs, E., Schieffelin, B. B. and Platt, M. L. (1979). Propositions across utterances and speakers. In E. Ochs and B. B. Schieffelin (eds), *Developmental Pragmatics* (pp. 251–68). New York: Academic Press.

Oelschlaeger, M. L. and Damico, J. S. (1998). Joint productions as a conversational strategy in aphasia. *Clinical Linguistics and Phonetics*, 12(6), 459–80.

(2000). Partnership in conversation: a study of word search strategies. *Journal of Communication Disorders*, 33(3), 205–25.

(2003). Word searches in aphasia: a study of the collaborative responses of communicative partners. In C. Goodwin (ed.), *Conversation and Brain Damage* (pp. 211–27). New York: Oxford University Press.

Orange, J. B., Kertesz, A. and Peacock, J. (1998). Pragmatics in frontal lobe dementia and primary progressive aphasia. *Journal of Neurolinguistics*, 11, 153–77.

Ozonoff, S., Pennington, B. F. and Rogers, S. J. (1991). Executive function deficits in high functioning autistic individuals: relationship to theory of mind. *Journal of Child Psychology and Psychiatry*, 32, 1081–106.

Panagos, J. M. and Prelock, P. A. (1982). Phonological constraints on the sentence production of language-disordered children. *Journal of Speech and Hearing Research*, 25, 171–7.

Panagos, J. M., Quine, M. E. and Klich, R. J. (1979). Syntactic and phonological influences on children's articulation. *Journal of Speech and Hearing Research*, 22, 841–8.

Panzeri, M., Semenza, C. and Butterworth, B. (1987). Compensatory processes in the evolution of severe jargon aphasia. *Neuropsychologia*, 25(6), 919–33.

Paradis, M. (1994). Neurolinguistic aspects of implicit and explicit memory: implications for bilingualism and SLA. In N. C. Ellis (ed.), *Implicit and Explicit Learning of Languages* (pp. 393–419). New York: Academic Press.

Paradis, M. (ed.). (1998a). *Pragmatics in Neurogenic Communication Disorders.* Special issue of the *Journal of Neurolinguistics* 11(1/2). Oxford: Elsevier.

Paradis, M. (1998b). The other side of language: pragmatic competence. *Journal of Neurolinguistics*, 11, 1–10.

(2003). Cerebral representation of language. In J. Verschueren and J.-O. Östman, J. Blommaert and C. Bulcaen (eds), *Handbook of Pragmatics* (pp. 1–20). Amsterdam: John Benjamins.

Paul, R., Augustyn, A., Klin, A. and Volkmar, F. R. (2005). Perception and production of prosody by speakers with autistic spectrum disorders. *Journal of Autism and Developmental Disorders*, 35(2), 205–20.

Paul, R. and Shriberg, L. D. (1982). Associations between phonology and syntax in speech-delayed children. *Journal of Speech and Hearing Research*, 25, 536–47.

Penke, M. (2003). On the morphological basis of syntactic deficits. *Brain and Language*, 87(1), 50–1.

Penn, C. (1985). The profile of communicative appropriateness. *South African Journal of Communication Disorders*, 32, 18–23.

(1999). Pragmatic assessment and therapy for persons with brain damage: What have clinicians gleaned in two decades? *Brain and Language*, 68, 535–52.

(2000). Clinical pragmatics and assessment of adult langauge disorders: product and process. In N. Müller (ed.), *Pragmatics and Clinical Applications* (pp. 107–24). Amsterdam: John Benjamins.

Pennington, B. and Ozonoff, S. (1996). Executive functions and developmental psychopathology. *Journal of Child Psychology and Psychiatry*, 37, 51–87.

Perez-Pereira, M. (1994). Imitations, repetitions, routines, and the child's analysis of language: insights from the blind. *Journal of Child Language*, 21(2), 317–38.

Perkins, L. (1995). Applying conversation analysis to aphasia: clinical implications and analytic issues. *Aphasiology*, 30(3), 372–83.

Perkins, L., Whitworth, A. and Lesser, R. (1997). *Conversation Analysis Profile for People with Cognitive Impairments (CAPPCI)*. London: Whurr.

(1998). Conversing in dementia: a conversation analytic approach. *Journal of Neurolinguistics*, 11, 33–53.

Perkins, M. R. (1983). *Modal Expressions in English*. London: Frances Pinter.

(1985). Discourse error analysis. In P. Roach (ed.), *Papers from the First Leeds English Language Teaching Symposium* (pp. 4–8). Leeds: Leeds University.

(1994). Repetitiveness in language disorders: a new analytical procedure. *Clinical Linguistics and Phonetics*, 8(4), 321–36.

(1998a). Is pragmatics epiphenomenal? evidence from communication disorders. *Journal of Pragmatics*, 29, 291–311.

(1998b). Review of H. H. Clark (1996) *Using Language* [Cambridge: Cambridge University Press]. *Child Language Teaching and Therapy*, 14(2), 214–16.

(1998c). The cognitive basis of pragmatic disability. In W. Ziegler and K. Deger (eds), *Clinical Phonetics and Linguistics* (pp. 195–202). London: Whurr.

(1999). Productivity and formulaicity in language development. In M. Garman and C. Letts and B. Richards and C. Schelletter and S. Edwards (eds), *Issues in Normal and Disordered Child Language: From Phonology to Narrative*. Special issue of *The New Bulmershe Papers* (pp. 51–67). Reading: University of Reading.

(2000). The scope of pragmatic disability: a cognitive approach. In N. Müller (ed.), *Pragmatics and Clinical Applications* (pp. 7–28). Amsterdam: John Benjamins.

(2001). Compensatory strategies in SLI. *Clinical Linguistics and Phonetics*, 15, 67–71.

(2002). An emergentist approach to clinical pragmatics. In F. Windsor, M. L. Kelly and N. Hewlett (eds), *Investigations in Clinical Phonetics and Linguistics* (pp. 1–14). New York: Lawrence Erlbaum.

(2003). Clinical pragmatics. In J. Verschueren, J.-O. Östman, J. Blommaert and C. Bulcaen (eds), *Handbook of Pragmatics: 2001 Installment* (pp. 1–29). Amsterdam: John Benjamins.

(2005a). Clinical pragmatics: an emergentist perspective. *Clinical Linguistics and Phonetics*, 19(5), 363–6.

(2005b). Pragmatic ability and disability as emergent phenomena. *Clinical Linguistics and Phonetics*, 19(5), 367–77.

Perkins, M. R., Body, R. and Parker, M. (1995). Closed head injury: assessment and remediation of topic bias and repetitiveness. In M. R. Perkins and S. J. Howard (eds), *Case Studies in Clinical Linguistics* (pp. 293–320). London: Whurr.

Perkins, M. R., Catizone, R., Peers, I. and Wilks, Y. (1999). Clinical computational corpus linguistics: a case study. In B. Maassen and P. Groenen (eds), *Pathologies of Speech and Language: Advances in Clinical Phonetics and Linguistics* (pp. 269–74). London: Whurr.

Perkins, M. R., Dobbinson, S., Boucher, J., Bol, S. and Bloom, P. (2006). Lexical knowledge and lexical use in autism. *Journal of Autism and Developmental Disorders*, 36, 795–805.

Perkins, M. R. and Firth, C. (1991). Production and comprehension of modal expressions by children with a pragmatic disability. *First Language*, 11, 61.

Perkins, M. R. and Howard, S. J. (1995). Principles of clinical linguistics. In M. R. Perkins and S. J. Howard (eds), *Case Studies in Clinical Linguistics* (pp. 10–35). London: Whurr.

Perkins, M. R. and Varley, R. (1996). *A Machine-Readable Corpus of Aphasic Discourse*. University of Sheffield: Department of Human Communication Sciences/Institute for Language, Speech and Hearing (ILASH).

Perner, J. (1998). The meta-intentional nature of executive functions and theory of mind. In P. Carruthers and J. Boucher (eds), *Language and Thought: Interdisciplinary Themes*. Cambridge: Cambridge University Press.

Peterson, C. C. and Siegal, M. (2000). Insights into theory of mind from deafness and autism. *Mind and Language*, 15(1), 123–45.

Peterson-Falzone, S., Hardin-Jones, M. and Karnell, M. (2001). *Cleft Palate Speech*, 3rd edition. St Louis: Mosby.

Phillips, C. E., Jarrold, C., Baddeley, A. D., Grant, J. and Karmiloff-Smith, A. (2004). Comprehension of spatial language terms in Williams syndrome: evidence for an interaction between domains of strength and weakness. *Cortex*, 40, 85–101.

Phillips, M. L., Drevets, W. C., Rauch, S. L. and Lane, R. (2003). Neurobiology of emotion perception. II: Implications for major psychiatric disorders. *Biological Psychiatry*, 54(5), 515–28.

Piaget, J. (1952). *The Origins of Intelligence in the Child*. London: Routledge.

Pinker, S. (1999). *Words and Rules: The Ingredients of Language*. London: Weidenfeld and Nicolson.

Pollard, C. and Sag, I. (1994). *Head-Driven Phrase Structure Grammar. Report No. CSLI-88-132*. Chicago, IL: Center for the Study of Language and Information, University of Chicago.

Poncet, M., Ali-Cherif, A., Joanette, Y. and Nespoulous, J.-L. (1984). Reference and modalization in a left-hander with a callosal disconnection and right hemianopia. In D. Caplan, A. R. Lecours and A. Smith (eds), *Biological Perspectives on Language* (pp. 264–9). Cambridge, MA: MIT Press.

Prelock, P. A. and Panagos, J. M. (1989). The influence of processing mode on the sentence productions of language-disordered and normal children. *Clinical Linguistics and Phonetics*, 3, 251–63.

Prinz, P. and Weiner, F. (1987). *The Pragmatics Screening Test*. Ohio: Psychological Corporation.

Prutting, C. A. and Kirchner, D. M. (1983). Applied pragmatics. In T. M. Gallagher and C. A. Prutting (eds), *Pragmatic Assessment and Intervention Issues in Language* (pp. 29–64). San Diego: College Hill Press.

Radford, J. and Tarplee, C. (2000). The management of conversational topic by a ten year old child with pragmatic difficulties. *Clinical Linguistics and Phonetics*, 14(5), 387–403.

Ramanathan, V. (1997). *Alzheimer's Discourse: Some Sociolinguistic Dimensions.* Hillsdale, NJ: Erlbaum.

Rapin, I. and Allen, D. A. (1983). Developmental language disorders: Nosologic considerations. In U. Kirk (ed.), *Neuropsychology of Language, Reading, and Spelling* (pp. 155–84). New York: Academic Press.

Redmond, S. M. (2004). Conversational profiles of children with ADHD, SLI and typical development. *Clinical Linguistics and Phonetics*, 18(2), 107–25.

Redmond, S. M. and Rice, M. L. (1998). The socioemotional behaviors of children with SLI: Social adaptation or social deviance? *Journal of Speech, Language and Hearing Research*, 41(3), 688–700.

Reilly, J. S., Bates, E. and Marchman, V. (1998). Narrative discourse in children with early focal brain injury. *Brain and Language.* (Special issue on *Discourse in Children with Anomalous Brain Development or Acquired Brain Injury*, (ed. Maureen Dennis), 61(3), 335–75.

Reilly, J., Klima, E. S. and Bellugi, U. (1990). Once more with feeling: affect and language in atypical populations. *Development and Psychopathology*, 2, 367–91.

Rein, R. P. and Kernan, K. T. (1989). The functional use of verbal perseverations by adults who are mentally retarded. *Education and Training in Mental Retardation*, 24(December), 381–9.

Renfrew, C. (1997). *The Bus Story Test: A Test of Narrative Speech*, 4th edition. Bicester: Winslow Press.

Rescher, N. (1968). *Topics in Philosophical Logic.* Dordrecht: Reidel.

Reuterskiöld-Wagner, C. and Nettelbladt, U. (2005). Tor: case study of a boy with autism between the age of three and eight. *Child Language Teaching and Therapy*, 21(2), 123–45.

Rhys, C. S. (2001). Interlocutor discourse practices in response to the word finding problems of an Alzheimer's patient. *Stem-, Spraak- en Taalpathologie*, 10(4), 233–47.

(2005). Gaze and the turn: a nonverbal solution to an interactive problem. *Clinical Linguistics and Phonetics*, 19(5), 419–31.

Ribeiro, B. T. (1994). *Coherence in Psychotic Discourse.* Oxford: Oxford University Press.

(1993). Framing in psychotic discourse. In D. Tannen (ed.), *Framing in Discourse* (pp. 77–113). Oxford: Oxford University Press.

Rice, M. L., Wexler, K. and Cleave, P. (1995). Specific language impairment as a period of extended optional infinitive. *Journal of Speech and Hearing Research*, 38, 850–63.

Ripich, D., Carpenter, B. D. and Ziol, E. W. (2000). Conversational cohesion patterns in men and women with Alzheimer's disease: a longitudinal study. *International Journal of Language and Communication Disorders*, 35(1), 49–64.

Ripich, D. N. and Terrell, B. Y. (1988). Patterns of discourse cohesion and coherence in Alzheimer's Disease. *Journal of Speech and Hearing Disorders*, 53, 8–15.

Robertson, L. C. and Rafal, R. (2000). Disorders of visual attention. In M. S. Gazzaniga (ed.), *The New Cognitive Neurosciences*, 2nd edition (pp. 633–49). Cambridge, MA: MIT Press.

Rochester, S. R., Martin, J. R. and Thurston, S. (1977). Thought-process disorder in schizophrenia: the listener's task. *Brain and Language*, 4, 95–114.

Rollins, P. R. and Snow, C. E. (1998). Shared attention and grammatical development in typical children and children with autism. *Journal of Child Language*, 25, 653–73.

Rondal, J. A. (1994). Exceptional language development in mental retardation: theoretical implications. In M. M. Leahy and J. L. Kallen (eds), *Interdisciplinary Perspectives in Speech and Language Pathology* (pp. 43–53). Dublin: School of Clinical Speech and language Studies, Trinity College Dublin.

Rosenberg, M. S. (1975). Factives that aren't so. *Papers from the 11th Regional Meeting of the Chicago Linguistics Society*, 475–86.

Rossen, M., Klima, E. S., Bellugi, U., Bihrle, A. and Jones, W. (1996). Interaction between language and cognition: evidence from Williams syndrome. In J. Beitchman, N. Cohen, M. Konstantareas and R. Tannock (eds), *Language, Learning and Behavior Disorders: Developmental, Biological and Clinical Perspectives* (pp. 367–92). Cambridge: Cambridge University Press.

Roth, D. and Leslie, A. M. (1991). The recognition of attitude conveyed by utterance: a study of preschool and autistic children. *British Journal of Developmental Psychology*, 9, 315–30.

Roth, F. P. and Spekman, N. J. (1984a). Assessing the pragmatic abilities of children: Part 1. Organizational framework and assessment parameters. *Journal of Speech and Hearing Disorders*, 49, 2–11.

(1984b). Assessing the pragmatic abilities of children: Part 2. Guidelines, considerations, and specific evaluation procedures. *Journal of Speech and Hearing Disorders*, 49, 12–17.

Ruffman, T., Slade, L., Rowlandson, K., Rumsey, C. and Garnham, A. (2003). How language relates to belief, desire, and emotion understanding. *Cognitive Development*, 18, 139–58.

Ruigendijk, E., Vasic, N. and Avrutin, S. (2006). Reference assignment: using language breakdown to choose between theoretical approaches. *Brain and Language*, 96(3), 302.

Russell, J. (ed.). (1997). *Autism as an Executive Disorder*. Oxford: Oxford University Press.

Russell, P. A., Hosie, J. A., Gray, C. D., Scott, C. and Hunter, N. (1998). The development of theory of mind in deaf children. *Journal of Child Psychology and Psychiatry*, 39(6), 903–10.

Ryalls, J. and Whiteside, J. (2006). An atypical case of Foreign Accent Syndrome. *Clinical Linguistics and Phonetics*, 20(2/3), 157–62.

Ryan, B. P. (2000). Speaking rate, conversational speech acts, interruption, and linguistic complexity of 20 pre-school stuttering and non-stuttering children and their mothers. *Clinical Linguistics and Phonetics*, 14(1), 25–51.

Sacks, H., Schegloff, E. A. and Jefferson, G. (1974). A simplest systematics for the organization of turn-taking for conversation. *Language*, 50(4), 696–735.

Sacks, O. (1995). *An Anthropologist on Mars: Seven Paradoxical Tales*. London: Picador.

Sahlén, B. and Nettelbladt, U. (1993). Context and comprehension: a neurolinguistic and interactional approach to the understanding of semantic-pragmatic disorder. *European Journal of Disorders of Communication*, 28, 117–40.

St James, P. J. and Tager-Flusberg, H. (1994). An observational study of humor in autism and Down syndrome. *Journal of Autism and Developmental Disorders*, 24(5), 603–17.

Salis, C. and Edwards, S. (2004). Adaptation theory and non-fluent aphasia in English. *Aphasiology*, 18(12), 1103–20.

Schegloff, E. A. (1996). Turn organization: one intersection of grammar and interaction. In E. Ochs, E. A. Schegloff and S. A. Thompson (eds), *Interaction and Grammar* (pp. 52–133). Cambridge: Cambridge University Press.

(1999). Discourse, pragmatics, conversation, analysis. *Discourse Studies*, 1(4), 405–35.

(2000). Overlapping talk and the organisation of turn-taking for conversation. *Language in Society*, 29, 1–63.

(2003). Conversation Analysis and communication disorders. In C. Goodwin (ed.), *Conversation and Brain Damage* (pp. 21–55). New York: Oxford University Press.

Schegloff, E. A., Jefferson, G. and Sacks, H. (1977). The preference for self-correction in the organization of repair in conversation. *Language*, 53, 361–82.

Schelletter, C. and Leinonen, E. (2003). Normal and language-impaired children's use of reference: syntactic versus pragmatic processing. *Clinical Linguistics and Phonetics*, 17(4–5), 335–43.

Scherer, K. R. (1986). Vocal affect expression: a review and a model for future research. *Psychological Bulletin*, 99(2), 143–65.

Schiffrin, D. (1994). *Approaches to Discourse*. Oxford: Blackwell.

Schuler, A. L. and Prizant, B. M. (1985). Echolalia. In E. Schopler and G. B. Mesibov (eds), *Communication Problems in Autism* (pp. 163–84). New York: Plenum.

Schwartz, M. F. (1987). Patterns of speech production deficit within and across aphasia syndromes: application of a psycholinguistic model. In M. Coltheart, G. Sartori and R. Job (eds), *The Cognitive Neuropsychology of Language* (pp. 163–99). Hove: Lawrence Erlbaum.

Scobbie, J. M. (2005). The phonetics–phonology overlap. *QMUC Speech Science Research Centre Working Paper* 1.

Scollon, R. (1979). A real early stage: An unzipped condensation of a dissertation on child language. In E. Ochs and B. B. Schieffelin (eds), *Developmental Pragmatics* (pp. 215–28). New York: Academic Press.

Searle, J. R. (1969). *Speech Acts*. Cambridge: Cambridge University Press.

(1976). A classification of illocutionary acts. *Language in Society*, 5, 1–23.

(1979). *Expression and Meaning.* Cambridge: Cambridge University Press.

Semel, E., Wiig, E. H. and Secord, W. (1987). *Clinical Evaluation of Language Fundamentals – Revised.* London: The Psychological Corporation.

Seung, H.-K. and Chapman, R. S. (2003). The effect of story presentation rates on story retelling by individuals with Down syndrome. *Applied Psycholinguistics*, 24, 603–20.

Shallice, T. (1988). *From Neuropsychology to Mental Structure.* Cambridge: Cambridge University Press.

Sherratt, S. M. and Penn, C. (1990). Discourse in a right-hemisphere brain-damaged subject. *Aphasiology*, 4(6), 539–60.

Shimamura, A. P. (1995). Memory and frontal lobe function. In M. S. Gazzaniga (ed.), *The Cognitive Neurosciences* (pp. 803–13). Cambridge, MA: MIT Press.

Shockey, L. (2003). *Sound Patterns of Spoken English.* Oxford: Blackwell.

Shriberg, L., Aram, D. and Kwiatkowski, J. (1997). Developmental apraxia of speech: 1. Descriptive and theoretical perspectives. *Journal of Speech Language and Hearing Research*, 40, 273–85.

Shriberg, L., Paul, R., McSweeny, J., Klin, A., Cohen, D. and Volkmar, F. (2001). Speech and prosody characteristics of adolescents and adults with high-functioning autism and Asperger syndrome. *Journal of Speech, Language, and Hearing Research*, 44, 1097–115.

Shriner, T. H., Holloway, M. S. and Daniloff, R. G. (1969). The relationship between articulatory deficits and syntax in speech defective children. *Journal of Speech and Hearing Research*, 12, 319–25.

Shulman, B. (1985). *Test of Pragmatic Skills.* Arizona: Communication Skill Builders.

Siegal, M. and Blades, M. (2003). Language and auditory processing in autism. *Trends in Cognitive Sciences*, 7(9), 378–80.

Siegal, M., Carrington, J. and Radel, M. (1996). Theory of mind and pragmatic understanding following right hemisphere damage. *Brain and Language*, 53(1), 40–50.

Silkes, J. P., McNeil, M. R. and Drton, M. (2004). Simulation of aphasic naming performance in non-brain-damaged adults. *Journal of Speech, Language and Hearing Research*, 47(3), 610–23.

Simmons-Mackie, N. and Damico, J. (1995). Communicative competence in aphasia: evidence from compensatory strategies. In M. Lemme (ed.), *Clinical Aphasiology.* Austin, TX: Pro-ed.

(1996). The contribution of discourse markers to communicative competence in aphasia. *American Journal of Speech-Language Pathology*, 5(1), 37–43.

(1997). Reformulating the definition of compensatory strategies in aphasia. *Aphasiology*, 11, 761–81.

Sinclair, J. M. and Coulthard, R. M. (1975). *Towards an Analysis of Discourse.* Oxford: Oxford University Press.

Sinclair, M. (1995). Fitting pragmatics into the mind: some issues in mentalist pragmatics. *Journal of Pragmatics*, 23, 509–39.

Slade, L. and Ruffman, T. (2005). How language does (and does not) relate to theory of mind: a longitudinal study of syntax, semantics, working memory and false belief. *British Journal of Developmental Psychology*, 23, 117–41.

Slugoski, B. R. and Wilson, A. E. (1998). Contribution of conversation skills to the production of judgmental errors. *European Journal of Social Psychology*, 28, 575–601.

Smith, B. R. and Leinonen, E. (1992). *Clinical Pragmatics: Unravelling the Complexities of Communicative Failure*. London: Chapman and Hall.

Smith, N. V. and Tsimpli, I.-M. (1995). *The Mind of a Savant: Language-Learning and Modularity*. Oxford: Blackwell.

Smith, S. T., Mann, V. A. and Shankweiler, D. (1986). Spoken sentence comprehension by good and poor readers: a study with the Token Test. *Cortex*, 22, 627–32.

Snow, D. (1996). A linguistic account of a developmental, semantic-pragmatic disorder: evidence from a case study. *Clinical Linguistics and Phonetics*, 10(4), 281–98.

  (2001). Imitations of intonation contours by children with normal and disordered language development. *Clinical Linguistics and Phonetics*, 15(7), 567–84.

Snow, P. and Douglas, J. (1999). Discourse rehabilitation following traumatic brain injury. In S. McDonald, L. Togher and C. Code (eds), *Communication Disorders Following Traumatic Brain Injury* (pp. 271–320). Hove: Psychology Press.

Snow, P., Douglas, J. and Ponsford, J. (1995). Discourse assessment following traumatic brain injury: a pilot study examining some demographic and methodological issues. *Aphasiology*, 9, 365–80.

Snowling, M. and Hulme, C. (1994). The development of phonological skills. *Philosophical Transactions of the Royal Society of London – Series B: Biological Sciences*, 346, 21–7.

Snyder, L. S. and Downey, D. M. (1991). The language–reading relationship in normal and reading-disabled children. *Journal of Speech and Hearing Research*, 34, 129–40.

Sorjonen, M.-L. (1996). On repeats and responses in Finnish. In E. Ochs and E. A. Schegloff and S. A. Thompson (eds), *Interaction and Grammar* (pp. 277–327). Cambridge: Cambridge University Press.

Sperber, D. (1996). *Explaining Culture: A Naturalistic Approach*. Oxford: Blackwell.

  (2002). In defense of massive modularity. In E. Dupoux (ed.), *Language, Brain and Cognitive Development: Essays in Honor of Jacques Mehler* (pp. 47–57). Cambridge, MA: MIT Press.

Sperber, D. and Wilson, D. (1995). *Relevance: Communication and Cognition*, 2nd edition. Oxford: Blackwell.

  (2002). Pragmatics, modularity and mind-reading. *Mind and Language*, 17, 3–23.

  (2005). Pragmatics. In F. Jackson and M. Smith (eds), *Oxford Handbook of Contemporary Analytic Philosophy* (pp. 468–501). Oxford: Oxford University Press.

Spitznagel, M. B. and Suhr, J. A. (2002). Executive function deficits associated with symptoms of schizotypy and obsessive-compulsive disorder. *Psychiatry Research*, 110(2), 151–63.

Springer, L., Miller, N. and Bürk, F. (1998). A cross-language analysis of conversation in a trilingual speaker with aphasia. *Journal of Neurolinguistics*, 11, 223–41.

Stackhouse, J. and Wells, B. (1997). *Children's Speech and Literacy Difficulties: A Psycholinguistic Framework*. London: Whurr.

Stemmer, B. (1999a). An on-line interview with Noam Chomsky: on the nature of pragmatics and related issues. *Brain and Language*, 68, 393–401.

Stemmer, B. (ed.). (1999b). *Brain and Language* 68, *1*. Special issue on *Pragmatics*. New York: Academic Press.

Stemmer, B. (forthcoming). Neuropragmatics. In M. J. Ball, M. R. Perkins, N. Müller, S. Howard (eds), *Handbook of Clinical Linguistics*. Oxford: Blackwell.

Stemmer, B., Giroux, F. and Joanette, Y. (1994). Production and evaluation of requests by right hemisphere brain-damaged individuals. *Brain and Language*, 47, 1–31.

Stemmer, B. and Joanette, Y. (1998). The interpretation of narrative discourse of brain-damaged individuals within the framework of a multilevel discourse model. In M. Beeman and C. Chiarello (eds), *Right Hemisphere Language Comprehension: Perspectives from Cognitive Neuroscience* (pp. 329–48). Mahwah, NJ: Lawrence Erlbaum.

Sternberg, R. J. (1995). *In Search of the Human Mind*. Orlando, FL: Harcourt Brace.

Stiles, W. B. (1992). *Describing Talk: A Taxonomy of Verbal Response Modes*. London: Sage.

Stojanovik, V. (2002). Williams syndrome, specific language impairment and modularity. Unpublished PhD, University of Sheffield.

Stojanovik, V., Perkins, M. R. and Howard, S. (2001). Language and conversational abilities in individuals with Williams syndrome: how good is good? *International Journal of Language and Communication Disorders (Supplement)*, 36, 234–9.

(2002). The language/cognition interface – lessons from Williams Syndrome and Specific Language Impairment. In E. Fava (ed.), *Clinical Linguistics: Theory and Applications in Speech Pathology and Therapy* (pp. 229–45). Amsterdam: John Benjamins.

(2004). Williams syndrome and specific language impairment do not support claims for developmental double dissociations and innate modularity. *Journal of Neurolinguistics*, 17, 403–24.

(2006). Linguistic heterogeneity in Williams Syndrome. *Clinical Linguistics and Phonetics*, 20(7–8), 547–52.

Stone, T. and Davies, M. (1996). The mental simulation debate: a progress report. In P. Carruthers and P. K. Smith (eds), *Theories of Theories of Mind* (pp. 119–37). Cambridge: Cambridge University Press.

Studdert-Kennedy, M. and Goodell, E. W. (1995). Gestures, features and segments in early child speech. In B. d. Gelder and J. Morais (eds), *Speech and Reading: A Comparative Approach* (pp. 65–88). Hove: Lawrence Erlbaum.

Sudhalter, V. and Belser, R. C. (2001). Conversational characteristics of children with Fragile X syndrome: tangential language. *American Journal on Mental Retardation*, 106(5), 389–400.

Surian, L., Baron-Cohen, S. and van der Lely, H. (1996). Are children with autism deaf to Gricean maxims? *Cognitive Neuropsychiatry*, 1(1), 55–71.

Tager-Flusberg, H. (1995). 'Once upon a ribbit': stories narrated by autistic children. *British Journal of Developmental Psychology*, 13, 45–59.

(1997). Language acquisition and theory of mind: contributions from the study of autism. In L. B. Adamson and M. A. Romski (eds), *Communication and Language Acquisition: Discoveries from Atypical Development* (pp. 135–60). Baltimore: Paul H. Brookes.

Tallal, P. and Piercy, M. (1973). Developmental aphasia: impaired rate of nonverbal processing as a function of sensory modality. *Neuropsychologia*, 12, 83–93.

Tallal, P., Stark, R. and Mellits, D. (1985). The relationship between auditory temporal analysis and receptive language development: evidence from studies of developmental language disorders. *Neuropsychologia*, 23, 527–34.

Tannock, R. and Schachar, R. (1996). Executive dysfunction as an underlying mechanism of behavior and language problems in attention deficit hyperactivity disorder. In J. Beitchman, N. Cohen, M. Konstantareas and R. Tannock (eds), *Language, Learning and Behavior Disorders: Developmental, Biological and Clinical Perspectives* (pp. 128–55). Cambridge: Cambridge University Press.

Tarling, K., Perkins, M. R. and Stojanovik, V. (2006). Conversational success in Williams syndrome: communication in the face of cognitive and linguistic limitations. *Clinical Linguistics and Phonetics*, 20(7–8), 583–90.

Tarplee, C. and Barrow, E. (1999). Delayed echoing as an interactional resource: a case study of a 3-year-old child on the autistic spectrum. *Clinical Linguistics and Phonetics*, 13(6), 449–82.

Taylor, R. (2000). Profiles of semantic-pragmatic disorder and the investigation of underlying psychological mechanisms. Unpublished Ph.D., University of Sheffield.

Temple, C. M., Almazan, M. and Sherwood, S. (2002). Lexical skills in Williams Syndrome: a cognitive neuropsychological analysis. *Journal of Neurolinguistics*, 15(6), 463–95.

Tényi, T., Herold, R., Szili, I. M. and Trixler, M. (2002). Schizophrenics show a failure in the decoding of violations of conversational implicatures. *Psychopathology*, 35, 25–7.

Tesak, J. (1994). Cognitive load and the processing of grammatical items. *Journal of Neurolinguistics*, 8(1), 43–8.

Thal, D., Wulfeck, B. and Reilly, J. S. (1993). *Brain and Language: A Cross-Population Perspective* The Annual Meeting of the American Speech–Language–Hearing Association, Anaheim, CA.

Thelen, E. and Smith, L. B. (1994). *A Dynamic Systems Approach to the Development of Cognition and Action*. Cambridge, MA: MIT Press.

Thomas, J. (1995). *Meaning in Interaction: An Introduction to Pragmatics*. London: Longman.

Thomas, M. S. C. (2003). Limits on plasticity. *Journal of Cognition and Development*, 4(1), 95–121.

(2005a). Characterising compensation. *Cortex*, 41, 434–42.

(2005b). Constraints on language development: insights from developmental disorders. In P. Fletcher and J. F. Miller (eds), *Development Theory and Language Disorders* (pp. 11–34). Amsterdam: John Benjamins.

Thomas, M. and Karmiloff-Smith, A. (2002). Are developmental disorders like cases of adult brain damage? Implications from connectionist modelling. *Behavioral and Brain Sciences*, 25, 727–88.

Thomas, M. S. C. and Karmiloff-Smith, A. (2003). Modeling language acquisition in atypical phenotypes. *Psychological Review*, 110(4), 647–82.

Thompson, C. K. (2003). Unaccusative verb production in agrammatic aphasia: the argument structure complexity hypothesis. *Journal of Neurolinguistics*, 16(2–3), 151–67.

Thompson, C. K., Fix, S. and Gitelman, D. (2002). Selective impairment of morphosyntactic production in a neurological patient. *Journal of Neurolinguistics*, 15(3–5), 189–207.

Thorndyke, P. W. (1977). Cognitive structures in comprehension and memory of narrative discourse. *Cognitive Psychology*, 9, 77–110.

Thurber, C. and Tager-Flusberg, H. (1993). Pauses in the narratives produced by autistic, mentally retarded, and normal children as an index of cognitive demand. *Journal of Autism and Developmental Disorders*, 23, 309–22.

Togher, L., Hand, L. and Code, C. (1999). Exchanges of information in the talk of people with traumatic brain injury. In S. McDonald, L. Togher and C. Code (eds), *Communication Disorders Following Traumatic Brain Injury* (pp. 113–45). Hove: Psychology Press.

Tomasello, M. (2000). The social-pragmatic theory of word learning. *Pragmatics*, 10(4), 401–13.

Tompkins, C. A., Blake, M. L., Baumgaertner, A. and Fassbinder, W. (2002). Characterising comprehension difficulties after right brain damage: attentional demands of suppression function. *Aphasiology*, 16, 559–72.

Tompkins, C. A., Bloise, C. G. R., Timko, M. L. and Baumgaertner, A. (1994). Working memory and inference revision in brain-damaged and normally aging adults. *Journal of Speech and Hearing Research*, 37, 896–912.

Tompkins, C. A., Lehman-Blake, M. T., Baumgaertner, A. and Fassbinder, W. (2001). Mechanisms of discourse comprehension impairment after right hemisphere brain damage: suppression in inferential ambiguity resolution. *Journal of Speech, Language, and Hearing Research*, 44, 400–15.

Tompkins, C. A. and Mateer, C. A. (1985). Right hemisphere appreciation of prosodic and linguistic indications of implicit attitude. *Brain and Language*, 24, 185–203.

Townshend, J. M. and Duka, T. (2003). Mixed emotions: alcoholics' impairments in the recognition of specific emotional facial expressions. *Neuropsychologia*, 41(7), 773–82.

Tranel, D., Bechara, A. and Damasio, A. (2000). Decision making and the somatic marker hypothesis. In M. S. Gazzaniga (ed.), *The New Cognitive Neurosciences*, 2nd edition (pp. 1047–61). Cambridge, MA: MIT Press.

Trautman, L. S., Healey, E. C., Brown, T. A., Brown, P. and Jermano, S. (1999). A further analysis of narrative skills of children who stutter. *Journal of Communication Disorders*, 32(5), 297–315.

Tsapkini, K., Jarema, G. and Kehayia, E. (2002). A morphological processing deficit in verbs but not in nouns: a case study in a highly inflected language. *Journal of Neurolinguistics*, 15(3–5), 265–88.

Tsimpli, I.-M. and Smith, N. (1998). Modules and quasi-modules: language and theory of mind in a polyglot savant. *Learning and Individual Differences*, 10(3), 193–215.

Uekermann, J., Daum, I., Peters, S., Wiebel, B., Przuntek, H. and Müller, T. (2003). Depressed mood and executive dysfunction in early Parkinson's disease. *Acta Neurologica Scandinavica*, 107, 341–8.

Ulatowska, H. K., Allard, L. and Chapman, S. B. (1990). Narrative and procedural discourse in aphasia. In Y. Joannette and H. H. Brownell (eds), *Discourse Ability and Brain Damage: Theoretical and Empirical Perspectives* (pp. 180–98). New York: Springer-Verlag.

Ulatowska, H. K. and Chapman, S. B. (1994). Discourse macrostructure in aphasia. In R. L. Bloom, L. K. Obler, S. De Santi and J. S. Ehrlich (eds), *Discourse Analysis and Applications: Studies in Adult Clinical Populations* (pp. 29–46). Hillsdale, NJ: Erlbaum.

Ullman, M. T., Pancheva, R., Love, T., Yee, E., Swinney, D. and Hickok, G. (2005). Neural correlates of lexicon and grammar: Evidence from the production, reading, and judgment of inflection in aphasia. *Brain and Language*, 93(2), 185–238.

Ullman, M. T. and Pierpont, E. I. (2005). Specific Language Impairment is not specific to language: the procedural deficit hypothesis. *Cortex*, 41, 399–433.

van der Lely, H. (2005). Domain-specific cognitive systems: evidence from Grammatical-SLI. *Trends in Cognitive Sciences*, 9(2), 53–9.

van der Lely, H. and Stollwerk, L. (1997). Binding theory and specifically language impaired children. *Cognition*, 62, 245–90.

van Lancker, D. (1987). Nonpropositional speech: neurolinguistic studies. In A. W. Ellis (ed.), *Progress in the Psychology of Language* (vol. III, pp. 49–118). Hillsdale, NJ: Erlbaum.

(1991). Personal relevance and the human right hemisphere. *Brain and Cognition*, 17, 64–92.

(2001). Is your syntactic component really necessary? *Aphasiology*, 15(4), 343–60.

van Lancker, D. R. and Canter, G. J. (1982). Impairment of voice and face recognition in patients with hemispheric damage. *Brain and Cognition*, 1, 185–95.

van Lancker, D., Cornelius, C. and Kreiman, J. (1989). Recognition of emotional-prosodic meanings in speech by autistic, schizophrenic, and normal children. *Developmental Neuropsychology*, 5, 207–26.

van Lancker, D. and Pachana, N. A. (1998). The influence of emotions on language and communication disorders. In B. Stemmer and H. A. Whitaker (eds), *Handbook of Neurolinguistics* (pp. 301–11). San Diego: Academic Press.

van Lancker, D. and Sidtis, J. J. (1992). The identification of affective-prosodic stimuli by left- and right-hemisphere-damaged subjects: all errors are not created equal. *Journal of Speech and Hearing Research*, 35, 963–70.

Van Leer, E. and Turkstra, L. (1999). The effect of elicitation task on discourse coherence and cohesion in adolescents with brain injury. *Journal of Communications Disorders*, 32(5), 327–49.

Varley, R. (2002). Science without grammar: scientific reasoning in severe agrammatic aphasia. In P. Carruthers, S. Stich and M. Siegal (eds), *The Cognitive Basis of Science* (pp. 99–116). Cambridge: Cambridge University Press.

Varley, R. and Siegal, M. (2000). Evidence for cognition without grammar from causal reasoning and 'theory of mind' in an agrammatic aphasic patient. *Current Biology*, 10, 723–6.

Verschueren, J. (1999). *Understanding Pragmatics*. London: Arnold.

Vihman, M. and Velleman, S. (2000). Phonetics and the origins of phonology. In N. Burton-Roberts, P. Carr and G. Docherty (eds), *Phonological Knowledge: Conceptual and Empirical Issues* (pp. 305–39). Oxford: Oxford University Press.

Violette, J. and Swisher, L. (1992). Echolalic responses by a child with autism to four experimental conditions of sociolinguistic input. *Journal of Speech and Hearing Research*, 35, 139–47.

Volden, J., Mulcahy, R. F. and Holdgrafter, G. (1997). Pragmatic language disorder and perspective taking in autistic speakers. *Applied Psycholinguistics*, 18, 181–98.

Wagner, C. R., Nettelbladt, U., Sahlén, B. and Nilholm, C. (2000). Conversation versus narration in pre-school children with language impairment. *International Journal of Language and Communication Disorders*, 35(1), 83–93.

Walker, J. P., Pelletier, R. and Reif, L. (2004). The production of linguistic prosodic structures in subjects with right hemisphere damage. *Clinical Linguistics and Phonetics*, 18(2), 85–106.

Weismer, S. E. (1996). Capacity limitations in working memory: the impact on lexical and morphological learning by children with language impairments. *Topics in Language Disorder*, 17, 33–44.

Wells, B. and Local, J. (1993). The sense of an ending: a case of prosodic delay. *Clinical Linguistics and Phonetics*, 7(1), 59–73.

Wells, B. and Peppé, S. (2003). Intonation abilities of children with speech and language impairments. *Journal of Speech, Language and Hearing Research*, 46, 5–20.

Wenzlaff, M. and Clahsen, H. (2004). Tense and agreement in German agrammatism. *Brain and Language*, 89(1), 57–68.

(2005). Finiteness and verb-second in German agrammatism. *Brain and Language*, 92(1), 33–44.

Werth, A., Perkins, M. and Boucher, J. (2001). 'Here's the Weavery looming up': verbal humour in a woman with high-functioning autism. *Autism*, 5(2), 111–25.

Wertz, R. T., Henschel, C. R., Auther, L. L., Ashford, J. R. and Kirshner, H. S. (1998). Affective prosodic disturbance subsequent to right hemisphere stroke: a clinical application. *Journal of Neurolinguistics*, 11, 89–102.

Whitehill, T. L. and Ciocca, V. (2000). Speech errors in Cantonese speaking adults with cerebral palsy. *Clinical Linguistics and Phonetics*, 14(2), 111–30.

Whitworth, A., Perkins, L. and Lesser, R. (1997). *Conversation Analysis Profile for People with Aphasia (CAPPA)*. London: Whurr.

Wilbur, R. (1977). An explanation of deaf children's difficulty with certain syntactic structures in English. *Volta Review*, 79, 85–92.

Wilcox, M. J. and Davis, G. A. (1977). Speech act analysis of aphasic communication in individual and group settings. In R. H. Brookshire (ed.), *Clinical Aphasiology Conference Proceedings* (pp. 166–74). Minneapolis, MN: BRK Publishers.

Wilkinson, R. (1995). Aphasia: conversation analysis of a non-fluent aphasic person. In M. R. Perkins and S. J. Howard (eds), *Case Studies in Clinical Linguistics* (pp. 271–92). London: Whurr.

Wilkinson, R., Beeke, S. and Maxim, J. (2003). Adapting to conversation: on the use of linguistic resources by speakers with fluent aphasia in the construction of turns at talk. In C. Goodwin (ed.), *Conversation and Brain Damage* (pp. 59–89). New York: Oxford University Press.

Wilks, Y. (1987). Relevance must be to someone. *Behavioral and Brain Sciences*, 10, 735–6.

Wilson, B. A., Baddeley, A. D. and Kapur, N. (1995). Dense amnesia in a professional musician following herpes simplex virus encephalitis. *Journal of Clinical Experimental Neuropsychology*, 17(5), 668–81.

Wilson, B. A., Cockburn, J. and Baddeley, A. (1985). *Rivermead Behavioural Memory Test*. Suffolk: Thames Valley Test Company.

Wilson, D. (2005). New directions for research on pragmatics and modularity. *Lingua*, 115, 1129–46.

Wilson, D. and Sperber, D. (1991). Pragmatics and modularity. In S. Davis (ed.), *Pragmatics: A Reader* (pp. 583–95). Oxford: Oxford University Press. (First published in Anne M. Farley, Peter T. Farley and Karl-Erik McCullough (eds) (1986). *The Chicago Linguistic Society Parasession on Pragmatics and Grammatical Theory*. Chicago: Chicago Linguistic Society.)

Wilson, J. and McAnulty, L. (2000). What do you have in mind? Beliefs, knowledge and pragmatic impairment. In N. Müller (ed.), *Pragmatics and Clinical Applications* (pp. 29–51). Amsterdam: John Benjamins.

Winner, E., Brownell, H., Happé, F., Blum, A. and Pincus, D. (1998). Distinguishing lies from jokes: theory of mind deficits and discourse interpretation in right hemisphere brain-damaged patients. *Brain and Language*, 62, 89–106.

Woolfe, T., Want, S. C. and Siegal, M. (2002). Signposts to development: Theory of Mind in deaf children. *Child Development*, 73(3), 768–78.

Wootton, A. J. (1989). Speech to and from a severely retarded young Down's syndrome child. In M. Beveridge, G. Conti-Ramsden and I. Leudar (eds), *Language and Communication in Mentally Handicapped People* (pp. 157–84). London: Chapman and Hall.

  (1999). An investigation of delayed echoing in a child with autism. *First Language*, 19(3), 359–81.

Wray, A. (2002). *Formulaic Language and the Lexicon*. Cambridge: Cambridge University Press.

Wray, A. and Perkins, M. R. (2000). The functions of formulaic language: an integrated model. *Language and Communication*, 20(1), 1–28.

Wulfeck, B., Bates, E. and Capasso, R. (1991). A crosslinguistic study of gramma-
    ticality judgements in Broca's aphasia. *Brain and Language*, 41(2), 311–46.
Wykes, T. and Leff, J. (1982). Disordered speech: differences between manics and
    schizophrenics. *Brain and Language*, 15, 117–24.
Yamada, J. (1990). *Laura: A Case for the Modularity of Language*. Cambridge,
    MA: MIT Press.
Yont, K. M., Snow, C. E. and Vernon-Feagans, L. (2001). Early communicative
    intents expressed by 12-month-old children with and without chronic otitis
    media. *First Language*, 21, 265–87.
    (2003). Is chronic otitis media associated with differences in parental input at 12
    months of age? An analysis of joint attention and directives. *Applied
    Psycholinguistics*, 24, 581–602.
Yule, G. (1996). *Pragmatics*. Oxford: Oxford University Press.
Zaidel, E. (1999). Language in the disconnected right hemisphere. In G. Adelman
    and B. H. Smith (eds), *Encyclopedia of Neuroscience*, 2nd edition
    (pp. 1027–32). Amsterdam: Elsevier.
Ziatas, K., Durkin, K. and Pratt, C. (2003). Differences in assertive speech acts
    produced by children with autism, Asperger syndrome, specific language
    impairment, and normal development. *Development and Psychopathology*,
    15, 73–94.

Index

adaptation theory 147
affect, *see* emotion
agrammatism 38–9, 118, 122
alcohol and stimulant abuse 85, 102
Alzheimer's disease, *see* dementia
amnesia 22, 91, 93, 95
amygdala damage 83
anomia 123–4
aphasia 15, 17, 22, 25, 28, 38–9, 59, 73–4,
    85, 91, 93, 95, 101, 102, 105, 114,
    115, 117–18, 120–1, 122, 125–7,
    128, 129–30, 131, 132–3,
    151, 153
    bilingual 91
artefact terms 79–80, 129
Asperger's syndrome, *see* autism
attention, *see* executive function
attention deficit hyperactivity disorder
    (ADHD) 85, 87
attitude 99–106, 140
    impairment of 102–4
    propositional 100–1
auditory perception 40, 42, 115–16, 129,
    140–1, 163–5
autism 15, 16–17, 18–19, 20, 22, 23–5, 28,
    56, 67, 74, 75–6, 78, 79–80, 81–2, 85,
    89, 92, 93, 97, 99, 102, 103, 104, 105,
    112, 114, 115, 117, 127, 131, 132, 141,
    150, 180
autistic spectrum disorder, *see* autism

Bates, Elizabeth 3, 14, 38, 46–7, 128
bilingualism 91
binding theory 39
bipolar disorder 102
blends 59
blindness, *see* visual impairment
brain plasticity 149–50

callosal disconnection 56, 102
cerebral palsy 112, 144
Clark, Andy 4, 45, 57, 66, 90

Clark, H. H. 4, 14, 48–9, 145, 152, 174–5,
    178, 181
cleft palate 112, 115–16, 144, 155
cognition 70–4, 79
cognitive impairment 162–5
cognitive overload 37–9, 40, 41–3, 149,
    152, 166
coherence 25–6, 132
cohesion 25–6, 132–3
commisurotomy 28
compensation, *see* compensatory
    adaptation
compensatory adaptation 6, 38–9, 47–8, 55,
    61–2, 65, 146–75, 181–2
    definition of 147–9
    interpersonal 171–5
    intrapersonal 165–70
    intrapersonal vs interpersonal
    151–5
    neurological basis of 149–51
competence and performance 37–8
competition model 37, 46–7, 64
comprehension difficulties 162
conceptual knowledge 37, 126
connectionism 37, 147, 182
consonant harmony 114
construction grammar 128
conversational implicature 11, 17–19, 20,
    70, 175
Conversation Analysis (CA) 4, 11, 27–30, 48,
    49, 151, 178, 180
coupled system 66

deafness, *see* hearing impairment
dementia 19, 22, 28, 85, 86–7, 93, 98, 102,
    127, 129, 132–3, 135–6
depression 85, 102
discourse 131–7
    impairment of 160
    and memory 135
    and pragmatics 21–2, 131–2
    procedural 133–4

discourse analysis
    and communication disorder 12–23
domains 52, 66–8, 177
double dissociation 35, 40
Down's syndrome 22, 28, 93, 98, 102, 110,
    133, 180
dynamic systems theory 37, 62
dysarthria 112, 144
dysexecutive syndrome 85
dysfluency 15, 152, 161
dyslexia 22, 114
dyspraxia 112
dysprosody 112

echolalia 89, 142, 153
elements 52, 62–4
ellipsis 119, 122
emergence 45–6
emergentist pragmatics, see pragmatics,
    emergentist
emotion 37, 99–106, 140
    impairment of 102–4
emotion–attitude continuum 100–1
emotional intelligence 99–100, 102
equilibrium 65, 66–8
executive function 37, 79, 82–90
    and central coherence 84
    and grammar 121
    impairment of 85–7
    and inference 84
    and memory 84–5, 90
    and Theory of Mind 83–4
eye gaze 28, 30–2, 130, 171–3

factive verb 73
fetal alcohol syndrome 22
focal brain injury 15, 22, 149
foreign accent syndrome 115
formulaic language 125, 135, 142, 152,
    168–9, 173
fragile X syndrome 22, 85, 121
frontal lobe deficit 19, 22

gesture 28–9, 53–4, 59, 60–1, 122, 140, 144,
    145, 170
glossectomy 52–3, 112, 115, 144, 155
glossomania 128

head-driven phrase structure
    grammar 128
hearing impairment 15, 22, 81, 89, 112, 121,
    136, 140–1, 143–4
hemidecorticate 22
herpes simplex encephalitis 85, 86
hydrocephalus 15, 22, 74, 132

inference 20, 37, 55, 72–6, 135
    bridging 72, 73, 75
    elaborative 72, 73, 75
    and executive function 84, 90
    impairment of 74
    logical 72, 73
    and memory 75
information structure 134
interactions 52, 64–5
interpersonal 60–1, 66–8, 178, 181
intonation, see prosody
intrapersonal 55, 66–8, 178, 181

joint action theory 14, 46, 48–9, 174–5

Karmiloff-Smith, Annette 3–4; see also
    neuroconstructivism

learning disability 22, 28, 79
lexical retrieval 25, 55, 66–7, 76, 123–4,
    127, 129–30, 140, 152, 154, 159,
    171–3
lexicon/lexis, see semantics

mania 22
Maxims of Conversation, see conversational
    implicature
memory 37, 39–40, 64, 90–8
    and executive function 84–5
    and inference 75
    declarative (explicit) 91–2
    episodic 91
    impairment of 93–7
    long-term 90, 91–2, 97
    long-term working 90
    medium-term 90, 91, 95–7
    procedural (implicit) 91–2
    savant 92
    semantic 91
    sensory 90
    short-term 90–1, 93–5, 97–8
    working 90
mental retardation, see learning
    disability
minimalist program 46, 118
mirror neurons 14, 77
modality 73–4, 79, 100–1, 104
modularity 5, 33–50, 147
    and grammar 117–18
    and phonology 111–12
    and pragmatics 36–7
morphology 37, 113–14, 117–20
motor neurone disease 28, 112, 144,
    145, 173
motor processing 143–5

multimodality 4, 49, 54, 58–60, 140, 145,
     177–8
multiple sclerosis 93, 98, 112, 127, 132

narrative 23–5, 134, 160
neuroconstructivism 3, 47–8, 150
neurolinguistics 10, 149–51
neuropragmatics 13–14
nonverbal communication 58–60

obsessive-compulsive disorder 85
optional infinitive 39

paragrammatisms 59
Parkinson's disease 85, 89, 102, 112, 144
perseveration 83, 86–7, 88
phonagnosia 141
phonologic-syntactic syndrome 113
phonology 37, 43, 109–16
     and memory 114–15
     impairment of 28, 81–2, 97, 109–10
posterior fossa tumour 22
posture 28, 30
pragmatic checklists/profiles 11–13
pragmatic language impairment (PLI) 13,
     28, 74, 75, 178, 180
pragmatics
     and cognition 14, 70–1
     and discourse 21–2
     and modularity 36–7
     as choices 57–61, 69
     component view 56–7
     definition 2, 4, 5, 9–10, 28, 30, 178,
        179–80
     emergentist 6–7, 44–5, 51–69, 176
     linguistic vs nonlinguistic 9–10
     normal vs abnormal 10–13
     perspectivist view 56–7
pragmatic theory 8–9, 28, 30–2, 178,
     179–80
presupposition 73
principles and parameters 118
procedural deficit hypothesis 39
propositional attitude 79, 100–1
prosody 37, 53, 63–4, 109–16
     impairment of 28, 103, 110, 112
prosopagnosia 142
psychosis 22, 28

reading 141
reference 25
Relevance Theory 4, 10–13, 17, 19–21, 36,
     67–8, 70, 175
repetitiveness 86, 89, 95–7
rhythm 54

right hemisphere damage (RHD) 15, 17, 19,
     23, 67, 73–4, 75, 79, 80, 84, 85, 102,
     103, 112, 115, 125, 127, 130, 132, 135,
     141, 142

schizophrenia 15, 19, 23, 79, 83, 85, 92, 93,
     102, 103, 127–8, 132
     and poetic language 128
semantic-pragmatic disorder 13, 23, 123,
     142–3
semantics 37, 114, 123–31
     and brain lateralization 124–5
     and memory 129
     impairment of 127–8, 159
sensorimotor systems 139–45
sign language 89, 144
social cognition 37
social inference theory 72
spatial neglect 142
speaker role 26–7
specific language impairment (SLI) 23, 28,
     39–40, 42–3, 53–4, 73, 74, 75, 79,
     91–2, 93, 105, 112, 113, 114–15, 118,
     119–20, 121, 127, 129, 132–3, 136–7,
     140, 141, 145, 146–7, 149–50, 151–2,
     165, 180
speech 64
Speech Act Theory 15–17, 70
split brain, see callosal disconnection
story grammar 25, 133
stuttering 23
sub-arachnoid haemorrhage 26–7
syntax 37, 40, 42, 43, 53, 117–23
     co-construction of 173–4
     impairment of 119–20, 157–8

temporal binding hypothesis 150
thematic role 38, 123
theory of mind 14, 37, 72, 76–82, 140, 150
     and executive function 83–4
     and grammar 121
     and hearing impairment 81, 141
     and language 80–1
     and modality 104
     impairment of 79–80
     theories of 77
topic 142
     bias 95–7, 98
     drift 86, 135, 160
     repetition 89, 95–7
Tourette's syndrome 85, 102
trace deletion 39
traumatic brain injury 15–16, 17, 19, 23, 26,
     28, 56, 74, 75, 79, 80, 84–5, 86, 88, 93,
     95–7, 98, 102, 103–4, 115, 127, 132

Turner syndrome 102
turntaking 116

verb argument structure 128
vertical constructions 173
visual impairment 121, 123, 140, 141–3
vocabulary, *see* semantics

weak central coherence 25, 74, 79, 150
wh- questions 81–2
Williams syndrome 23, 28–9, 40–1, 97,
    105–6, 115, 119, 126, 128, 132, 142, 180
word finding, *see* lexical retrieval
word meaning deafness 129
writing 64–5, 141